Money in the Modern World

Josef Jílek / Roman Matoušek

Money in the Modern World

PETER LANG
Frankfurt am Main · Berlin · Bern · Bruxelles · New York · Oxford · Wien

Bibliographic Information published by the Deutsche Nationalbibliothek
The Deutsche Nationalbibliothek lists this publication in the Deutsche Nationalbibliografie; detailed bibliographic data is available in the internet at http://dnb.d-nb.de.

Cover Design:
Olaf Gloeckler, Atelier Platen, Friedberg

ISBN 978-3-631-59118-5

www.peterlang.de

Contents

Preface

The book tries to explain the framework of the money, liquidity and monetary policy in major countries (the USA, the Eurozone, Japan and the United Kingdom). Even if the book is based on the contemporary banking practice, it comes from careful examination of historical development of opinions on money, liquidity and monetary policy. The authors are of the view that the best way how to demonstrate the money and liquidity (and the financial system as a whole) is through financial statements (balance sheet and income statement) which are based on accounting. Thus any operation is clarified through double-entry record.

The first part of the book concentrates on money, namely on money aggregates, creation and extinction of money, decision-making of banks/clients about whether or not to grant/accept loans, issue of debt and equity securities by commercial banks and clients and flow of money as a result of cross-border investments.

The second part focuses on liquidity and reserve requirements. Further, two examples of the banking system (without and including central bank) are shown. These examples help to understand the effects of the currency and of the reserve requirements on the financial positions of economic sectors (commercial banks, enterprises, government, households and central bank). Consequently, the attention is devoted to the basics of financial statements, three structures of central bank's balance sheet, examples of the central bank's financial statements, administration of the international reserves and seigniorage.

The third part concentrates on the practice of monetary policy according to the monetary policy framework: monetary policy instruments, operating targets, intermediate targets and ultimate targets. Inflation targeting follows as many central banks decided to use explicit monetary policy targets in the 1990s. Monetary policy relies on a chain of economic relations allowing the central bank to influence inflation. Thus, transmission mechanism plays the central role in monetary policy. It works through credit, entrepreneurial, expenditure and foreign exchange channels. Subsequently, the topics are monetary policy rules, foreign exchange interventions and dollarization. The issue is closed with description of monetary policy in the major countries.

The last part outlines the payment systems. It is an extension of the first part and begins with interbank payment systems and forms of bank payments. Further, gross and net payment systems are explained. Finally, payment systems in the major countries are described.

Acknowledgements

Many people have played a part in the genesis of this book. Practitioners, academics and students who have made suggestions including Charles Goodhart (Norman Sosnow Professor of Banking and Finance, London School of Economics), L. Randall Wray (Professor of Economics, University of Missouri-Kansas City), Lex Hoogduin (Head of Research de Nederlandsche Bank, Professor of Monetary Economics and Financial Institutions), Huw Pill (Head of Division, Monetary Policy Stance, European Central Bank), Jonathan Thomas (Monetary Assessment and Strategy Division, Bank of England), Frederic Gielen (Lead Financial Management Specialist, The World Bank Group) and Jaroslav Kucera (International Monetary Fund).

Part I: Money

1 Money as monetary aggregates

1.1 Definition of Money

What is money? What can be designated as "money"? Such questions are asked by many people including central bankers. The reason is that people are eager to know it and that the main objective of almost every central bank is to maintain the price stability. In order to achieve this target, people and central banks need to know the quantity of money in the economy. For general public money generally indicates anything acceptable as a legal tender in repaying debts and a store of value.

Any money represents for one entity claim (financial asset) and for the other entity payable (financial liability) at the same time. There are a lot of relationships between creditors and debtors in the economy but only some relationships are considered as money. Money mostly refers to some relationships where the debtors are banks and the creditors are non-bank entities. Relationships where both the debtors and the creditors are banks are not called "money" but "liquidity". However not all claims of non-bank entities, which are at the same time bank liabilities, are covered by the definition of money. **Therefore, money (monetary aggregates) is a subset of all relationships between creditors and debtors in the whole economy and more specifically a subset of all relationships between non-bank creditors and bank debtors.** Money as debt instruments represents a subset of financial instruments.[1]

Banks as debtors ensure high credibility of debtor-creditor relationship. Such money is sometimes referred to as "**bank money**", **"money stock"** or "**money supply**" but we mostly use the simple term "**money**". There are some exceptions to the above mentioned definition of money. For example some central banks include in broad monetary aggregates also some securities issued by some non-bank entities. For example aggregate M3 of the Eurozone covers also money market fund shares and units as well as debt securities with a maturity of up to two years).

1 According to International Financial Reporting Standards (IFRS), a financial instrument is any contract that gives rise to a financial asset of one entity and a financial liability or equity instrument of another entity.

More specifically the term "money" covers (Figure 1.1):

- Currency (banknotes and coins) held by the public (households and enterprises) and government, i.e. currency in circulation; and
- Accounting money held by the public and government.

The accounting money represents book entries on current accounts (checking accounts, demand deposits or sight deposits), term accounts (time deposits, term deposits) and saving accounts. In other words, money represents some liabilities of central bank to the public and government (currency in circulation[2]) and some liabilities of commercial banks to the public (current accounts, term accounts and savings accounts). The definition of money does not comprise liabilities of commercial banks to other banks, i.e. the liquidity. Nowadays, the currency in circulation represents only a small portion of the total money stock. Thus talking about money, we mean primarily the money in the form of book entries.

Looking on **central bank liabilities** only the currency in circulation (i.e. banknotes and coins held by the public and government) contributes to the money stock (monetary aggregate M0). We have to point out that the currency in circulation consists only of the coins and banknotes outside of the central bank and commercial banks. Currency held by commercial banks in their vaults is usually excluded from the definition of money. Other liabilities of the central bank to its clients[3] (including government) do not contribute to the monetary aggregates. The same holds for liabilities of central bank to commercial banks (liquidity).

Money represents the purchasing power of economic agents (households, enterprises and government). It is supposed that purchasing power of money is strongly related to total expenses and total production of goods and services in the whole economy. **Estimations of future price changes** determine the longing of economic agents to hold money at the expense of other financial and real assets (i.e. it determines the velocity of money). If there is **strong inflation** or inflation expectation, agents seek to minimize holdings of almost all kinds of money, and the velocity of money accelerates. Consequently, agents replace money by holdings of other financial and real assets. If prices are expected to remain **stable**, agents generally hold more money and less other financial and real assets, and the velocity of money decelerates. In the case of **deflation** and deflation expectation, holdings of money are very lucrative, and holdings of other financial and real assets are minimized. The velocity of money decelerates.

---

2 This exactly holds when central bank issues both banknotes and coins. However, in some countries coins are issued by the treasury department.

3 Clients are considered the non-bank entities in this book.

The reason is that even if holding of money does not bear any or very low nominal interest, it yields positive real income.

The question of monetary policy is which monetary aggregate influence the price level, i.e. which monetary aggregate has the best correlation with the price level. **There is no satisfactory monetary aggregate that can help us find reliable and stable relation between money and the price level.** Diverse money items fit the moneyness differently. Thus central bank sets several definitions of money (monetary aggregates).

Figure 1.1 Simplified chart of monetary aggregates M0, M1 and M2 in the balance sheets of central bank and commercial banks

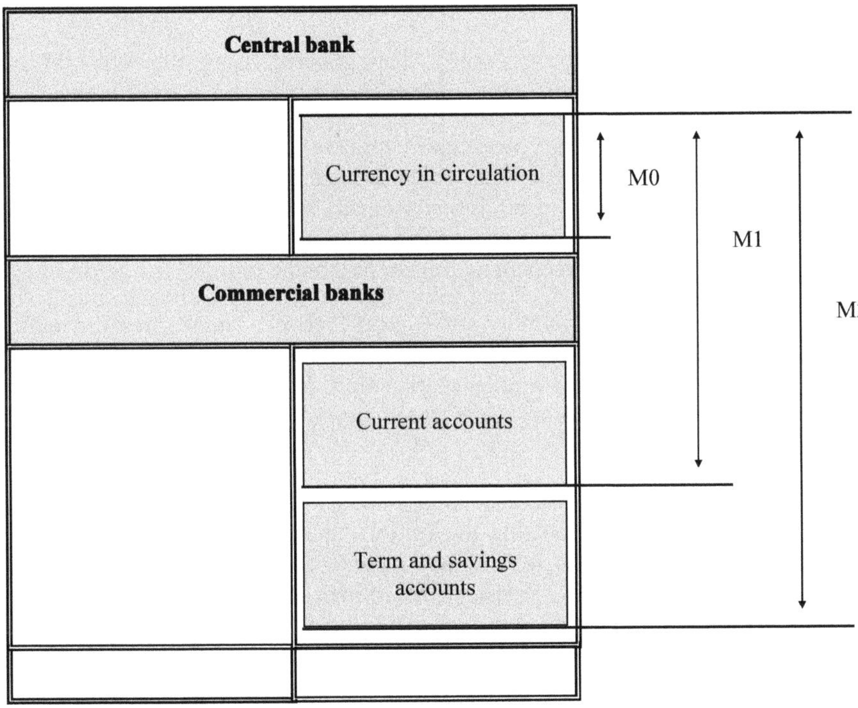

1.2 Monetary aggregates

There is no unique measure of money. The stock of money is usually measured by the **monetary aggregates**, such as M0, M1, or M2. Monetary aggregates generally cover some debts of central bank and commercial banks[4]. There are some exceptions to this rule. For example some broad monetary aggregates cover money market fund shares and units as a high degree of liquidity make these instruments close substitutes for deposits. The interbank deposits (i.e. deposits commercial bank versus commercial bank and deposits commercial bank versus central bank) are excluded from the definitions of money. It follows the fact that during the accounting consolidation of the whole banking system these deposits are cancelled. **Interbank deposits do not influence purchasing power of the public and thus price level.**

Monetary aggregates are generally characterized as follows:

- Monetary aggregates are usually distinguished using the letter M in connection with the digits ranging from 0 to 3 (sometimes even higher);
- The ranking of monetary aggregates follows the degree of liquidity, i.e. the ease and convenience with which an asset can be converted to a medium of exchange or used for payments. Lower digits correspond to higher liquidity. The aggregate marked by a higher number generally contains the whole precedent aggregate plus some of the less liquid assets;
- In some cases, the liquidity differences between aggregates are quite small. For example, the conversion from M1 to the liquid parts of broader aggregates, such as the money market unit, is very easy. These conversions take usually place when the opportunity costs of holding M1 change;
- Currency in circulation is usually denoted as M0 and it is represented by coins and banknotes outside the central bank, treasury department and commercial banks, i.e. it does not include coins and banknotes in the vaults of central bank, treasury department and commercial banks. It contains both the currency in circulation held by residents as well as by non-residents, for these two parts of currency are indistinguishable. Currency on circulation is generally regarded as liquid as deposits on current accounts;

---

4 Under the term "commercial bank" we refer in this book any financial institution which is legally allowed to accept monetary deposits from the public and government. It is "depository institutions" in the USA and "credit institutions" in Eurosystem

- Broader monetary aggregates are usually more stable than the narrow ones, for broader aggregates are less affected by the conversions between the components of money stock (such as the conversions between the current accounts and the term accounts);

- Narrow money M1 has the best correlation with the purchasing power of the public and thus with the price level. The reason is that it doesn't contain the money which is used by the public as a store of value (i.e. money that is not used for the purchases of goods and services). The broader money M2 and M3 cannot be used so easily for immediate purchases for the premature withdrawal from term accounts are usually penalized. The restrictions involve the need for advance notification, delays, penalties or fees;

- Term accounts also usually provide higher yields, which lead to their higher popularity;

- In some countries monetary aggregates (with the exception of currency in circulation) contain only financial instruments held by the country **residents**, for only this money is said to impact the domestic inflation. If we study monetary aggregates in different countries, we really observe that non-residential deposits do not make part of domestic aggregates in many countries. On the other hand in some countries (e.g. the USA) some of monetary aggregates include the deposits of domestic residents (U.S. citizens) in foreign countries; and

- Monetary aggregates in some countries can differ substantially even if they bear the same code. There are continuous changes in definitions of monetary aggregates within individual countries.

1.3 Monetary aggregates in the USA

In the United States **the Federal Reserve System** (the Fed) tracks and reports three monetary aggregates of depository institutions, i.e. commercial banks and thrift institutions (savings and loan associations, savings banks and credit unions): M0, M1 and M2 (Table 1.1).

The aggregate M1 consists of money, which is used primarily for immediate payments, that is of currency in circulation, traveler's checks, demand deposits and other checkable deposits. The Federal Reserve float is not included. The aggregate M2 consists of M1 plus savings deposits (including money market deposit accounts), small-denomination time deposits, retail money market mutual funds. Households primarily hold the M2.

Table 1.1 Monetary aggregates in the USA according to the Fed

Monetary aggregate	**Definition**
M0	o Currency outside the U.S. Treasury, Federal Reserve Banks and the vaults of depository institutions
M1	o M0 o Traveler's checks of nonbank issuers o Demand deposits at commercial banks (excluding those amounts held by depository institutions, the U.S. government, foreign banks and official institutions) less cash items in the process of collection and Federal Reserve float other checkable deposits (OCDs), consisting of negotiable order of withdrawal (NOW) and automatic transfer service (ATS) accounts at depository institutions, credit union share draft accounts, demand deposits at thrift institutions
M2	o M1 o Savings deposits (including money market deposit accounts) o Small-denomination time deposits (time deposits in amounts of less than $100,000), less individual retirement account (IRA) and Keogh balances at depository institutions o Balances in retail money market mutual funds, less IRA and Keogh balances at money market mutual funds
M3[a]	o M2 o Balances in institutional money market mutual funds o Large-denomination time deposits (time deposits in amounts of $100,000 or more) o Repurchase agreement (RP) liabilities of depository institutions, in denominations of $100,000 or more, on U.S. government and federal agency securities o Eurodollars held by U.S. addressees at foreign branches of U.S. banks worldwide and at all banking offices in the United Kingdom and Canada; large-denomination time deposits, RPs and Eurodollars exclude those amounts held by depository institutions, the U.S. government, foreign banks, official institutions and money market mutual funds
Money holders does not include US government, US and foreign depository institutions, foreign official institutions and money market mutual funds	
Nonresidents are included	

[a] Publication of the monetary aggregate M3 discontinued in March 2006.
Source: http://www.federalreserve.gov.

Till March 2006 the Fed also had published monetary aggregate M3. It was M2 plus balances in institutional money market mutual funds, large-denomination time deposits, large repurchase agreement liabilities of depository institutions on U.S. government and federal agency securities and Eurodollars held by U.S. addressees at foreign branches of U.S. banks worldwide. The reason for termination of M3 is that M3 did not appear to carry any additional information about economic activity that was not already embodied in M2, and they were not necessary for the monetary policy. According to the Fed the costs of collecting the underlying data outweighed the benefits.

1.4 Monetary aggregates in the Eurozone

The **Eurozone** is formed by 16 countries which have introduced euro as a final step of the third phase of Economic and Monetary Union (EMU), namely by Austria, Belgium, Cyprus, Finland, France, Germany, Greece, Ireland, Italy, Luxembourg, Malta, the Netherlands, Portugal, Slovakia, Slovenia and Spain. The **Eurosystem** consists of European Central Bank (ECB) and national central banks of those countries that have accepted euro. For determination of monetary aggregates the ECB uses the balance sheet of Eurosystem and the consolidated balance sheet of the so-called monetary financial institutions (MFIs). MFIs are the central banks, credit institutions and other institutions accepting deposits (and close substitutes of deposits) from non-financial institutions – residents of the EU. The number of MFIs amounts to approximately 10 000. The complete list of MFIs could be found on the website of the European Central Bank (http://www.ecb.int).

Table 1.2 Monetary aggregates in the Eurozone according to the ECB

Monetary aggregate	Definition
M0	○ Currency in circulation
M1	○ M0 ○ Overnight deposits
M2	○ M1, ○ Deposits with an agreed maturity of up to two years ○ Deposits redeemable at notice of up to three months
M3	○ M2 ○ Repurchase agreements ○ Money market fund shares and units ○ Debt securities with a maturity of up to two years
Money holders does not include central government and MFIs	
Nonresidents are excluded form money holders	

Source: http://www.ecb.int

ECB reports four monetary aggregates: M0, M1, M2 and M3 (Table 1.2). The definitions of aggregates are very simple. The aggregate M1 includes currency in circulation as well as balances which can immediately be converted into currency or used for cashless payments, i.e. overnight deposits. The aggregate M2 comprises M1 and, in addition, deposits with a maturity of up to two years and deposits redeemable at a period of notice of up to three months. The aggregate M3 covers M2, repurchase agreements, money market fund shares and units and debt securities with a maturity of up to two years issued by the MFI sector.

1.5 Monetary aggregates in Japan

Bank of Japan reports now four main monetary aggregates: M0, M1, M2 and M3 from the date of last revision in April 2008 (Table 1.3).

Table 1.3 Monetary aggregates in Japan according to the Bank of Japan

Monetary aggregate	Definition	Money issuers
M0	o Currency in circulation	
M1	o M0 o Demand deposits (current deposits, ordinary deposits, saving deposits, deposits at notice, special deposits and deposits for tax payments) less checks and notes held by financial institutions	all depository institutions (financial institutions surveyed for M2, Japan Post Bank, The Shinkumi Federation Bank, Shinkumi Banks, The Rokinren Bank, Labour Banks, Prefectural Credit Federations of Agricultural Cooperatives, Agricultural Cooperatives, Prefectural Credit Federations of Fishery Cooperatives and Fishery Coops)
M2	o M0 o Deposits	Bank of Japan, domestically licensed banks (excluding Japan Post Bank), foreign banks in Japan, Shinkin Central Bank, shinkin banks, Norinchukin Bank and Shoko Chukin Bank
M3	o M2 o Time deposits + fixed savings + installment savings + foreign currency deposits o Certificates of deposits (CDs)	the same as those of M1
Money holders does not include central government, depository institutions, insurance companies, government financial institutions, securities companies, *Tanshi* companies, etc.		
Nonresidents are excluded form money holders		

Source: http://www.boj.or.jp

It reported similar monetary aggregates: M0, M1, M2+CD and M3+CDs till then. The revision had little effect on the most widely watched monetary aggregate M2. The definitions are not so simple as in the case of the Eurozone.

The aggregate M1 consists of currency in circulation and demand deposits (current deposits, ordinary deposits, saving deposits, deposits at notice, special deposits and deposits for tax payments) less checks and notes held by financial institutions. The range of money issuers covers all depository institutions. The aggregate M2 comprises of currency in circulation and all deposits. But the range of money issuers is narrower. It consists only of Bank of Japan, domestically licensed banks (excluding Japan Post Bank), foreign banks in Japan, Shinkin Central Bank, shinkin banks, Norinchukin Bank and Shoko Chukin Bank. The aggregate M3 is composed of M2, time deposits plus fixed savings plus installment savings plus foreign currency deposits and certificates of deposits (CDs). The range of money issuers is the same as those of M1.

1.6 Monetary aggregates in the United Kingdom

The Bank of England publishes its own monetary aggregates: M0 (monetary base), retail M4 (known also as M2) and M4 (broad money) (Table 1.4) and also estimates of the Eurozone aggregates M1, M2 and M3. The relation between the UK measures and the euro-area monetary aggregates is quite complex.

The origins of M0 date back to March 1981, when it was described as the monetary base. Commercial banks' operational deposits with the Bank of England constitute a tiny component of M0. The aggregate Retail M4 comprises of non-bank and non-building society holdings of notes and coins plus sterling retail deposits with UK banks and building societies. The aggregate M4 consists of Retail M4 plus other private sector sterling interest bearing deposits at banks and building societies plus sterling certificates of deposit plus other paper issued by banks and building societies of not more than five years' original maturity.

Table 1.4 Monetary aggregates in the United Kingdom according to the Bank of England

Monetary aggregate	Definition
M0	○ Sterling notes and coin in circulation outside the Bank of England (including those held in banks' and building societies' tills) ○ Banks' operational deposits with the Bank of England
Retail M4 (M2)	○ Non-bank and non-building society holdings of notes and coins, ○ Sterling retail deposits with UK banks and building societies
M4	○ Retail M4 ○ Other private sector sterling interest bearing deposits at banks and building societies ○ Sterling certificates of deposit ○ Other paper issued by banks and building societies of not more than five years' original maturity
Money holders does not include central government, banks and building societies, public corporations and local government	
Nonresidents are excluded form money holders	

Source: http://www.bankofengland.co.uk

2 Creation and Extinction of Money I

In this and the next sections, we will explain the fundamental principle of the contemporary banking system. Without the perfect knowledge of this principle, we will not be able to understand correctly the modern monetary policy. The synonymous terms for "creation and extinction of money" are the terms "issue and redemption of money". We will also mention payment operations (even if it is a topic of a separate chapter), issue of debt and equity securities, and flow of money as a result of cross-border investments.

2.1 Where, how and when does the money create and become extinct

The importance of this question is extremely high. We have already seen that the core of modern money transactions takes the form of book entries. The **explanation of money creation must start with accounting money and not with currency.** In order to make the understanding of money creation easier, let us suppose that all currency is deposited with commercial banks and commercial banks have transferred this currency to their clearing accounts with central bank. To put it another way, all payments take the form of transfers between bank accounts. This is a realistic assumption since currently most of the money transactions are settled through current accounts, i.e. without currency. The questions are: where, how and when does the money create and become extinct?

First, let us answer the question **"where does the creation and extinction of money take place"? Money both originates and ends in commercial banks in the form of accounting money**. Only after creation of accounting money, it can be converted into currency. Money originates only as accounting money.

Our second question is "**how does the money create, and how does it become extinct**"? There is no need for production of goods and rendering of services when the money is created or extinct.

The money creates in commercial banks through:

- Loans granted by banks to non-bank entities;
- Interest paid on deposits and other liabilities of banks (e.g. debt securities) to non-bank entities;
- Assets (debt and equity securities, tangible and intangible assets etc.) and services purchased by banks from non-bank entities;

- Wages and salaries paid to bank employees, management and statutory individuals; and
- Dividends and royalties paid by banks.

These operations will be described in following subsections. As we will see, the money does not originate because of foreign investments if we consider consolidated money stock of both countries. The majority of money originates by means of loans. The remaining four sources of money creation are not generally considered to be substantial. Commercial banks thus generate money from nothing. Central bank is trying to influence the loan activity of commercial banks, and in this way it indirectly controls the quantity of money stock in some extent. It does it through the regulation of interest rates, and it cannot do anything else. Herein the true alchemy of modern money lies.

The money becomes extinct in commercial banks through:

- Repayments of loans (including interest) to banks by non-bank entities;
- Sale of assets (debt and equity securities, tangible and intangible assets etc.) by banks to non-bank entities; and
- Issue of own equity and debt securities by banks to non-bank entities.

The majority of money becomes extinct by means of loans repayments.

There are three relations between money creation and money extinction:

- Money creation exceeds money extinction. In this case broad monetary aggregates (e.g. M2) increases over time;
- Money creation equals money extinction. In this case broad monetary aggregates (e.g. M2) is constant over time; and
- Money extinction exceeds money creation. In this case broad monetary aggregates (e.g. M2) decline over time.

Money is always denominated in a certain currency (e.g. dollar, euro, yen and pound) and the same holds for newly created money. Commercial banks can create money **denominated in whatever currency**. For instance, any U.S. bank can issue loans denominated not only in U.S. dollars but also in euros, yens, pounds etc. Commercial banks do not have to issue only loans in domestic currency but also loans in currency of any other country. Similarly, a commercial bank can use whatever currency for paying of interests, wages, salaries, dividends and royalties, as well as for purchasing assets.

Not only commercial banks grant loans, purchase assets, and pay out wages, salaries, dividends and royalties. Non-bank entities perform all of these activities as well. However, non-bank entities do not create money. Current definitions of money thus do not contain all debt relationships. Non-bank entities can never spend more than the actual balance of their bank accounts. On the contrary, **commercial banks can provide loans, pay interests, wages, salaries, dividends and royalties and purchase assets virtually without any limit.** In all of these transactions, commercial banks credit accounts of its partners.

The creation and extinction of money takes place solely because of transaction **between commercial banks and its clients** and not because of transactions between banks. If a bank grants a loan to another bank, and it consequently charges interests on it, or if it purchases assets from another bank, or it pays dividends to another bank, there is no impact on the aggregate stock of money, i.e. no additional money is created. Similarly, money does not cease to exist when one bank repays loan or if it sells assets to another bank or pays dividends to another bank. Similarly, money does not arise in any transaction between a commercial bank and the central bank (e.g. when central bank buys the foreign currency from commercial bank). Interbank transactions affect liquidity. This fact results from the current definition of money.

Furthermore, money is not created or extinct in the course of transaction (payment) between clients of one commercial bank as well as in the course of transactions (payment) between clients of two different commercial banks. The exception is when a transaction takes place between a resident and a non-resident. Such transaction influences monetary aggregates. To put it another way, money is created when the bank credits the account of its client in absence of operation debiting other client's account operated by the same bank (this would be an example of the intra-bank transaction) or by any other bank (this would represent the interbank transaction). Therefore, money is not generally created when one client receives payment from another one.

The creation of money corresponds mainly to the loan expansion and not to the coinage or to the printing of notes. The money is created because of every newly granted loan or every purchase of any asset from bank client or every payment of interest, wage, salary, dividend or royalty by a bank. In each of this case, the overall balance of the current accounts rises, i.e. the money stock rises.

This reality corresponds to the commonly used accounting principles. The accounting of the former mentioned operations differs substantially in the case of banks and non-bank entities. In the course of money creation operations (e.g. granting loans), the bank credits the account of its client. In the course of the reverse operations, the bank debits the account of its client. In banks, these operations result in entries in both asset and liabilities side of the balance sheet i.e., newly granted loans increase both assets and liabilities at the same time. In the accounting of non-bank entities, these operations affect only the structure of assets. This is the only (even if considerable) difference between the accounting of banks and non-bank entities.

At this moment, we have only one question left. **When does the creation and extinction of money take place?** Our answer is very simple. Money originates at the same time when the bank adds a specific amount of money (e.g. the amount of loan) to its client's accounts. Similarly, money becomes extinct at the moment when reverse operations take place.

Issue of money was never under the direct control of central bank. Central bank has never possessed the issue monopoly. Central bank has solely the monopoly to issue the currency for commercial banks in exchange for the liquidity of commercial banks (in some countries, e.g. in the USA, the monopoly right to issue coins lies in the hands of the Department of the Treasury). Central bank issues new money only as far as it operates as a commercial bank (e.g. when central bank grants loans to non-bank entities).

Central bank has neither the quantity of currency nor the quantity of accounting money under direct control. Even if t**he issue monopoly of currency is usually held by central bank, central bank cannot influence the quantity of currency (including currency in circulation). Central bank can influence the amount of accounting money through the credit channel of monetary policy transmission mechanism by increasing or decreasing interest rates.**

If some commercial bank anticipates increasing withdrawals of currency by its clients, it simply purchases currency from central bank in exchange for its liquidity with central bank. Liquidity with central bank represents the balance of clearing accounts that commercial bank holds with central bank. Hence, the quantity of currency can never be set by central bank, but exclusively by the demand of clients of commercial banks. Because currency does not bear interest, most agents minimize their holdings of currency. Agents prefer other financial or real assets in exchange for currency because the income from holding other financial assets or real assets as well as from production of goods and rendering of services is usually positive.

2.2 Loans granted by banks to non-bank entities

2.2.1 Principles of money creation through loans

We commence this part by reviewing the basic difference between accounting of banks and non-bank entities. Let us start with Example 2.1 where a non-bank entity (let us call it A) grants a loan to another non-bank entity (B). In this case, money is not created. The unit A simply transforms one of its assets (sum on its current account of $1,000) to another asset (loans granted of $1,000). The total assets of unit A do not change.

On the contrary, when in Example 2.2 bank grants a loan to its client (non-bank entity) then the bank's total assets increase by the loaned amount. The bank creates both the completely new asset (loans granted of $1,000) and the new liability (deposit on client's current account of $1,000). In other words, bank debits the account "loans granted" and credits the "current account".

Example 2.1 Non-bank entity grants a loan to non-bank entity

1) Non-bank entity A grants a loan of $1,000 to non-bank entity B

Non-bank entity A granting a loan

Current account with bank

Initial balance	1) $1,000

Loans granted

1) $1,000	

Non-bank entity B accepting a loan

Current account with bank

1) $1,000	

Loans accepted

	1) $1,000

Example 2.2 Bank grants a loan to its client (non-bank entity)

1) The bank grants a loan of $1,000 to its client

Bank granting a loan

Loans granted		Client's current account	
1) $1,000			1) $1,000

Client accepting a loan

Current account with bank		Loans accepted	
1) $1,000			1) $1,000

Creation of money by granting loans is in any case followed by the next step, when client makes payment by:

- Transfer of money from its current account to the current account of another client of the same bank or to current account of the another client of another bank through some payment system or through correspondent banking; or

- Withdrawal of coins or banknotes from its current account with subsequent transfer of coins or banknotes to some non-bank entity.

Without this payment there would be no reason for granting a loan.

The fundamental difference between granting loans by non-bank entities and by banks follows from the definition of money. Money originates in banks mainly as a result of their loan activities. As we shall see later, this fundamental principle has many theoretical and practical consequences. **For loans create money (deposits),** direction of this causality is more than clear. At the same time when the non-bank entity receives the loan, it receives the money on its current account. This is the moment when the non-bank entity can start using newly created money. Every new loan granted by a bank to a non-bank entity of some amount represents the creation of new money of the same amount. This simple fact was well described already by Knut Wicksell in 1898[5] and Hartley Withers in 1909[6].

Thus every loan represents for the bank one accounting operation, namely the occurrence of claim on the asset side against creation of money (on the client's current account) on a liability side of the bank's balance sheet. Similarly, on the client's balance sheet, new loan represents one accounting operations, namely the money on the current account (claim on the bank) on the asset side and the acceptance of loan on the liabilities side (payables to the bank).

There are many bank loans by many banks and subsequent payments in the banking system. If some commercial bank expands more in loans than in deposits (i.e. it observes the outflow of deposits to other banks), it must fill up the difference by accepting loans or deposits at the interbank market. In such a case, there is certainly another commercial bank which is expanding more in deposits than in loans (such a bank is attractive for depositors) and which can grant loans or deposits to other banks on interbank market.

The ability of commercial banks to create money is endless, i.e. the resources of any bank are unlimited. Loan expansion can never reach its end. Let's see the current development of monetary aggregates in the USA, the Eurozone, Japan and the United Kingdom. It is solely the decision of any commercial bank how much money it creates. Every newly granted loan increases both the assets and liabilities in the amount of loan granted (Figure 2.1). Money is created of the same amount. The same amount is added to assets and liabilities of non-bank entities.

Nevertheless, the loan expansion stops any moment somewhere. Commercial banks grant loans primarily to clients with the highest credit rating, e.g. to corporates with the AAA rating. Subsequently, they grant loans to clients with lower rating (AA) and so forth. Figure 2.2 shows that the loan expansion is in any moment constrained, for example to loans to clients with rating down to B. Naturally, the risk aversion of some banks might be stronger. Such banks refuse to grant loans already to BBB or BB clients.

---

5 Wicksell, Knut: *Interest and Prices*. Kelley, New York 1898.
6 Withers, Hartley: *The Meaning of Money*. Smith and Elder, London 1909.

Figure 2.1 New loans and new deposits

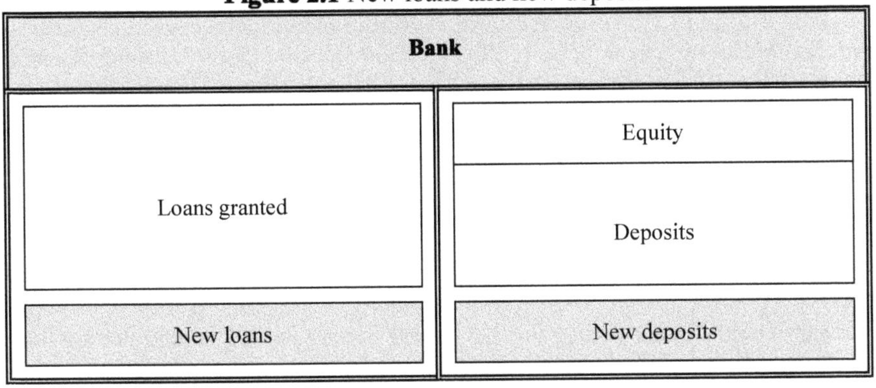

Figure 2.2 Loan expansion constraints

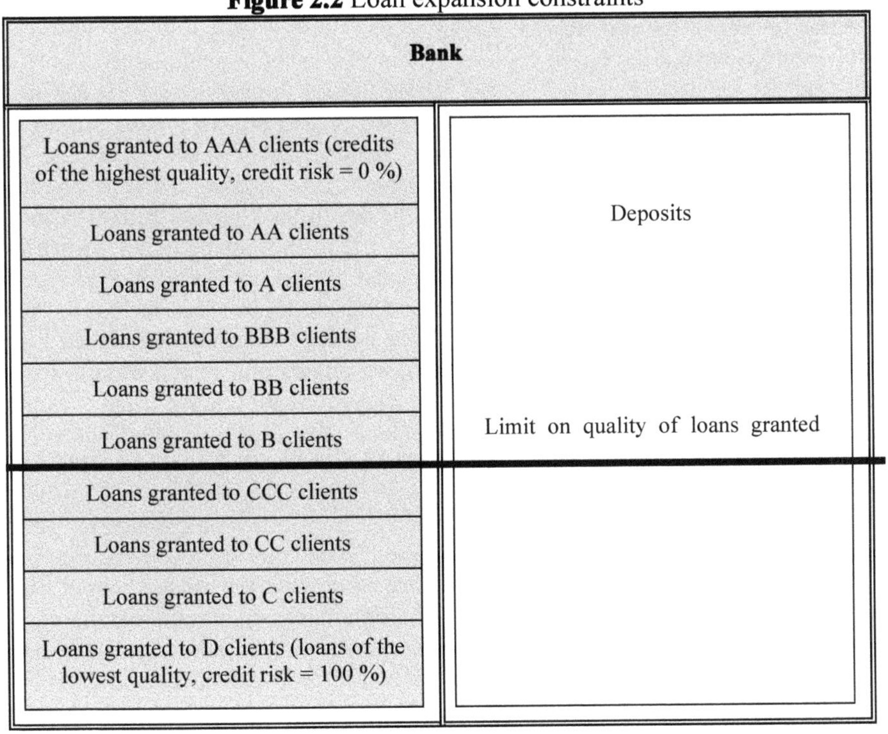

On the contrary, some banks follow relaxed loan policy and they grant loans even to CCC and CC clients. It is only up to the individual commercial bank to estimate correctly whom it is willing to lend money. Only the bank decides which economic activity guarantees high probability of repayment of the loan. We shall see later that central bank can influence the loan activity of commercial banks by means of short-term interest rates regulation.

Commercial banks make loans in order to maximize their profits. If commercial banks were granting loans only to their best clients, they wouldn't reach the maximum profit possible. Loans to the best clients yield low interest for such loans are granted for approximately interbank interest rate. On the other hand, loans granted to less credible clients entail higher credit risk and higher interest rate (exceeding interbank market interest rate). Higher interest rates generate higher income. But at the same time, commercial banks granting risky loans are forced to create higher amount of allowances, since there is a higher probability of debtors' default. Theory of loans assumes that **interest income higher than interest income corresponding to the interbank interest rate should be more or less balanced by allowances**. It is up to individual bank to evaluate properly individual client's risks and to decide whether yes or not to grant a loan.

In order to make the best loans possible (in terms of credit risk), banks compete for credible clients (borrowers). Business history of these clients should be transparent. Is is supposed that credible clients will be willing and able to repay their debts. However, there are a limited number of such clients and an infinite number of non credible clients. Non credible clients will not be either willing or able to repay their debts. Among them, related parties are considered to represent the worst ones, hence the rule "never lend money to your friends." Thus even if theoretically the amount of loans that banks can grant is unlimited, in practice, however, it is limited by their credit risk aversion. Default of high-risky clients is highly probable. Loans to clients with lower ratings are dangerous not only to individual banks but also to the banking system as a whole. Bank regulation should try to prevent banks from granting such loans.

Evolution of the loan development is cyclical, i.e. it follows the business cycle. During the period of recovery and expansion, banks are more optimistic, and grant, therefore, more loans. The importance of credit risk management is suppressed. Conversely, during the time of recession, banks must write-off the loans granted during the recovery and expansion. Recession is also the time when banks grant fewer loans, and the importance of credit risk management rises. This rule holds regardless of the fact that credit officers are paid both for quality and quantity of loans. The competitive environment forces them to increase their market share.

We have seen already that every newly granted loan constitutes for the bank and for the non-bank entity a simultaneous increase of both assets and liabilities. To put it another way, creation of asset and creation of liability represents for the bank and for the non-bank entity two inseparable processes. From the point of view of the bank the amount granted is added to client's current account. Following payment from this account represents solely the reduction of payer's current account balance and an increase of recipient's current account balance. **Payments between current accounts do not change the aggregate money stock (aggregate quantity of money), i.e. payments do not change the aggregate balance of deposits.** This holds for payments both through the clearing systems (clearinghouses) and through the correspondence banking systems. Clearinghouses have evolved to meet requirements of modern banking systems in order to facilitate payments. Clearing centers can be organized and operated (but not necessarily) by central banks.

2.2.2 Primary and secondary allocation of money

At this moment we have necessary information to answer the question: "Why do banks exist?" Banks decide whom they will grant loans, i.e. who will get the chance to start new business or to follow the current bsiness, and who will not get such a chance. In order to maximize their profits, banks grant loans only to those entities which convince them that their plans are realistic, and that they will be able to repay debts. This will be the case of entities who intend producing saleable products or services. The ultimate decision about products and services to be produced will be taken by the market anyway. By deciding whom to grant loans banks realize the **primary money allocation to entities (households, enterprises and government)**. Banks do exist to stimulate economic activity of households, enterprises and government.

Secondary allocation of money (i.e. the allocation of money created through primary allocation) takes place on the money and capital markets, where enterprises try to attract investors possessing enough money in banks (created as a result of primary allocation of money). Some investors provide this money (deposits) for a definite period of time (in the form of debt securities like bonds, notes or bills) or for an indefinite period of time (in the form of equity securities – shares). Investors expect enterprises to produce goods and services that they will get paid for. This will allow enterprises to repay the principal plus interests or to pay dividends. Investors take these steps since they expect income exceeding the risk-free interest (e.g. interest paid on government securities). This is also the case of entrepreneurs who employ their own savings. Secondary allocation of money (i.e. the issue of debt and equity securities) does not influence the money stock. Some countries (e.g. the United States) heavily rely on secondary allocation of money through capital market.

The market-oriented economy thus creates a really ingenious system in which many agents are concerned in decisions about funding of production of goods and services. It follows the natural human desire for wealth. Financial environment determines economic activity. This is what differentiates market-oriented economy from the centrally planned one.

The analysis clearly demonstrates that banks are not financial intermediaries. Loans represent the bilateral relation between the bank and its client and not trilateral relation through intermediary.

2.2.3 Impaired loans

There is one critical factor discouraging banks from granting whatever amount of loans. It is **credit risk** of the borrower – risk of impairment (loss) caused by the borrower's default, i.e. failure in meeting her obligation imposed by the contract. If the loan gets impaired, the bank has to account for loss due to impairment (directly of through the allowance account). Example (2.3) demonstrates the successive creation of allowances (of the amount of $200 and $800) of a loan of $1,000. The loan was completely written off since the client did not repay even a part of the principal. In this case the total loss of the bank equals the whole amount of $1,000 (in fact, the loss is even higher because of accumulated interests).

If the loan is repaid, only the accrued interest is recorded in the income statement (as income), whereas in the case of default, the whole amount of outstanding loan is recorded in the income statement (as expense). It is evident that the impairment loss of loans can cause severe losses of bank and in extreme case even bankruptcy of the bank (as long as the bank is not saved using money of taxpayers). If this is a case of more banks in one country, there is banking crisis.

Loan allowance equals the reduction of the value of the loan by reason of increased credit risk of the borrower. This means that a **loan is not depreciated due to the movement in risk-free interest rate (yield curve)**. Therefore, entities do not account for allowances for debt instruments issued by state and central banks in OECD countries.

The initial amount granted P_0 equals the sum of discounted cash flows C_i using the original risk yield to maturity (i.e. effective interest rate) ${}_0r$ that equals zero-risk yield to maturity ${}_{b,0}r$ plus the risk premium ${}_0\Delta r$ associated with the borrower:

Example 2.3 Successive creation of loan allowances

1) Bank grants a credit of $1,000 to its client
2) Bank creates the first allowance amounting to $200
3) Bank creates the second allowance amounting to $800
4) Bank writes the credit off

Bank granting a loan

Loans granted

1) $1,000	4) $1,000

Client's current account

	1) $1,000

Allowances

4) $1000	2) $200 3) $800

Impairment loss

2) $200 3) $800	

$$P_0 = \sum_{i=1}^{n} \frac{C_i}{(1+{}_0r)^{t_i}} = \sum_{i=1}^{n} \frac{C_i}{(1+{}_{b,0}r+{}_0\Delta r)^{t_i}}$$

The increased risk of borrower's default (within the length of contract) can be expressed by two different methods.

The **first method** is based on discounting the nominal values of cash flows C_i using the enhanced risk premium from ${}_0\Delta r$ to ${}_1\Delta r$. Thus the impairment loss (allowance) is the difference between P_a and P_b:

$$allowance = P_a - P_b = P_a - \sum_{i=1}^{n} \frac{C_i}{(1+{}_{b,0}r+{}_1\Delta r)^{t_i}}$$

P_a stands for the initial loan amount granted P_0 increased by the accrued interest (using the effective interest method) and decreased by loan repayments. P_b stands for the sum of nominal cash flows C_i discounted using the new risk yield to maturity ${}_1r$ that is zero-risk yield to maturity ${}_{b,0}r$ plus the new (higher) risk premium ${}_1\Delta r$ associated with the borrower.

In the **second method** the estimates of future cash flows $C_{i,e}$ are discounted by the original risk yield to maturity (i.e. effective interest rate) ${}_0r$ that equals zero-risk yield to maturity ${}_{b,0}r$ plus the risk premium ${}_0\Delta r$ associated with the borrower and thus receiving P_c. Then the impairment loss (allowance) is the difference between P_a and P_c:

$$allowance = P_a - P_c = P_a - \sum_{i=1}^{n} \frac{C_{i,e}}{\left(1 + {}_{b,0}r + {}_0\Delta r\right)^{t_i}}$$

Both methods should result in the same amount of allowance.

Let us take the following example. Bank granted a loan of $1,000,000 with the three yearly annuity payments of $381,748. The one-year zero-risk interest rate equals ${}_{b,0}r_{0,1} = 3.50\%$, two-years zero-risk interest rate equals ${}_{b,0}r_{0,2} = 3.82\%$, and three-years zero-risk interest rate equals ${}_{b,0}r_{0,3} = 4.11\%$. The yield to maturity of a loan (i.e. the effective interest rate) is ${}_0r = 7.10\%$, since:

$$\$1,000,000 = \frac{\$381,748}{1+r} + \frac{\$381,748}{(1+r)^2} + \frac{\$381,748}{(1+r)^3}$$

Whence ${}_br = 7.10\%$.

If the loan with the same annuity of $381,748 was granted to a zero-risk entity, the amount of loan granted would be $1,061,309, since:

$$\frac{\$381,748}{1+0.0350} + \frac{\$381,748}{(1+0.0382)^2} + \frac{\$381,748}{(1+0.0411)^3} = \$1,061,309$$

The zero-risk yield to maturity (the zero-risk effective interest rate) ${}_{b,0}r$ would thus equal 3.90%, since:

$$\$1,061,309 = \frac{\$381,748}{1+{}_br} + \frac{\$381,748}{(1+{}_br)^2} + \frac{\$381,748}{(1+{}_br)^3}$$

Whence ${}_br = 3.90\%$.

This means that the original risk premium ${}_0\Delta r$ of the borrower equals 3.20% (= 7.10% − 3.90%).

Alternatively, we can calculate the original risk premium ${}_0\Delta r$ of the borrower in the following way:

$$\$1{,}000{,}000 = \frac{\$381{,}748}{1+0.0350+{}_0\Delta r} + \frac{\$381{,}748}{(1+0.0382+{}_0\Delta r)^2} + \frac{\$381{,}748}{(1+0.0411+{}_0\Delta r)^3}$$

Whence ${}_0\Delta r = 3.20\%$.

Let the one-year zero-risk interest rate after one year equal ${}_{b,1}r_{0,1} = 4.50\%$, and two-years zero-risk interest rate equal ${}_{b,0}r_{0,2} = 4.82\%$. The current risk premium of the borrower exceeds the original one and reach ${}_1\Delta r = 5.2\%$ (e.g. the borrower's financial situation has worsen). Under the effective interest rate method, the loan value after one year (right after the first repayment) is $689,252, since:

$$\frac{\$381{,}748}{1+0.0710} + \frac{\$381{,}748}{(1+0.0710)^2} = \$689{,}252$$

The loan value, considering the higher risk premium and original zero-risk yield to maturity, is $670,627, since:

$$\frac{\$381{,}748}{1+0.0390+0.0520} + \frac{\$381{,}748}{(1+0.0390+0.0520)^2} = \$670{,}627$$

Using **the first method** the allowance equals $18,625 (i.e. 2.7% of the accounting value), since:

$$\text{Allowances} = \$689{,}252 - \$670{,}627 = \$18{,}625$$

The fair value of a loan is $663,372, since:

$$\frac{\$381{,}748}{1+0.0450+0.0520} + \frac{\$381{,}748}{(1+0.0482+0.0520)^2} = \$663{,}372$$

It is necessary to highlight that **loan allowance** can not be assessed as the difference between the loan value (under the effective interest rate method) and fair value of the loan, but the difference between the loan value (under the effective interest rate method) and discounted value of cash flows calculated using the new risk yield to maturity, which equals the original zero-risk yield to maturity plus the increased risk premium associated to borrower.

Alternatively, allowances can be assessed using the estimated cash flows. In such a case, cash flows are discounted by the original risk yield to maturity. For example, we can estimate the reduction of first repayment from the nominal value of \$381,748 to \$380,000 (i.e. the decrease by 0.5%) and a reduction of second repayment from the nominal value of \$381,748 to \$362,257 (i.e. the decrease by 5.1%). The value of loan hence equals \$670,627, since:

$$\frac{\$380,000}{1+0.0710}+\frac{\$380,000}{(1+0.0710)^2}=\$670,627$$

Using **the second method** allowance equals \$18,625.

The first method of assessing allowances is based on the estimate of the risk premium, and the second method is based on the estimate of future cash flows. However, both of these values are hard to estimate. The allowance value depends on several factors such as default in payments, financial situation of the borrower and others. Bank regulation in individual countries may set specific rules on loan allowances. Regulators may impose the allowances computed as a percentage of the unsecured value of the loan.

2.2.4 Corporate loans

The nature of loan contract implies that bank cannot control activities of an entity to which it has lent money. Enterpreise thus has to:

- Convince the bank of her project's profitability and ability to run their business in a way capable of repaying the loan;
- Be ready to share costs of a potential business failure;
- Provide adequate security.

Most corporate projects do not fit the conditions for bank financing. The quality of the majority of proposed projects is not high enough, and financing of them would pose high risks to the banks. Many of corporates who apply for loans are hardly indebted or characterized by low equity and insufficient labour productivity. Hence, the profitability of these entities would be too low to ensure smooth and full repayments. Usually, opinions on the quality of proposed project differ substantially from the bank and from the corporates point of view.

Some corporates believe that it is enough to have a:

- Splendid business idea;
- Excellent technology or industrial capacity to carry out the project;
- Not binding confirmations of potential processor of delivered goods and services;
- Estimates of future development based on unreasonably optimistic numbers.

Some projects can be designed in a way that even small changes of input prices or demand would cause severe losses and thus inability to repay loans. Such projects do not fit standards of prudent financing. Applicants for a loan sometimes highlight benefits that the project would represent to regional employment.

Conversely, banks must require reasonable demand for delivered goods and services, measures against unpredictable decrease in demand and changes of input prices, sound history of both company and its management, documented competence of managers, market research and so forth. Success of corporate operations depends primarily on abilities of its management. The project financing represents one of special kinds of corporate loans, whose repayments come only from returns of the established capacity.

In order to lower or transfer credit risk, banks often require **credit risk mitigation instruments**. They demand guarantees or collateral (financial collateral, real estate etc.) or they use credit derivatives. However, such instruments create new risks, such as legal risk. The key feature of any instrument is its legal enforceability in any relevant legal system.

2.2.5 Household loans

Household loans represent mainly consumer loans, mortgage loans, credit cards and overdrafts. Banks evaluate their clients using diverse systems of credit scoring. These systems are continuously recalibrated based on the new loan observations. A process of granting loans to households is based on a complex survey of number of parameters. This holds practically for any kind of loans, even for loans that can be granted immediately.

Consumer loan is intended for households who can use it to purchase consumer goods. Non-bank entities can offer it as well. The massive increase of consumer loans occurs worldwide.

Mortgage loan represents the loan granted for the purpose of purchase of real estate. Repayment of such a loan is secured by the mortgage right.

Credit card is the payment card indicating that its holder is allowed to draw a loan. Holder of credit card can purchase goods and services or draw money up to a certain limit (credit line). Such a loan can be repaid partly or fully before the end of interest-free period. Interest rates, yearly fees and terms of maturity differ substantially among issuers. The major disadvantage of credit card is the high interest charged on the amount of a loan drawn. The credit line is frequently related to the month salary and to the credit scoring.

The main advantage of the bank credit card lies in the interest-free period, usually lasting from 30 to 45 days and starting at the date of purchase. During the interest-free period borrower can repay his debt without any additional interest. Such an option thus represents to credit card holder the advantageous access to a free short-term loan. The interest-free period applies only to payments and not to ATM withdrawals. Interest on withdrawal is charged immediately. Credit cards are also usually connected to some of international payment systems (e.g. Visa or MasterCard).

Banks compete to attract more households. However, the massive rise of these loans represents serious danger for the whole economy. It engangers banks especially in a moment when the economy starts to slow down. In the boom banks do not take these risks seriously. As long as households receive regular incomes, they are capable of repaying their debts. However, as soon as the economy slows down and people start loosing their jobs, banks start to face serious problems.

2.2.6 Finance lease

Corporate and household loans can be granted also in the form of a lease. Banks usually do not grant these loans directly but through their subsidiaries (controlled and financed by banks). International Financial Reporting Standards (IFRS) define **lease** as an agreement whereby the lessor conveys to the lessee in return for a payment or series of payments the right to use an asset for an agreed period of time. There are two basic kinds of a lease, namely the financial lease and operating lease. **Finance (capital) lease** is a lease that transfers substantially all the risks and rewards incidental to ownership of an asset. Title may or may not eventually be transferred. All other kinds of a lease represent the **operating lease**. Classification of a lease does not depend on the legal form of a contract.

According to Generally Accepted Accounting Principles of the United States (US GAAP), lease shall be considered as finance lease if it meets at least one of the following four criteria:

- The lease transfers ownership of the property to the lessee by the end of the lease term;
- The lease contains a bargain purchase option;
- The lease term is equal to 75 % or more of the estimated economic life of the leased property; or
- The present value of at the beginning of the lease term of the minimum lease payments equals or exceeds 90 % of the excess of the fair value of the leased property to the lessor at the inception of the lease.

In substance the finance lease is considered a loan granted by lessor to lessee and the asset is regarded as collateral. From the point of view of the lessee the asset is recorded on the asset side against to liabilities.

In the case of **operating lease** the lessor books received payments uniformly as income and the lessee books provided payments uniformly as expenses.

Sale and leaseback stands for the sale of an asset and the leasing back of the same asset. The lease payment and the asset sale price are usually interdependent because they are negotiated as a package.

2.2.7 Legal environment

Legal environment represents one of the key features determining the loan granting process. Banks can grant loans more easily in countries where the legal system provides good protection of creditors. On the contrary, if the legal environment allows obligors avoiding successfully fulfillment of their obligations, banks will be granting loans much more carefully.

2.2.8 External credit rating

Corporate credit risk rating represents a very complicated process. Professional investors seek, therefore, to find the way to simplify it. In contrast to Europe, The United States relies substantially on the financing through capital market. That is the reason for the expansion of specialized companies offering the external credit rating services of individual debt instruments, companies and countries. Among the most popular rating agencies are Standard & Poor's, Moody's, FitchIBCA, Duff & Phelps and Thomson Financial BankWatch.

Credit rating assesses the probability that the debt will not be repaid or the probability of the default of some debt, company or country. But rating agencies do not use probability of default but rather some systems of symbols. It seems politically sensitive if S&P have announced, for instance “The probability of country X’s bankruptcy within the next five years is 3.88%“. Probability of default varies depending on actual world economic conditions, political changes and so forth. The interpretation of a downgraded rating is very easy: rating agency concluded that the probability of insolvency of a debt, company or country has increased.

Agencies evaluate some **debt issues, companies, government agencies, local governments and central governments (countries).** Financial experts and commentators often use ratings as indicators of the creditworthiness of debt issuers rather than indicators of the quality of the debt instruments themselves. This is reasonable because it is rare for two different debt instruments issued by the same company to have different ratings. Indeed, when rating agencies announce ratings they often refer to companies, not individual bond issues.

Corporate rating is based on company’s size, relative value of debt to business activity and profits. Rating agencies consider also other features of rather qualitative substance. They weight individual indicators differently. For example, Moody’s accentuates the issuer’s overall debt burden and cash flows, while Standard & Poor’s concentrates on issuer’s business environment. Such differences result in different ratings. In the United States, rating agencies currently evaluate approximately eight thousands of non-bank institutions (among which about five hundreds obtained rating equal or better than AA–), while in Europe agencies evaluate only six hundreds institutions (among which about eighty obtained rating equal or better than AA–). Long-term rating accentuate profitability and business sector and short-term ratings emphasize solvency.

To evaluate **debts** rating agencies consider the type of security, seniority in the case of default and limits for further debts. Debt rating is related to a particular debt and not solely to the issuing company. One company can, therefore, issue several debts of different ratings. This allows company to raise funds for riskier projects. What matters is the correct interpretation of a rating. Credit rating does not reflect market prices, expected income, or investor’s risk preferences. It evaluates solely the default risk of a debt. Ratings of debt instruments do not represent recommendation to buy or sell securities. Leading agencies evaluate securities by type of issuer and by political stability. Ratings from renowned agencies are usually very expensive. However, institutional investors looking for high rated securities in their portfolios require it. Nowadays, credit rating represents necessary condition to attract key investors.

Standard & Poor's (S&P) evaluates certain debts, companies, government agencies, local governments and countries based on current borrower's credibility (including guarantees and insurance). It assesses risk of default that might occur at any time from now until the date of maturity. It takes into account probabilities of all future events. S&P's rating is based on:

- Probability of default (regarding borrower's capacity to repay both principal and interest in a full amount and in time);
- Essentials of the debt instrument; and
- Legal and contractual protection of creditor including its relative position in the case of borrower's bankruptcy. This protection follows from the local bankruptcy law and from other legal regulations.

To indicate the probability of default, S&P uses rating of the borrower's senior debt. If there is no such debt, S&P derives the rating implicitly. Subordinated debts usually obtain lower ratings than senior debts. This practice reflects the relatively better enforceability of senior debts in the case of bankruptcy. When corporate issues substantial amount of secured debt, its unsecured debt is rated closed to the rating of subordinated debts.

The best rating of S&P is AAA. Financial instruments with this rating are considered to have almost no probability of default in the near future. The next rating is AA. After that come A, BBB, BB, B and CCC. The Moody's ratings corresponding to S&P' AAA, AA, A, BBB, BB, B and CCC are Aaa, Aa, A, Baa, Ba, B and Caa respectively. To create finer rating categories S&P' divides its AA category into AA+, AA and AA– and its A category into A+, A, and A– etc. Similarly Moody's divides its Aa category into Aa1, Aa2 and Aa3, and its A into A1, A2 and A3 etc. Only the S&P AAA and Moody's Aaa categories are further divided.

Rating categories from AAA to BBB– (S&P) and from Aaa to Baa3 (Moody's) are referred to as **investment grades**. Originally rating agencies were using this term only to indicate bonds suitable for investment of banks and insurance companies. Ratings below BBB– (S&P) and below Baa3 (Moody's) are considered to represent **speculative grades**. These debts can have quality collateral. However, uncertainties (about what can happen in the case of exposition to negative conditions) outweigh any collateral. The commonly used term "junk bonds" corresponds approximately to speculative grades.

If the real or implicit rating of senior debt is AAA, subordinated and junior debts are rated AAA or AA+. If the real or implicit rating of senior debt is lower than

AAA but higher than BB+, subordinated and junior debts are rated one grade lower. If, for example, rating of senior debt is A, subordinate debt is usually rated A–. If the real or implicit rating of senior debt is or lower than BB+, subordinated and junior debts are rated two grades lower.

S&P also evaluates **short-term debts** (debts with original maturity of up to 365 days, including commercial papers) by estimating probability of proper repayment. Short-term rating consists of categories from A–1 to D.

2.2.9 Internal credit rating

In a majority of loan contracts, creditors (especially banks) need to rely on their own internal ratings. In banks, responsibility for internal ratings lies in the hands of credit officers. They try to identify all relevant criteria on borrower's credibility. However, there are no standard criteria generally applicable to all clients. Individual criteria are weighted, but the weights assigned cannot be easily standardized. At the end of credit rating process, creditor adds up the weighted criteria and gets one single number. Although this technique looks easily understandable and readily applicable, it is characterized by considerable subjective evaluation of loan officers. Their decisions are unique and unrepeatable by any other persons.

In the case of companies, loan officers evaluate for example the industry characteristics, company characteristics, management, historical earnings, financial conditions, plans and prospects. Each characteristic has its own risk weight. They can also use the international scoring sheet designed for loans granted to client from foreign countries. In this case, ratings are based particularly on classification of projects alone for such clients do not usually have any history. Officers should also consider sovereign risk and currency risk, i.e. borrower's capacity to repay debts denominated in a specific currency.

Credit scoring is used to rate and monitor individuals before and after the loan is granted. It usually consists in static analysis of current and former clients. The process of credit scoring is analogous to the internal credit ratings of companies. First, creditor sets relevant criteria, and consequently it weights them. Among the main criteria are: age, sex, marital status, number of children, length of current employment and the length of current contract. One can observe that creditors usually ascribe higher credibility to women than men. Consequently, loan officers add up all weighted criteria and he gets one single number. Scoring and weighting of individual criteria depends on the concrete market segment, i.e. credit instruments (credit cards, consumer loans etc.), regions, maturities and size of the loans.

2.2.10 Information about the borrower's financial conditions

Information about the borrower's financial standing represents the core of decision-making process about whether or not to grant a loan. If this information is distorted, institution could face serious troubles. Accounting statements should notify their users (investors, lenders, regulators and public) about the financial standing of the entity. Nevertheless, accounts do not usually provide all information necessary for good decisions of its users since these accounts concentrate primarily on the past and usually do not provide non-financial information.

The existing Generally Accepted Accounting Principle of the United States (US GAAP) and International Financial Reporting Standards (IFRS) hold equally for all entities regardless their size. **Any operation has the same risks and the same benefits in any entity.** There is a strong effort to integrate US GAAP and IFRS.

Bookkeeping represents burden that entities must suffer. Authorities should, therefore, implement such accounting that would not hit them too hard. To put it another way, accounting should be transparent, not too costly and endowed with clear rules. Everybody would easily orientate in financial statements and the costs of bookkeeping and audit should not amount too high. Such accounting also supports competitiveness of companies in a worldwide scale.

Auditors should evaluate and approve final accounts. Managers generally prefer rather benevolent auditors. In the United States, however, popularity of "nice" auditors resulted in several significant business collapses, such as Enron and WorldCom bankruptcies in 2002. In Europe, this was the case of Vivendi, Ahold, or Parmalat.

2.3 Interest paid on deposit and other liabilities of banks to non-bank entities

Interest rates that commercial banks charge on clients' loans and other claims (on the asset side of the banks' balance sheet) usually exceed interest rates on interbank money market (e.g. LIBOR, EURIBOR). The more clients are credible, the less the interest rate exceeds interbank money market. Banking competition represents the factor determining this excess. On the other hand, the interest rates paid on clients' deposit accounts balances and other liabilities (e.g. on the issued debt securities) hardly exceed the interbank interest rate. The difference between the average interest rate on debt assets and debt liabilites represents the so-called **credit spread**. Credit spread generates the substantial part of profit for many banks.

The Example 2.4 continues from the Example 2.2. Let us suppose that the inter-bank interest rate is 6%, interest rate paid on deposits is 4%, and the interest rate charged on loans is 8%. Commercial bank granted a loan of $1,000. It follows that the yearly interest profit generated by this loan is $40 (= $80 – $40). This profit matches precisely the clients' interest loss of $40. This example shows that interests paid on deposits represent another way of money creation. Interests paid by banks on deposits represent new money.

Example 2.4 Bank creates money by paying interest from deposit

1) Bank grants loan of $1,000 to its client
2) Bank pays yearly interest (from deposit) of $40 on client's current account (interest rate 4 %)
3) Bank charges yearly interest (on loan) of $80 on loan account (interest rate 8 %)

Bank granting a loan

Loans granted	
1) $1,000 3) $80	

Client's current account	
	1) $1,000 2) $40

Interest expense	
2) $40	

Interest income	
	3) $80

Client accepting a loan

Current account	
1) $1,000 2) $40	

Loans accepted	
	1) $1,000 3) $80

Interest expense	
3) $80	

Interest income	
	2) $40

3 Creation and Extinction of Money II

This section follows with the issue of creation and extinction of money.

3.1 Assets and services purchased by banks from non-bank entities

Although the major part of money originates in banks by means of granting loans, money also originates when the bank purchases assets (debt and equity securities, tangible and intangible assets etc.) and services from non-bank entities. Let's suppose that the bank is buying three kinds of assets, namely debt securities, equity securities, real estate and also services.

Purchase of debt securities (bills, notes, bond, bills of exchange) issued by non-bank entity does not differ economically from granting a loan by bank to non-bank entity. The difference between loans and debt securities is only in legal forms of these operations, and in the fact that securities are generally much more negotiable than loans. In an Example 3.1, the bank purchases debt securities directly from issuer (i.e. on the primary market) for $1,000. This sum is added to issuer's current account.

Example 3.1 Bank purchases debt securities from its client on the primary market

1) Bank purchases debt securities from its client for $1,000

Bank buying debt securities

Debt securities purchased		Client's current account	
1) $1,000			1) $1,000

Client issuing debt securities

Current account		Debt securities issued	
1) $1,000			1) $1,000

The economic result of this operation is the same as in the case of granting a loan by the bank. In both cases, a bank increases its claim against client's current account, and a client increases current account against its liabilities by $1,000. The balance sheet amount of both a bank and a client has increased by the same amount.

Let us suppose that the bank purchases **equity securities** (shares) issued by non-bank entity. Example 3.2 shows that bank credits issuer's current account by $1,000. The balance sheet of both a bank and a client has increased by the same amount. Economically, the purchase of equity securities differs from purchase of debt securities. The operation does not increase claims of the bank but its share in client's net assets (client's assets reduced by client's liabilities). The balance sheet amount of both a bank and a client has increased by the same amount.

In an example 3.3 bank purchases other assets (real estate) from its client. To pay for this real estate, the bank credits seller's (client's) current account by $1,000. Client replaces one of its assets (real estate) by another asset (cash on current account). The balance sheet amout of commercial bank has increased by $1,000, and the balance sheet of client has remained unchanged.

Example 3.2 Bank purchases equity securities from its client on the primary market

1) Bank purchases equity securities from its client for $1,000

Bank buying equity securities

Equity securities purchased	
1) $1,000	

Client's current accounts	
	1) $1,000

Client issuing equity securities

Current account	
1) $1,000	

Equity securities issued (equity)	
	1) $1,000

Example 3.3 Bank purchases real estate from its client

1) Bank purchases real estate from its client for $1,000

Bank buying real estate

Real estate	
1) $1,000	

Client's current account	
	1) $1,000

Client selling real estate

Current account	
1) $1,000	

Real estate	
Initial balance	1) $1,000

Finally, the bank purchases services from its client (Example 3.4). To pay for these services, the bank credits provider's current account. By contrast to preceding examples, however, bank records this payment as expenses into the income statement. Similarly, client records the payment as income in her income statement.

3.2 Buy back of banks' own securities from non-bank entities

The bank can issue debt and equity securities which can be purchased back by its clients. Example 3.5 shows the bank buying back its own securities for $1,000 from its client. The bank pays by crediting client's current account. The buy back of debt securities represents the exchange of one banks' liability (issued securities) for another banks' liability (client's current account). The new liability matches the definition of money. The buy back of equity securities represents the exchange of banks' equity for banks' liability (current account).

Example 3.4 Bank purchases services from its client

1) Bank purchases services from its client for $1,000

Bank purchasing service

	Client's current account
Expenses - services	

Client's current account

Debit	Credit
	1) $1,000

Expenses - services

Debit	Credit
1) $1,000	

Client providing service

Current account	
	Income - services

Current account

Debit	Credit
1) $1,000	

Income - services

Debit	Credit
	1) $1,000

Thus there are two possibilities:

- In the case of buy back of equity securities and debt securities which do not match the definition of broad money the money stock increases by the amount equal to price of securities purchased, i.e. by $1,000; or
- In the case of buy back of debt securities which match the definition of broad money the money stock is not changed.

Example 3.5 Bank buys back its own securities from its client

1) Bank pays $200 for securities purchased back from its client on its current account

Bank

Client's current account

	1) $200

Securities issued

1) $200	Initial balance

Client

Current account

1) $200	

Securities purchased

Initial balance	1) $200

3.3 Payments of wages and salaries to bank employees, management and statutory individuals

Money is also created when a bank pays wages and salaries to its employees, management and statutory individuals (Example 3.6). This way is similar to purchases of services from clients.

Example 3.6 Bank pays wages and salaries to its employees

1) Bank pays wages and salaries to its employees of $1,000

<table>
<tr><th colspan="2">Bank paying wages and salaries</th></tr>
<tr><td></td><td><table><tr><th colspan="2">Client’s current account</th></tr><tr><td></td><td>1) $1,000</td></tr></table></td></tr>
<tr><td><table><tr><th colspan="2">Expenses - labour</th></tr><tr><td>1) $1,000</td><td></td></tr></table></td><td></td></tr>
</table>

<table>
<tr><th colspan="2">Employee providing work</th></tr>
<tr><td><table><tr><th colspan="2">Current account</th></tr><tr><td>1) $1,000</td><td></td></tr></table></td><td></td></tr>
<tr><td></td><td><table><tr><th colspan="2">Income - employment</th></tr><tr><td></td><td>1) $1,000</td></tr></table></td></tr>
</table>

3.4 Payments of dividends and royalties

Money is also created by dividend and royalty payments to the bank’s non-bank shareholders and management (paying dividends to its banking shareholders bank does not represent creation of money as it changes only interbank liquidity). It is similar to the purchase of services (Example 3.7). However, in this case the bank debits its retained earnings. Dividend and royalty payments affect the structure of balance sheet and not the income statement.

Example 3.7 Bank pays dividends and royalties to its non-bank shareholders and management

1) Bank pays dividends and directors' fees of $1,000

Bank paying dividends and royalties

Client's current account

	1) $1,000

Retained earnings

1) $1,000	Initial balance

Shareholders or management

Current account

1) $1,000	

Income - dividends

	1) $1,000

3.5 Extinction of money

As we have already mentioned above, the money becomes extinct in commercial banks through reverse processes to the money creation:

- Repayments of loans (including interest) to banks by non-bank entities;
- Sale of assets (debt and equity securities, tangible and intangible assets etc.) and services by banks to non-bank entities; and
- Issue of own equity and debt securities by banks to non-bank entities.

3.5.1 Repayment of loans to banks by non-bank entities

Repayment of a loan (Example 3.8) is reversal process to granting a loan (Example 2.2). The bank credits the account "loans granted" and debits the "current account" by amount of principal and interest ($1,080). Loan repayment results in simultaneous decrease of both assets and liabilities of the bank.

Example 3.8 Client (non-bank entity) repays a loan to bank

1) Bank grants a loan of $1,000 to its client
2) Bank pays yearly interest from deposit of $40 on client's current account (interest rate 4 %)
3) Bank charges yearly interest (on loan) of $80 on loan account (interest rate 8 %)
4) Client repays both loan ($1,000) and corresponding interest ($80)

Bank granting a loan

Loans granted	
1) $1,000	4) $1,080
3) $80	

Client's current account	
4) $1,080	1) $1,000
	2) $40

Interest expense	
2) $40	

Interest income	
	3) $80

Client accepting a loan

Current account with bank	
1) $1,000	4) $1,080
2) $40	

Loans accepted	
4) $1,080	1) $1,000
	3) $80

Interest expense	
3) $80	

Interest income	
	2) $40

Balance sheet amout of the bank have decreased by $1,080. Similarly, balance sheet amout of the client have decreased by $1,080 as both assets (current account with bank) and liabilities (loans accepted) have lowered. As the banks loans granted, and deposits have become extinct, money has become extinct as well (Figure 3.1).

As the interest rates on loans exceed interest rates on deposits, clients have to pay more money then they have borrowed plus interest on deposits. To repay loan, client needs to “earn” money in its business, i.e. to convince other clients to pay its. The interest spread generates commercial banks’ profits. Commercial bank’s profit represents a very interesting topic for discussion.

In the Example 3.8, we have observed that, in its simplified version, commercial bank’s profit equals the difference between interest on loans granted and interest on current account. Therefore, in hypothetical case **even if all borrowers use deposits of all clients to repay their debts, there still remain some claims of commercial banks. This claim equals the difference between interests on loans and interests on deposits. But borrowers have no remaining money to repay it.**

It follows that the “too fat” banks are undesirable, for they “stretch” borrowers. On the other hand, however, economy neither needs the “too weak” banks, e.g. banks with a large amount of impaired loans (loans whose repayments are very unlikely).

Figure 3.1 Extinction of loans and deposits

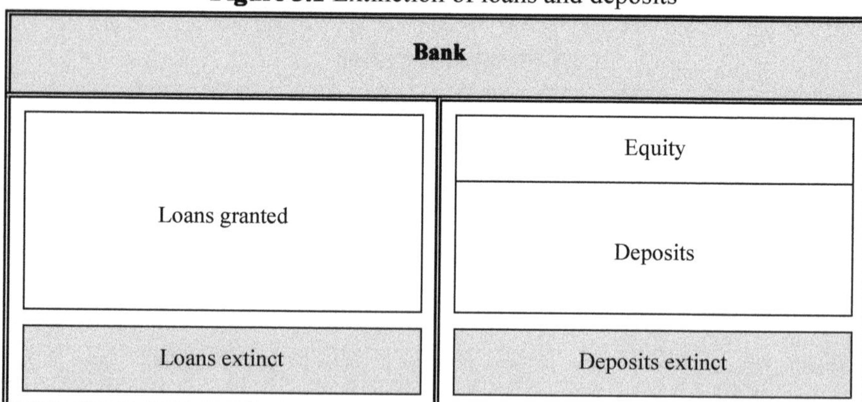

3.5.2 Assets and services sold by banks to non-bank entities

Money also becomes extinct when the bank sales assets (debt and equity securities, tangible and intangible assets etc.) and services to non-bank entities. Let's suppose that the bank is selling three kinds of assets, namely debt securities (Example 3.9), equity securities (Example 3.10), real estate (Example 3.11) and also services (Example 3.12).

Example 3.9 Bank sales back debt securities to its client on the primary market

1) Bank purchases debt security from its client for $1,000
2) Bank pays yearly interest from deposit of $40 on client's current account (interest rate 4 %)
3) Bank accounts yearly interest (on debt security) of $80 (interest rate 8 %)
4) Client purchases back debt security for $1,080

Bank buying debt securities

Debt securities purchased		Client's current account	
1) $1,000 3) $80	4) $1,080	4) $1,080	1) $1,000 2) $40

Interest expense		Interest income	
2) $40			3) $80

Client issuing debt securities

Current account with bank		Debt securities issued	
1) $1,000 2) $40	4) $1,080	4) $1,080	1) $1,000 3) $80

Interest expense		Interest income	
3) $80			2) $40

Example 3.10 Bank sales back equity securities to its client on the primary market

1) Bank purchases equity security from its client for $1,000
2) Bank pays yearly interest from deposit of $40 on client's current account (interest rate 4 %)
3) Bank accounts yearly increase of fair value of equity security of $80
4) Client purchases back equity security for $1,080

Bank buying equity securities

Equity securities purchased	
1) $1,000 3) $80	4) $1,080

Client's current account	
4) $1,080	1) $1,000 2) $40

Interest expense	
2) $40	

Profit from securities	
	3) $80

Client issuing equity securities

Current account with bank	
1) $1,000 2) $40	4) $1,080

Equity securities issued	
4) $1,080	1) $1,000

Interest income	
	2) $40

Example 3.11 Bank sales real estate to its client

1) Bank sales real estate for $1,000

Bank buing real estate

Real estate

Initial balance	1) $1,000

Client's current account

1) $1,000	Initial balance

Client selling real estate

Current account

Initial balance	1) $1,000

Real estate

1) $1,000	

Example 3.12 Bank sales services to its client

1) Bank sales services for $1,000

Bank selling service	
	Client's current account 1) $1,000 | Initial balance
	Income - services | 1) $1,000

Client purchasing service	
Current account Initial balance | 1) $1,000	
Expense - services 1) $1,000 |	

3.5.3 Issue of banks' own equity and debt securities to non-bank entities

Let us examine the impact of the issue of debt and equity securities by commercial banks. Example 3.13 shows the bank issuing securities for $1,000 to its client. The issued securities are sold to bank's client, who pays for it with money from its current account. The issue of debt securities represents the exchange of one banks' liability (client's current account) for other banks' liability (issued securities). The new liability can match the definition of money. The issue of equity securities represents the exchange of banks' liability (client's current account) for banks' equity. Equity does not match the definition of money.

Example 3.13 Bank issues securities to its client

1) Client pays $200 for securities to bank from his account with this bank

Bank

Assets: (empty)

Liabilities:

Client's current account	
1) $200	Initial balance

Securities issued	
	1) $200

Client

Assets:

Current account	
	1) $200

Securities purchased	
1) $200	

Liabilities: (empty)

Thus there are two possibilities:

- In the case of issue of equity securities and debt securities which do not match the definition of broad money the money stock decreases by the amount equal to price of securities sold, i.e. by $1,000; or
- In the case of issue of debt securities which match the definition of broad money the money stock is not changed.

3.6 Payments between clients of one commercial bank

There is a question how payments between clients of one commercial bank influence money stock. According to Example 1.14 client X pays $1,000 for the real estate to client Y. Both clients have current accounts in the same bank. Client X orders bank to transfer money from his account to the account of client Y. Alternatively client X draws a cheque to client Y who presents it to the bank. The bank consequently debits the current account of client X, and credits the current account of client Y. When we talk about payment from client X to client Y we mean the final transfer of money. Client Y becomes creditor of the bank. It follows that **the payment does not change money stock.**

3.7 Domestic currency payments between clients of two commercial banks

Payments between clients of two commercial banks denominated in the domestic currency are more complicated. In an Example 3.15 client X, which has its current account with bank A, pays $1,000 for to client Y, who has its current account with bank B. Client X orders bank to transfer money from its account to account of client Y, or client X draws a cheque to client Y who presents it to bank B.

The payment consists in three successive operations:

- Bank A debits current account of client X, and credits its clearing account with the clearing house (asset side of the balance sheet);
- Clearing house transfers liquidity from bank A's clearing account to bank B's clearing account; and
- Bank B credits current account of client Y, and debits its clearing account.

It follows that **the payment does not change money stock.**

Example 3.14 Payment between clients of one commercial bank

1) Client X pays $1,000 to client Y for real estate

Commercial bank

Client X's current account

1) $1,000	Initial balance

Client Y's current account

	1) $1,000

Client X buying real estate

Current account

Initial balance	1) $1,000

Real estate

1) $1,000	

Client Y selling real estate

Current account

1) $1,000	

Real estate

Initial balance	1) $1,000

Example 3.15 Domestic currency payment between clients of two commercial banks through clearing house

1) Bank A debits current account of client X against its clearing account
2) Clearing house transfers liquidity from clearing account of bank A to the clearing account of bank B
3) Bank B credits current account of client Y against its clearing account

Bank A

Clearing account with clearing house

Initial balance	1) $1,000

Client X's current account

1) $1,000	Initial balance

Client X

Current account with bank A

Initial balance	1) $1,000

Real estate

1) $1,000	

Bank B

Clearing account with clearing house

3) $1,000	

Client Y's current account

	Initial balance 3) $1,000

Example 3.15 Continuation

Client Y

Current account with bank B

3) $1,000	

Real estate

Initial balance	3) $1,000

The clearing house

Clearing account of bank A

2) $1,000	Initial balance

Clearing account of bank B

	2) $1,000

3.8 Foreign currency payments between clients of two commercial banks

Payments between clients of two commercial banks denominated in the foreign currency are even more complicated. Until now, we have not assumed the cross-border payments. We have supposed that both banks and their clients are residents of the same country. How would the situation look like if client X pays $1,000 from current account with its bank A (both client X and bank A are in the USA) to client Y's current account with bank B (both client Y and bank B are in the Eurozone). Example 3.16 illustrates foreign currency cross-border payment between clients of two commercial banks. We suppose that payment is carried out through vostro account of payer's bank. For example U.S. investor purchases real estate in the Eurozone for $1,000.

The transaction consists of two successive operations:

- Bank A debits current account of client X, and credits vostro account of bank B held in bank A; and

- Bank B credits current account of client Y, and debits its nostro account in bank A.

It is evident that **the aggregate money stock in the USA has decreased by $1,000 whereas the aggregate money stock in the Eurozone has increased by $1,000.** The amount of $1,000 is balanced by the receivable of the Eurozone bank from U.S. bank (but this receivable does not make part of neither Eurozone money nor U.S. money). We have to point out once more that when we talk about payments from client X to client Y we mean solely the final transfer of money. Client Y becomes creditor of bank B who becomes creditor of bank A. Payments denominated in any other currency follow the same pattern.

We can conclude that cross-border investments affect money stock in both countries. **Money stock in the country of investor decreases, and the money stock of country attracting the investment increases. Money stock of individual countries thus depends on the inflows and outflows of money**. It is evident that cross-border investments do not cause the real creation of money. The sum of money stock remains constant. What changes, is the relative distribution of money stock among countries. In the first country money stock decreases while in the second country money stock increases.

Example 3.16 describes the so-called **correspondent banking**. It is a situation when one bank has the current account in another bank, and through this account banks manage payments of their clients (or their own payments). In the first bank, this account is called nostro account, and in the second one, it is called vostro account. Terms nostro account and vostro account thus stand for one sole account – once from the point of view of the first bank and once from the point of view of the second bank.

Nostro account is the Latin expression for "our" account, for the account of one bank held in the other (usually foreign) bank. It is on the asset side of balance sheet. The bank that has an account in another bank to is called respondent bank. **Vostro account** is the Latin expression for "your" account i.e., for the account of another (usually foreign) bank held in a bank. It is on the liabilities side of balance sheet. The bank, in which another bank holds its accounts, is also called correspondent bank. Vostro account is also called nostro account.

In Example 3.16 payments between clients of banks is carried out through the current account of bank B in bank A (through vostro account of payer's bank). This payment could also be realized through the current account of bank A in bank B (through nostro account of payer's bank). Such situation can one easily imagine. Both of these cases suppose the correspondent relation between bank A and bank B. However, this is not always the case. If there is no such relation, payment operations must go through another bank in the United States or in the Eurozone through the corresponding local payment system. In the United States it is the Fedwire, automated clearing house (ACHs) and other clearing houses. In the Eurozone it is the TARGET and many other clearing houses.

Example 3.16 Foreign currency cross-border payment between clients of two commercial banks

1) Client X (U.S. resident) pays $1,000 for real estate to client Y (Eurozone resident)

Bank A in the USA

Client X's current account

1) $1,000	Initial balance

Vostro account of bank B

	1) $1,000

Client X in the USA

Current account with bank A

Initial balance	1) $1,000

Real estate

1) $1,000	

Bank B in the Eurozone

Nostro account with bank B

1) $1,000	

Client Y's current account

	1) $1,000

Client Y in the Eurozone

Current account with bank B

1) $1,000	

Real estate

Initial balance	1) $1,000

Part II: Liquidity

4 Liquidity and reserve requirements

Some central banks still impose reserve requirements (required reserves) on commercial banks. The reasons for their existence are of rather historical and technical character than economic. Reserve requirements consist in the obligation of commercial bank to hold a certain balance (liquidity) on its clearing accounts (nostro accounts) at central bank so that the average liquidity of any bank during a period is equal or higher than the reserve requirement of this commercial bank. Some central banks allow commercial banks to include in this obligation the currency held in their vaults. The amount of reserve requirement is calculated as the reserve ratio (set by central bank) multiplied by the volume of commercial bank's reservable liabilities (the so-called reserve base).

Reserve requirements in many countries historically decline. In some countries reserve requirements do not exist anymore (e.g. in Canada, Denmark, Mexico, New Zealand, Norway and Sweden). Originally, there was no interest paid on required reserves. But central banks in countries, where required reserves were not abandoned yet, started to pay the interest on them. Interest is mostly based on interbank interest rates. In some countries, one part of reserves does not bear interest, and the other part does.[7]

4.1 Liquidity and bank reserves

Liquidity is generally the term for balances on interbank (commercial banks and central banks) current accounts but not balances on interbank term accounts. For the liquidity of commercial banks on central bank's current account (clearing account) is often used the term **bank reserves**. Liquidity and bank reserves are subject to the interbank market (interbank loans and deposits). The interbank market represents market for liquidity including bank reserves. Interbank loans and deposits are not usually collaterised. What is very important is that **liquidity (including bank reserves) in not part of money (monetary aggregates).**

Clearing account is the account of commercial bank at central bank to fulfil reserve requirements and to conduct interbank domestic currency payments. Banks with the excess of bank reserves (in relation to reserve requirements) lend these bank reserves (usually without collateral) to other banks for the interbank

7 This topic is comprehensively covered in chapter 6 of Bindseil, Ulrich: *Monetary Policy Implementation: Theory Past and Present.* Oxford University Press, Oxford 2004.

interest rate (LIBOR, EURIBOR etc.). Banks can also deposit the excess reserves at central bank for the interest rate lower to the interbank interest rates paid on deposits of the same maturity.

In the United States, bank reserves of depository institutions with Fed are called **federal funds**. The interbank market is called **federal funds market**. The overnight interest rate of this market is called **overnight federal funds rate**. The most of interbank loans and deposits are overnight, even if interbank term deposits exist as well. U.S. depository institutions thus borrow bank reserves usually for only one day, i.e. they pay it back at the beginning of the next workday. Bank reserves, as well as its distribution among individual depository institutions, changes every day. Smaller banks are usually lending bank reserves to bigger ones. The overnight federal funds rate is the key rate of monetary policy.

Bank reserves consist of required and excess reserves. Some central banks set the amount of required clearing reserves, since the account with central bank is also used for clearing (payment) operations. The excess reserves (sometimes also called surplus reserves or free reserves) represent the excess of commercial bank's bank reserves over required reserves. Regarding the fact that excess reserves often do not bear interest (even if required reserves do) commercial banks seek to minimize them.

Reserve ratio represents the required ratio of bank reserves and reservable liabilities.

The bank reserves of commercial banks at central bank are influenced by the following operations between central bank and commercial banks and their clients:

- Currency withdrawals and currency deposits of commercial banks in central bank, e.g. when client asks for currency withdrawal from its bank. When clients withdraw currency from commercial banks then commercial banks have to withdraw currency from central bank. In substance withdrawal of currency from central bank by commercial bank represents central bank's issue debt security bearing zero interest. Commercial banks seek to minimize their holdings of currency because they do not bear interest. Commercial banks pay for currency with their reserves. The increase of currency decreases bank reserves. Conversely, the decrease of currency increases bank reserves (Example 4.1);

Example 4.1 Decrease of bank reserves through commercial bank's withdrawal of currency from central bank

1) Client withdraws currency of $1,000 from its current account
2) Bank A withdraws currency of $1,000 from its clearing account

Bank A

Currency in circulation	
2) $1,000	1) $1,000

Clearing account with central bank	
Initial balance	2) $1,000

Client's current account	
1) $1,000	Initial balance

Central bank

Currency in circulation	
	2) $1,000

Clearing account of bank A	
2) $1,000	Initial balance

Client

Currency in circulation	
1) $1,000	

Current account with bank A	
Initial balance	1) $1,000

- Payments between central bank and commercial bank in domestic currency (Example 4.2); and
- Payments between central bank and client of commercial bank in domestic currency (Example 4.3).

Currency withdrawals by central bank's clients do not impact bank reserves (Example 4.4).

In addition, there are operations which have impact on bank reserves but the central bank is not a partner of such operations:

- Payments between clients (including government) of central bank and clients of commercial bank in domestic currency (Example 4.5); and
- Payments between clients (including government) of central bank and commercial banks in domestic currency (Example 4.6).

Example 4.2 Decrease of bank reserves through commercial bank's payment to central bank

1) Commercial bank pays $1,000 to central bank

Bank A

Clearing account with central bank		Liabilities	
Initial balance	1) $1,000	1) $1,000	Initial balance

Central bank

Claims		Clearing account of bank A	
Initial balance	1) $1,000	1) $1,000	Initial balance

Example 4.3 Decrease of bank reserves through client's payment to central bank via commercial bank

1) Client pays $1,000 to central bank through its current account with bank A

Bank A

Clearing account with central bank	
Initial balance	1) $1,000

Client's current account	
1) $1,000	Initial balance

Central bank

Claims	
Initial balance	1) $1,000

Clearing account of bank A	
1) $1,000	Initial balance

Client

Current account with bank A	
Initial balance	1) $1,000

Liabilities	
1) $1,000	Initial balance

Example 4.4 Bank reserves unchanged through central bank's client withdrawal of currency

1) Client of central bank withdraws currency of $1,000 from central bank

Central bank

Currency

	1) $1,000

Client's current account

1) $1,000	Initial balance

Clearing accounts

	Initial balance

Client

Currency in circulation

1) $1,000	

Current account with central bank

Initial balance	1) $1,000

Example 4.5 Decrease of bank reserves through payment of client of commercial bank to client of central bank

1) Client X of commercial bank A pays $1,000 to client Y of central bank

Bank A

Clearing account with central bank

Initial balance	1) $1,000

Client X's current account

1) $1,000	Initial balance

Central bank

Clearing account of bank A

1) $1,000	Initial balance

Client Y'current account

	1) $1,000

Client X

Current account with bank A

Initial balance	1) $1,000

Liabilities

1) $1,000	Initial balance

Client Y

Current account with central bank

1) $1,000	

Receivables

Initial balance	1) $1,000

Example 4.6 Decrease of bank reserves through payment of commercial bank to client of central bank

1) Bank A pays $1,000 to client of central bank

Bank A

Clearing account with central bank

Initial balance	1) $1,000

Liabilities

1) $1,000	Initial balance

Central bank

Clearing account of bank A

1) $1,000	Initial balance

Client's current account

	1) $1,000

Client

Current account with central bank

1) $1,000	

Receivables

Initial balance	1) $1,000

Payment operations between clients of commercial banks do not change bank reserves (Example 3.15). Bank reserves remains also unchanged in the case of payments (resulted from interbank operations) between commercial banks in domestic currency via central bank. In example 4.7 bank B grants a loan $1,000 to bank A. In both cases, we observe only the transfers of bank reserves between commercial banks and not changes of the total bank reserves at central bank.

Example 4.7 Bank reserves unchanged through payment between two commercial banks via central bank

1) Bank B pays $1,000 to bank A

Bank A

Clearing account with central bank

1) $1,000	

Loan accepted

	1) $1,000

Central bank

Clearing account of bank A

	1) $1,000

Clearing account of bank B

1) $1,000	Initial balance

Bank B

Clearing account with central bank

Initial balance	1) $1,000

Loans granted

1) $1,000	

Examples 4.1 to 4.3, 4.5 and 4.6 illustrate decreases of bank reserves at central bank. Reverse operations that increase bank reserves are not mentioned here.

Let's pay attention to banks' loan activity directed on clients. **Loan activity of commercial banks does not change bank reserves directly**. There is no direct relationship between amount of loans granted to clients and bank reserves. Granting new loan to a client results only in the creation of a new asset (loans granted) and a new deposit (money). But new deposits are reservable liabilities that with some time delay require on commercial banks to hold higher bank reserves. That's the indirect relationship between loan activity and bank reserves. Commercial banks' reserves at central bank thus slightly increase (in proportion to reserve ratio that generally does not exceed a few percents). But this indirect relationship does not hold true in some cases. Deposits can be converted into nonreservable liabilities (e.g. equity instruments). **In such a case there is neither direct nor indirect relationship between loan activity of commercial banks and bank reserves.**

Central bank fulfils the role of banker to the government in many countries. Then central bank operates government accounts. This is generally the main source of bank reserve fluctuations. If, for instance, clients of commercial banks pay taxes, bank reserves decreases (Example 4.5). Conversely, if government sends money to clients of commercial banks, bank reserves rises. Similar effects are created by the issue of treasury bills, notes and bonds (bank reserves decreases) and its repayments (bank reserves increases).

Foreign exchange operations of central bank affect bank reserves in a similar way. When central bank sells foreign currency for domestic currency then commercial bank that buys foreign exchange pays from its clearing account at central bank. Hence, the bank reserves of banking sector decreases. Conversely when central bank buys foreign currency for domestic currency then commercial bank that sells foreign exchange is paid on its clearing account at central bank. Hence, the bank reserves of banking sector rises.

The total amount of bank reserves varies on a daily basis. Bank reserves are influenced by payments initialized by commercial banks, their clients, clients of central bank, and by payments activated by central bank itself. Variations of many factors are easily predictable. Many fluctuations result from seasonal effects. For example, the volume of currency in circulation increases before the end of the year. During the Christmas time, households need to hold more currency for shopping. The balance on government accounts in central bank varies seasonally with dates of tax and social security payments.

Central bank imposes the reserve requirements, and then central bank regulates bank reserves by means of open market operations (buying or selling bank reserves) in order to achieve bank reserves slightly exceeding reserve requirements (excess reserves should be positive). Commercial banks themselves have only a little chance to influence bank reserves. Open market operations thus represent rather defensive operations. The central bank uses them to compensate other operations that affect bank reserves.

The amount of excess reserves should be neither too low (in such case, the lack of bank reserves pushes the short-term interbank interest rates up) nor too high (in this case, the abundance of bank reserves pushes the short-term interbank interest rates down). The key aspect is the fact that the short-term interbank interest rate cannot be determined by the excess reserves but only by the decision of central bank about the level of short-term interbank interest rate. In many cases it is the rate under which central bank regulates the bank reserves. The optimal amount of excess reserves can be derived only by the practice of central bank which is based on the interbank money market. Whatever theory seems useless.

As the total amount of bank reserves of any bank varies on a daily basis, any commercial bank establishes reserves (liquidity) management department. It should be noted that if some bank finds itself with the lack of bank reserves, there is the other bank with excess of bank reserves. The first bank can borrow bank reserves from the second bank. Central bank regulates only the total amount of bank reserves in such a way that commercial banks as a whole are able to meet reserve requirements. When managing its bank reserves, commercial bank must take into account primarily major payments of its clients (both provided and received). It is obvious that at the end of each workday some banks find themselves with the unpredicted excess of reserves and some banks with the unpredicted lack of reserves. Experience shows that the more banks in the system the bigger the amount of everyday total excess reserves.

There are many different ways how central banks regulate bank reserves by open market operations. One possible way for central bank is to provide bank reserves by means of collaterised loan to commercial bank (Example 4.8). Example 4.9 illustrates the absorption of bank reserves. Central bank offers to commercial bank to put its bank reserves on term account with the central bank. It is again evident that open market operations do not affect commercial banks' loan activity directed on clients.

Example 4.8 Central bank providing bank reserves by means of collaterised loan granted to a commercial bank

1) Central bank grants collaterised loan of $1,000 to commercial bank

Commercial bank			
Clearing account with central bank		Loans from central bank	
1) $1,000			1) $1,000

Central bank			
Loans granted		Clearing account of bank A	
1) $1,000			1) $1,000

Commercial banks use their bank reserves to settle interbank payments. But reserve requirements in individual countries are historically decreasing, and in some countries they do not exist at all. To settle properly payments many banks now need temporary reserve balances exceeding required reserves. Overdrafts of clearing accounts are forbidden. To secure continuous operation of payment system, commercial banks thus often need to ask for **collaterised intraday lending facility**. Otherwise payments from their clearing accounts would face problems. Banks would easily lose its credibility, clients would leave it, and some banks would even turn bankrupt. Central banks generally do not provide uncollaterised facilities. This issue will be developed further.

Example 4.9 Central bank absorbing bank reserves by means of term account offered to a commercial bank

1) Commercial bank transfers $1,000 from clearing account on a term account with central bank

Commercial bank

Clearing account with central bank

Initial balance	1) $1,000

Term account with central bank

1) $1,000	

Central bank

Clearing account of bank A

1) $1,000	Initial balance

Term account of bank A

	1) $1,000

4.2 Role of reserve requirements

Reserve requirements perform two functions:

- Taxation of commercial banks; and
- Commercial bank's reserve cushions at central bank.

Reserve requirements as t**axation of commercial banks** represent the profit of central bank (and thus the profit of the government) and the loss of commercial banks. Reserve requirements perform this function only if central bank does not pay interest on reserve requirements or if the interest rate on reserve requirements (interest paid to the central bank) is lower than interest on the interbank market. On the other hand we shall consider the fact that central banks provide number of services (including the supervision) for free.

Taxation can be derived from interest that would be paid on bank reserves if they are placed on interbank market:

$$\textit{taxation} = (r - r_r) \text{ x } \textit{reserve ratio} \text{ x } \textit{reserve base}$$

Where: r interbank interest rate and
r_r interest rate applicable on reserve requirements.

There is zero taxation if interest rate applicable on reserve requirements is the same as interbank interest rate. In the Example 1.42 (Chapter 5) taxation is:

$$\textit{taxation} = (0.06 - 0.00) \text{ x } 0.0324 \text{ x } \$1{,}050 \textit{ billion} = \$2.05 \textit{ billion}$$

Implementation of the zero-interest bearing reserve requirement represents to central bank an additional profit of $2.05 billion. If the interest rates on clients' assets and liabilities remain unchanged, profits of commercial banks would fall by the same amount, i.e. by $2.05 billion. In fact, commercial banks will rather transfer the decrease of profit on their customers, i.e. on households and enteprises. They lower interest on deposits, and they increasue interest on loans granted. Regardless competition, this is exactly what commercial banks generally do. While some borrowers have the access to loans from non-bank entities, other borrowers have no other chance than to stay with banks and pay higher interest. Implementation (or rise) of reserve requirements thus makes bank loans less attractive. Anyway, **the implementation of zero-interest-bearing reserve requirements causes higher taxation of households and enterprises** as it increases the credit spread between interest rates on loans and interest rates on deposits.

"Bank reserves tax" influences commercial banks and their clients. It motivates clients (both borrowers and depositors) to evade this system. Moreover, banks always seek to minimize their bank reserves by means of new products that allow for similar services but do not require bank reserves. There is a number of ways how to evade bank reserves. Banks can use the off-balance sheet operations or can offer of non-reservable deposits or transfers of reservable deposits to other banking institutions (particularly subsidiaries) or even non-bank institutions.

Reserve requirements also serve as **reserve cushions** of commercial banks at central bank. This function becomes important when the individual bank faces unpredictable withdrawals of deposits by clients. Example 4.1 illustrates decrease of the total of bank reserves through commercial bank's withdrawal of currency from central bank initiated by the withdrawal of currency by clients from commercial bank. Example 4.10 describes transfer of client's money in domestic currency within two current accounts with two banks through the clearinghouse (this example is very similar to Example 3.15). Even if in this case total amount of bank reserves remains unchanged, the bank reserves of the first bank decrease, and the bank reserves of the second bank increase.

When facing increased currency withdrawals or money transfers to other banks, commercial bank needs:

- To borrow bank reserves from other commercial banks (if these banks are willing to lend bank reserves it);
- To borrow bank reserves from central bank (but central banks is willing to grant only collaterised loans, i.e. commercial bank have to transfer acceptable collateral to central bank); or
- To sell its assets (usually bank starts selling the most liquid asset, like securities).

Many bankruptcies of commercial banks are trigerred by insufficient bank reserves of commercial banks. This is the main reason for the implementation of reserve requirements. Requirements are set either by law or by moral suasion in the way that every commercial bank transfer part of its assets into bank reserves on its account at central bank. However, the cause of insufficient bank reserves (and the primary cause of bankruptcies) is always to be found in inability of bank to meet withdrawals of deposits, i.e. a conversion of deposits into currency and a transfer of deposits from one bank to another. To avoid such situations, banks were trying to window-dress their annual reports by increasing their holdings of currency and liquid assets.

As an alternative to reserve requirements, several central banks have imposed the **liquid asset ratio** (LAR). It is a proportion of total assets readily convertible into cash. These liquid assets are bank reserves, currency held by commercial banks (vault cash), balances of nostro accounts, cheques in the process of collection and treasury bonds easily convertible into currency (e.g. T-bills).

Example 4.10 Transfer of client's money in domestic currency within two current accounts with two banks

1) Client transfers $1,000 from its current account with bank A to its current account with bank B

Bank A

Clearing account with central

Initial balance	1) $1,000

Client's current account

1) $1,000	Initial balance

Bank B

Clearing account with central bank

1) $1,000	

Client's current account

	1) $1,000

Central bank

Clearing account of bank A

1) $1,000	Initial balance

Clearing account of bank B

	1) $1,000

Client

Current account with bank A

Initial balance	1) $1,000

Current account with bank B

1) $1,000	

However LAR features certain shortcomings. As these assets are to be held, it could not be used to secure withdrawals. Besides, whatever decline (even if temporary) in liquid assets under the required level is considered to signal weakness or troubles of a bank. Compulsory holdings of the less yielding assets also negatively affect profits of banks. LAR requirements have restrained competitiveness in banking sector, and they sometimes even motivated bank to take riskier actions in order to restore its original profitability. In several cases LAR was misused to fiscal purposes.

Reserve requirements were often considered to represent one of the **monetary policy instruments** used to influence the loan expansion of commercial banks, i.e. the creation of money and subsequently the final target of monetary policy (price stability, long-term economic growth and employment). To put it another way, changes in reserve requirements were supposed to stimulate or restrain amount of loans granted. The raise of reserve requirement was expected to slow down the loan activity and hence the overall economic activity. Nowadays we know that this causality doesn't hold. Monetary policy tools consists solely in the open market operations that central bank employs to manage short-term interest rates. Reserve requirements thus have no monetary effects, for it has nothing common with commercial bank's loan activity. It was confirmed by Moore in 1984[8], Goodhart in 1989[9] etc.

---

8 Moore, Basil. J.: Contemporaneous Reserve Accounting: Can Reserve be Quality-Constrained? Journal of Post Keynesian Economics, 1984, 7(1), 103-113. According to Moore: "It has only recently been recognized that the conventional view, that the growth of monetary aggregated can be "controlled" through a quantity-constrained process over the sources of bank reserves, represents a fundamental analytical misunderstanding of the nature of the money supply process. In credit-money as distinct from commodity-money economies, the money stock is determined basically by the demand for bank credit, which governs the volume of bank intermediation (Hicks, 1977; Kaldor, 1982; Moore 1984). Banks are price-setters and quantity-takers in both their retail loan and deposit markets, and they use the wholesale markets, where they are price-takers and quantity-setters, to lend or borrow any net excess sources or uses of funds (Willis, 1982). As a result bank earning asset decisions are largely independent of their reserve positions."

9 Goodhart, Charles: The Conduct of Monetary Policy, The Economic Journal, 1989, 99(396), 293-346. According to Goodhart: "The historical stability of the banks' reserve ratio had depended on the willingness of the authorities always to supply extra cash on demand at an interest rate chosen by the authorities. If the authorities should shift the operational form of the system, by refusing banks' access to cash freely at any price, the banks' desired reserve ratio might experience a major shift, and could then become much more variable. There would be a long transition period, from regime to regime, in which it would be hard to select an appropriate level of base money, and the variability of the banks' reserve/deposit ratio under the new system could be so large as to prevent any improvement in monetary control, while at the same time losing grip on interest rates."

4.3 Examples of reserve requirements

In this section, we will make brief overview of the reserve requirements of the Fed, the European Central bank, the Bank of Japan and the Bank of England.

4.3.1 Fed

According to the Fed regulation (as at 1 January 2009) there are three reserve ratios (amounts for net transaction amounts are adjusted each year according to a formula specified by the act):

- **0 %** for net transaction accounts from $0 million to $10.3 million non-personal time deposits and euro-currency liabilities;
- **3 %** for net transaction accounts from $10.3 million to $44.4 million; and
- **10 %** for net transaction accounts from $44.1 million.

Net transaction accounts are total transaction accounts less amounts due from other depository institutions and less cash items in the process of collection. Total transaction accounts consists of demand deposits, automatic transfer service (ATS) accounts, NOW accounts, share draft accounts, telephone or preauthorized transfer accounts, ineligible bankers acceptances and obligations issued by affiliates maturing in seven days or less.

Required reserves must be held in the form of vault cash and, if vault cash is insufficient, also in the form of a deposit with a Federal Reserve Bank. An institution that is a member of the Federal Reserve System must hold that deposit directly with a Reserve Bank. An institution that is not a member of the System can maintain that deposit directly with a Reserve Bank or with another institution in a pass-through relationship. Reserve requirements are imposed on commercial banks, savings banks, savings and loan associations, credit unions, U.S. branches and agencies of foreign banks, Edge corporations and agreement corporations. **Historically reserve requirements were not remunerated.** Beginning October 2008, the Federal Reserve Banks pay interest on required reserves and excess reserves. In the first half of 2009 interest rate was set on level 0.25 %.

4.3.2 European Central Bank

According to the ECB regulation credit institutions are subject to reserve requirements. The reservable liabilities include deposits and debt securities issued. Liabilities to other credit institutions subject to the ECB's reserve requirments are excluded from reservable liabilities.

A reserve ratio of **0 %** is applied to the following liabilities:

- Deposits with agreed maturity over two years;
- Deposits with period of notice over two years;
- Repos; and
- Debt securities issued with maturity over two years.

A reserve ratio of **2.0 %** is applied to the following liabilities:

- Overnight deposits;.
- Deposits with agreed maturity or period of notice up to 2 years;
- Debt securities issued with maturity up to 2 years; and
- Money market paper.

A lump sum of €100 000 is deducted from the calculated reserve requirement. **Reserve requirements are remunerated at the of the ECB rate for the main refinancing operations.**

4.3.3 Bank of Japan

Reserve requirements system in Japan is complicated. There is a wide range of reserve ratios (**from 0.05 to 1.3 %)** for specific deposits and debt securities. **Reserve requirements are not remunerated.**

4.3.4 Bank of England

In May 2006 the Bank of England has introduced system of voluntary bank reserves for banks and building societies. There were 41 reserve scheme members at that time. Members should maintain a level of reserves within a ±1% range around a target that they choose, averaging across reserves balances at the end of each calendar day over the maintenance period. **Reserve requirements are remunerated up to the top of target band at official rate of the Bank of England.**

5 Examples of banking systems

5.1 Example of banking system without central bank

In order to make the concept of the banking system more concrete, let's imagine hypothetical economy, and let's divide it into four separate sectors, namely commercial banks, enterprises, government and households. This system does not contain central bank yet. Central bank will be included into the model further. This system would operate in a similar way as if the central bank were included. Let interest rates are regulated by another central institution. First, we will introduce the simplest case in the Example 5.1 (beginning of the year) and Example 5.2 (end of the year).

Let's suppose that commercial banks finance both enterprises and government. Commercial banks, at the beginning of the year, grant loans to enterprises amounting to \$1,000 billion carrying the interest rate of 8 % (transaction No. 1). Governments usually issue treasury bonds. In our case, government issues bonds for \$200 billion with yield to maturity of 6 %. Commercial banks then buy these bonds (transaction No. 2). There are loans granted and treasury bonds purchased on asset side of the commercial bank's balance sheet. Amounts credited to current accounts belonging to enterprises and government represent their liabilities (banks pays on these liabilities interest rate of 4 %). In the balance sheets of government and enterprises, loans and bonds issued (sold) represent liabilities and received amounts of money represent assets.

At the beginning of the year all real assets (real estate, machinery and so forth) are in possession of households and that these households are not indebted. At the beginning of the year, enterprises purchase real assets from households for \$1,000 billion (transaction No. 3). Real assets thus shift from the balance sheet of households into balance sheet of enterprises. Conversely, deposits shift from the balance sheet of enterprises into balance sheet of households.

In addition, government distributes at the beginning of the year all its cash (held with commercial banks) to households (salaries of state employees, social benefits and so forth). In other words, government transfers \$200 billion from its balance sheet to the balance sheet of households (transaction No. 4). This amount represents expenses of government and income of households. Households' equity increases by the same amount.

Example 5.1 Balance sheets of commercial banks, enterprises, government and households at the beginning of the year

1) Loans of $1,000 billion from commercial banks to enterprises
2) Issue of treasury bonds of $200 billion sold to commercial banks
3) Purchase of real assets of $1,000 billion by enterprises from households
4) Transfer of $200 billion from government to households

Commercial banks	
Loans granted to enterprises (r = 8 %) 1) + $1,000 billion	~~Enterprises deposits (r = 4 %)~~ ~~1) + $1,000 billion~~ ~~3) – $1,000 billion~~
Treasury bonds purchased (r = 6 %) 2) + $200 billion	~~Government deposits (r = 4 %)~~ ~~2) + $200 billion~~ ~~4) – $200 billion~~
	Households' deposits (r = 4 %) 3) + $1,000 billion 4) + $200 billion

Enterprises	
~~Deposits with commercial banks (r = 4 %)~~ ~~1) + $1,000 billion~~ ~~3) – $1,000 billion~~	Loans from commercial banks (r = 8 %) 1) + $1,000 billion
Real assets 3) $1,000 billion	

Example 5.1 Continuation

Government	
Deposits with commercial banks (r = 4 %) 2) + $200 billion 4) – $200 billion	Treasury bonds sold (issued) (r = 6 %) 2) + $200 billion
4) Expense of transferring government deposits with commercial banks to households **$200 billion**	

Households	
~~Real assets~~ ~~$1,000 billion~~ ~~3) – $1,000 billion~~	Equity $1,000 billion
Deposits with commercial banks (r = 4 %) 3) + $1,000 billion 4) + $200 billion	
	4) Income from transferring government deposits with commercial banks to households **$200 billion**

At this moment, commercial bank's assets consist of loans granted to enterprises and treasury bonds, and liabilities consist of household's deposits. Assets of enterprises consist of real assets, and liabilities consist of loans from commercial banks. Government loss from redistribution is $200 billion, and its liabilities contain only treasury bonds. Households' income is $200 billion, and their assets consist of deposits with commercial banks.

Example 5.2 Balance sheets of commercial banks, enterprises, government and households at the end of the year

1) Loans of $1,000 billion from commercial banks to enterprises
2) Issue of treasury bonds of $200 billion sold to commercial banks
3) Purchase of real assets of $1,000 billion by enterprises from households
4) Transfer of $200 billion from government to households

Commercial banks

Loans granted to enterprises (r = 8 %) 1) + $1,000 billion **(+80)**	~~Enterprises deposits (r = 4 %)~~ ~~1) + $1,000 billion~~ ~~3) - $1,000 billion~~
Treasury bonds purchased (r = 6 %) 2) + $200 billion **(+12)**	~~Government deposits (r = 4 %)~~ ~~2) + $200 billion~~ ~~4) - $200 billion~~
	Households' deposits (r = 4 %) 3) + $1,000 billion **(+40)** 4) + $200 billion **(+8)**
Interest expense **$48 billion**	**Interest income** **$92 billion**

Enterprises

~~Deposits with commercial banks (r = 4 %)~~ ~~1) + $1,000 billion~~ ~~3) - $1,000 billion~~	Loans from commercial banks (r = 8 %) 1) + $1,000 billion
Real assets 3) $1,000 billion	
Interest expense **$80 billion**	

Example 5.2 Continuation

Government	
Deposits with commercial banks (r = 4 %) 2) + \$200 billion 4) – \$200 billion	Treasury bonds sold (issued) (r = 6 %) 2) + \$200 billion
4) Expense of transferring government deposits with commercial banks to households **\$200 billion** **Interest expense** **\$12 billion**	

Households	
~~Real assets~~ ~~\$1,000 billion~~ ~~3) – \$1,000 billion~~	Equity \$1,000 billion
Deposits with commercial banks (r = 4 %) 3) + \$1,000 billion 4) + \$200 billion	
	4) Income from transferring government deposits with commercial banks to households **\$200 billion** **Interest income** **\$48 billion**

How do the sectors look like **one year later** (Example 5.2)? It is necessary to concentrate primarily on expense and income of each sector. Net interest income of commercial banks is \$44 billion (the difference between gross interest income \$92 billion and gross interest expense \$48 billion), entrepreneurial interest expense is \$80 billion, government interest expense is \$12 billion, and households' interest income is \$48 billion. **The sum of incomes and expenses in the whole**

economy is, naturally, zero as the interest income of one sector represent interest expense of other sectors. Similarly it must hold that interest expense of one entity corresponds to interest income of another entity.

5.2 Example of banking system with central bank

Now, we introduce central bank into the banking system. Central bank's principal role is to conduct monetary policy, i.e. to regulate short-term interbank market interest rates in order to influence inflation. Central bank regulates the short-term interbank market interest rate and from it the whole range of interest rates in the economy is derived. Central bank also issues currency and can impose reserve requirements.

5.2.1 Central bank without currency and reserve requirements

Let the central bank enter the system described in the Examples 5.1 and 5.2. The first deal of central bank can be the purchase of the riskless financial assets from commercial banks (e.g. purchase of treasury bonds). Central bank buys treasury bonds from commercial banks and credits their clearing accounts with the amount equal to the value of purchased bonds. In the Example 5.3 (beginning of the year) central bank purchases treasury bonds for $200 billion (transaction No. 5). Let balances of commercial banks' current accounts held with central bank bear the riskless interest rate of 6 %. For the reason of simplicity we suppose that this interest rate is the same as yield to maturity of treasury bonds (plain yield curve).

How do the sectors look like **one year later** (Example 5.4)? It is evident that both interest expense and interest income of each sector do not differ from the situation described in the Example 5.2. Expense and income of each sector is the same as if central bank is not present in the system. Net interest income of commercial banks is $44 billion, entrepreneurial interest expense is $80 billion, government interest expense is $12 billion, and households' interest income is $48 billion. **The sum of incomes and expenses in the whole economy is, naturally, zero as the interest income of one sector represent interest expense of other sectors.**

It is evident that the establishment of central bank affects neither interest expense nor interest income of any sector. **The central bank's profit is zero, and it has no influence on other sectors.** The establishment of central bank neither rises nor lowers interest expense and interest income of any sector. What are the benefits of central bank? Central bank conducts monetary policy i.e., it regulates short-term interbank market interest rates. In our examples **it regulates the in-**

terest paid on commercial banks' deposits held with central bank. Herein lies fundamental of the interest rates regulation. There was no regulator of interest rates in our preceding Examples 5.1 and 5.2. We have been working with interest rates of 4, 6 and 8 %, but there was no mechanism to anchor it. The introduction of central bank helped solve this problem. It is the crucial benefit of central bank.

The second benefit from establishment of central bank is the possibility to create central payment system. Commercial banks thus do not need to hold many nostro accounts with one another anymore. Every commercial bank can have only one account in central bank (the so-called clearing account). Via these accounts, commercial banks can operate their client payments (if both clients have their accounts with commercial banks) and interbank payments. Central bank generally operates payments denominated in domestic currency. Central bank influences balances oon clearing accounts by means of open market operations. Its objective is to affect balances of clearing accounts so that it is neither too small (otherwise, interest rates could be pushed very high) nor too large (in this case interest rates could fall to zero). It is necessary that the short-term interbank interest rates are not determined by the excess bank reserves but exclusively by the interest rate used to supply or absorb bank reserves (e.g. interest rate on commercial banks' deposits held with central bank as in Examples 5.3 and 5.4).

5.2.2 Central bank with currency and no reserve requirements

Let's suppose further that the legislature delegates to central bank a privilege to issue currency (banknotes and coins), and forbids it to any other entity. **Banknotes and coins issued by central bank represent debt securities bearing zero interest.** The amount of banknotes and coins issued depends exclusively on the demand of households, enterprises, commercial banks and government. All entities (households, enterprises, commercial banks and government) seek to minimize their holdings of currency. Let the whole amount of currency lies in the hands of households, and let the households demand currency of $150 billion. Central bank hence according to the Example 5.5 (beginning of the year) sells banknotes and coins to commercial banks for $150 billion (transaction No. 6). This amount is also deducted from commercial banks' clearing accounts held with central bank. Commercial banks thus exchange part of its assets (deposits with central bank) for currency. The balance sheet total of any sector remains unchanged.

Example 5.3 Balance sheets of commercial banks, enterprises, government, households and central bank (without currency and reserve requirements) at the beginning of the year

1) Loans of $1,000 billion from commercial banks to enterprises
2) Issue of treasury bonds of $200 billion sold to commercial banks
3) Purchase of real assets of $1,000 billion by enterprises from households
4) Transfer of $200 billion from government to households
5) Purchase of treasury bonds of $200 billion by central bank from commercial banks

Commercial banks

Loans granted to enterprises (r = 8 %) 1) + $1,000 billion	~~Enterprises deposits (r = 4 %)~~ ~~1) + $1,000 billion~~ ~~3) – $1,000 billion~~
~~Treasury bonds purchased (r = 6 %)~~ ~~2) + $200 billion~~ ~~5) – $200 billion~~	~~Government deposits (r = 4 %)~~ ~~2) + $200 billion~~ ~~4) – $200 billion~~
Deposits with central bank (r = 6 %) 5) + $200 billion	Households' deposits (r = 4 %) 3) + $1,000 billion 4) + $200 billion

Enterprises

~~Deposits with commercial banks (r = 4 %)~~ ~~1) + $1,000 billion~~ ~~3) – $1,000 billion~~	Loans from commercial banks (r = 8 %) 1) + $1,000 billion
Real assets 3) $1,000 billion	

Example 5.3 Continuation

Government	
~~Deposits with commercial banks (r = 4 %)~~ ~~2) + $200 billion~~ ~~4) – $200 billion~~	Treasury bonds sold (issued) (r = 6 %) 2) + $200 billion
4) Expense of transferring government deposits with commercial banks to households **$200 billion**	

Households	
~~Real assets~~ ~~$1,000 billion~~ ~~3) – $1,000 billion~~ Deposits with commercial banks (r = 4 %) 3) + $1,000 billion 4) + $200 billion	Equity $1,000 billion
	4) Income from transferring government deposits with commercial banks to households **$200 billion**

Central bank	
Treasury bonds purchased (r = 6 %) 5) + $200 billion	Deposits from commercial banks (r = 6 %) 5) + $200 billion

Example 5.4 Balance sheets of commercial banks, enterprises, government, households and central bank (without currency and reserve requirements) at the end of the year

1) Loans of $1,000 billion from commercial banks to enterprises
2) Issue of treasury bonds of $200 billion sold to commercial banks
3) Purchase of real assets of $1,000 billion by enterprises from households
4) Transfer of $200 billion from government to households
5) Purchase of treasury bonds of $200 billion by central bank from commercial banks

Commercial banks

Loans granted to enterprises (r = 8 %) 1) + $1,000 billion **(+80)**	~~Enterprises deposits (r = 4 %)~~ ~~1) + $1,000 billion~~ ~~3) – $1,000 billion~~
~~Treasury bonds purchased (r = 6 %)~~ ~~2) + $200 billion~~ ~~5) – $200 billion~~	~~Government deposits (r = 4 %)~~ ~~2) + $200 billion~~ ~~4) – $200 billion~~
Deposits with central bank (r = 6 %) 5) + $200 billion **(+12)**	Households' deposits (r = 4 %) 3) + $1,000 billion **(+40)** 4) + $200 billion **(+8)**
Interest expense **$48 billion**	**Interest income** **$92 billion**

Enterprises

~~Deposits with commercial banks (r = 4 %)~~ ~~1) + $1,000 billion~~ ~~3) – $1,000 billion~~	Loans from commercial banks (r = 8 %) 1) + $1,000 billion **(+80)**
Real assets 3) $1,000 billion	
Interest expense **$80 billion**	

Example 5.4 Continuation

Government	
~~Deposits with commercial banks (r = 4 %)~~ ~~2) + $200 billion~~ ~~4) – $200 billion~~	Securities sold (issued) (r = 6 %) 2) + $200 billion **(+12)**
4) Expense of transferring government deposits with commercial banks to households **$200 billion** **Interest expense** **$12 billion**	

Households	
~~Real assets~~ ~~$1,000 billion~~ ~~3) – $1,000 billion~~ Deposits with commercial banks (r = 4 %) 3) + $1,000 billion **(+40)** 4) + $200 billion **(+8)**	Equity $1,000 billion
	4) Income from transferring government deposits with commercial banks to households **$200 billion** **Interest income** **$48 billion**

Central bank	
Treasury bonds purchased (r = 6 %) 5) + $200 billion **(+12)**	Deposits from commercial banks (r = 6 %) 5) + $200 billion **(+12)**
Interest expense **$12 billion**	**Interest income** **$12 billion**

Example 5.5 Balance sheets of commercial banks, enterprises, government, households and central bank (with currency and without reserve requirements) at the beginning of the year

1) Loans of $1,000 billion from commercial banks to enterprises
2) Issue of treasury bonds of $200 billion sold to commercial banks
3) Purchase of real assets of $1,000 billion by enterprises from households
4) Transfer of $200 billion from government to households
5) Purchase of treasury bonds of $200 billion by central bank from commercial banks
6) Purchase of currency of $150 billion by commercial banks from central bank
7) Withdrawal of currency of $150 billion by households from commercial banks

Commercial banks	
Loans granted to enterprises (r = 8 %) 1) + $1,000 billion	~~Enterprises deposits (r = 4 %)~~ ~~1) + $1,000 billion~~ ~~3) – $1,000 billion~~
~~Treasury bonds purchased (r = 6 %)~~ ~~2) + $200 billion~~ ~~5) – $200 billion~~	~~Government deposits (r = 4 %)~~ ~~2) + $200 billion~~ ~~4) – $200 billion~~
Deposits with central bank (r = 6 %) 5) + $200 billion 6) –$150 billion	Households' deposits (r = 4 %) 3) + $1,000 billion 4) + $200 billion 7) –$150 billion
~~Currency (r = 0 %)~~ ~~6) + $150 billion~~ ~~7) – $150 billion~~	

Enterprises	
~~Deposits with commercial banks (r = 4 %)~~ ~~1) + $1,000 billion~~ ~~3) – $1,000 billion~~	Loans from commercial banks (r = 8 %) 1) + $1,000 billion
Real assets 3) $1,000 billion	

Example 5.5 Continuation

Government	
~~Deposits with commercial banks (r = 4 %)~~ ~~2) + $200 billion~~ ~~4) – $200 billion~~	Securities sold (issued) (r = 6 %) 2) + $200 billion
4) Expense of transferring government deposits with commercial banks to households **$200 billion**	

Households	
~~Real assets~~ ~~$1,000 billion~~ ~~3) – $1,000 billion~~	Equity $1,000 billion
Deposits with commercial banks (r = 4 %) 3) + $1,000 billion 4) + $200 billion 7) – $150 billion	
Currency (r = 0 %) 7) + $150 billion	
	4) Income from transferring government deposits with commercial banks to households **$200 billion**

Central bank	
Treasury bonds purchased (r = 6 %) 5) + $200 billion	Deposits from commercial banks (r = 6 %) 5) + $200 billion 6) – $150 billion
	Currency (r = 0 %) 6) + $150 billion

Example 5.6 Balance sheets of commercial banks, enterprises, government, households and central bank (with currency and without reserve requirements) at the end of the year

1) Loans of $1,000 billion from commercial banks to enterprises
2) Issue of treasury bonds of $200 billion sold to commercial banks
3) Purchase of real assets of $1,000 billion by enterprises from households
4) Transfer of $200 billion from government to households
5) Purchase of treasury bonds of $200 billion by central bank from commercial banks
6) Purchase of currency of $150 billion by commercial banks from central bank
7) Withdrawal of currency of $150 billion by households from commercial banks

Commercial banks	
Loans granted to enterprises (r = 8 %) 1) + $1,000 billion **(+80)**	~~Enterprises deposits (r = 4 %)~~ ~~1) + $1,000 billion~~ ~~3) – $1,000 billion~~
~~Treasury bonds purchased (r = 6 %)~~ ~~2) + $200 billion~~ ~~5) – $200 billion~~	~~Government deposits (r = 4 %)~~ ~~2) + $200 billion~~ ~~4) – $200 billion~~
Deposits with central bank (r = 6 %) 5) + $200 billion **(+12)** 6) –$150 billion **(-9)**	Households' deposits (r = 4 %) 3) + $1,000 billion **(+40)** 4) + $200 billion **(+8)** 7) –$150 billion **(-6)**
~~Currency (r = 0 %)~~ ~~6) + $150 billion~~ ~~7) – $150 billion~~	
Interest expense **$42 billion**	**Interest income** **$83 billion**

Enterprises	
~~Deposits with commercial banks (r = 4 %)~~ ~~1) + $1,000 billion~~ ~~3) – $1,000 billion~~	Loans from commercial banks (r = 8 %) 1) + $1,000 billion
Real assets 3) $1,000 billion	
Interest expense **$80 billion**	

Example 5.6 Continuation

Government	
~~Deposits with commercial banks (r = 4 %)~~ ~~2) + $200 billion~~ ~~4) – $200 billion~~	Securities sold (issued) (r = 6 %) 2) + $200 billion
4) Expense of transferring government deposits with to households $200 billion **Interest expense** **$12 billion**	

Households	
~~Real assets~~ ~~$1,000 billion~~ ~~3) – $1,000 billion~~	Equity $1,000 billion
Deposits with commercial banks (r = 4 %) 3) + $1,000 billion **(+40)** 4) + $200 billion **(+8)** 7) – $150 billion **(-6)**	
Currency (r = 0 %) 7) + $150 billion	
	4) Income from transferring government deposits with to households $200 billion **Interest income** **$42 billion**

Central bank	
Treasury bonds purchased (r = 6 %) 5) + $200 billion	Deposits from commercial banks (r = 6 %) 5) + $200 billion **(+12)** 6) – $150 billion **(-9)**
	Currency (r = 0 %) 6) + $200 billion
Interest expense **$3 billion**	**Interest income** **$12 billion**

Further commercial banks sell the whole amount of currency to households (transaction No. 7). Households receive currency in exchange for the part of their deposits held with commercial banks. The households' current accounts decrease by $150 billion. The balance sheet total of commercial banks decreases by the same amount, and the balance sheet total of any other sectors remains unchanged.

How do the sectors look like **one year later** (Example 5.6)? In comparison to Examples 5.2 and 5.4, the net interest income of commercial banks decreased from $44 billion to $41 billion (i.e. by $3 billion), entrepreneurial interest expense remains unchanged ($80 billion), government expense is $12 billion, and households' interest income decreased from $48 billion to $42 billion (i.e. by **$6 billion**). On the other hand, central bank's interest expense decreased by **$9 billion. The sum of incomes and expenses in the whole economy is, naturally, zero as the interest income of one sector represent interest expense of other sectors.**

It is clear that the privilege to issue currency of central bank substantially changes redistribution of interest expense and interest income among sectors. **Since the currency does not bear interest, the net income of central bank increased from zero to $9 billion.** This net income results solely from privilege of central bank at the market. Other entities cannot achieve this benefit. **Such an income must necessarily represent the expense of other entities. Enterprises loose $3 billion, and households loose $6 billion.**

Central bank is the public sector agency. The right to issue currency by central bank represents:

- **Taxation of commercial banks**, even if commercial banks does not hold any vault cash. This taxation consists in the fall of households' deposits with commercial banks and in the equivalent fall of interest-bearing deposits of commercial banks held with central bank. In our example this taxation is $3 billion; and

- **Taxation of households and enterprises.** This taxation consists in the falling households' and entrepreneurial deposits with commercial banks in exchange for currency. In our example this taxation equals $6 billion.

The taxation makes the profit of central bank. **It is evident that taxation results from the central bank's privilege to issue currency, and therefore this taxation should be redistributed to the government budget.** However, legislation usually sets that central bank does not transfer this particular item but the whole profit, as it performs other state functions as well. The profit of $9 billion mentioned hereinbefore is the so-called **seigniorage.**

Theoretically, **currency need not exist at all**. Deposits on current accounts of households, enterprises and government can perform the same functions (medium of exchange and store of value) as currency itself. Central bank would save its expense of printing banknotes and coinage. Households, enterprises, government and commercial banks would also save their safekeeping expense. All payments would be cashless, i.e. in the form of transfers between clients' and commercial banks' accounts.

5.2.3 Central bank with currency and reserve requirements

The issue of currency does not represent the only central bank's monopoly. Another privilege of the central bank consists in the option to impose reverve requirements and in the option not to pay (or to pay less then on interbank market) interest on commercial banks' deposits with central bank. In preceding chapter, we have supposed that these deposits yield the interest rate of 6 %. Legislature on central banks in some countries allows central banks not to pay this interest (or to use interest rate lower than the interbank interest rate). Since the zero-interest-bearing deposits are not favourable, commercial banks seek to minimize such holdings. If deposits become mandatory, they are call reserve requirements (see section 1.3). Central bank usually sets it as a percentage of client deposits (deposits of household and enterprises) in commercial banks. Let's suppose (Examples 5.7 and 5.8) that reserve requirements are $34 billion (operation No. 8) and that reserve base consists solely of client deposits. Hence the reserve ratio reach 3.24 % (= $34 billion / $1,050 billion).

In Examples 5.7 (beginning of the year) and 5.8 (end of the year) **reserve requirements do not bear interest**. The calculation in section 4.2 shows that **the taxation through zero-interest-bearing reserve requirements is $2.05 billion**. Central bank's interest expense decreased from $3 billion to $0.95 billion, i.e. by $2.05 billion. If there is no change of interest paid and charged on client deposits and loans, the implementation of zero-interest-bearing reserve requirements would affect adversely profit of commercial banks. Their interest income lowers from $83 billion to $80.95 billion, i.e. by $2.05 billion. This sum corresponds to the central bank's additional profit.

Example 5.7 Balance sheets of commercial banks, enterprises, government, households and central bank (with currency and reserve requirements) at the beginning of the year

1) Loans of $1,000 billion from commercial banks to enterprises
2) Issue of treasury bonds of $200 billion sold to commercial banks
3) Purchase of real assets of $1,000 billion by enterprises from households
4) Transfer of $200 billion from government to households
5) Purchase of treasury bonds of $200 billion by central bank from commercial banks
6) Purchase of currency of $150 billion by commercial banks from central bank
7) Withdrawal of currency of $150 billion by households from commercial banks
8) Imposition of reserve requirements of $34 billion by central bank on commercial banks

Commercial banks	
Loans granted to enterprises (r = **8.1 %**) 1) + $1,000 billion	~~Enterprises deposits (r = 4 %)~~ ~~1) + $1,000 billion~~ ~~3) – $1,000 billion~~
~~Treasury bonds purchased (r = 6 %)~~ ~~2) + $200 billion~~ ~~5) – $200 billion~~	~~Government deposits (r = 4 %)~~ ~~2) + $200 billion~~ ~~4) – $200 billion~~
Deposits with central bank (r = 6 %) 5) + $200 billion 6) –$150 billion 8) – $34 billion	Households' deposits (r = **3.9 %**) 3) + $1,000 billion 4) + $200 billion 7) –$150 billion
~~Currency (r = 0 %)~~ ~~6) + $150 billion~~ ~~7) – $150 billion~~	
Required reserves (r = 0 %) 8) + $34 billion	

Enterprises	
~~Deposits with commercial banks (r = 4 %)~~ ~~1) + $1,000 billion~~ ~~3) – $1,000 billion~~	Loans from commercial banks (r = **8.1 %**) 1) + $1,000 billion
Real assets 3) $1,000 billion	

Example 5.7 Continuation

Government	
~~Deposits with commercial banks (r = 4 %)~~ ~~2) + $200 billion~~ ~~4) – $200 billion~~	Securities sold (issued) (r = 6 %) 2) + $200 billion
4) Expense of transferring government deposits with to households $200 billion	

Households	
~~Real assets~~ ~~$1,000 billion~~ ~~3) – $1,000 billion~~	Equity $1,000 billion
Deposits with commercial banks (r = **3.9 %)** 3) + $1,000 billion 4) + $200 billion 7) – $150 billion	
Currency (r = 0 %) 7) + $150 billion	
	4) Income from transferring government deposits with to households $200 billion

Central bank	
Treasury bonds purchased (r = 6 %) 5) + $200 billion	Deposits from commercial banks (r = 6 %) 5) + $200 billion 6) – $150 billion 8) – $34 billion
	Currency (r = 0 %) 6) + $150 billion
	Required reserves (r = 0 %) 8) + $34 billion

Example 5.8 Balance sheets of commercial banks, enterprises, government, households and central bank (with currency and reserve requirements) at the end of the year

1) Loans of $1,000 billion from commercial banks to enterprises
2) Issue of treasury bonds of $200 billion sold to commercial banks
3) Purchase of real assets of $1,000 billion by enterprises from households
4) Transfer of $200 billion from government to households
5) Purchase of treasury bonds of $200 billion by central bank from commercial banks
6) Purchase of currency of $150 billion by commercial banks from central bank
7) Withdrawal of currency of $150 billion by households from commercial banks
8) Imposition of reserve requirements of $34 billion by central bank on commercial banks

Commercial banks

Loans granted to enterprises (r = **8.1 %**) 1) + $1,000 billion **(+8.1)**	~~Enterprises deposits (r = 4 %)~~ ~~1) + $1,000 billion~~ ~~3) – $1,000 billion~~
~~Treasury bonds purchased (r = 6 %)~~ ~~2) + $200 billion~~ ~~5) – $200 billion~~	~~Government deposits (r = 4 %)~~ ~~2) + $200 billion~~ ~~4) – $200 billion~~
Deposits with central bank (r = 6 %) 5) + $200 billion **(+12)** 6) –$150 billion **(-9)** 8) – $34 billion **(-2.05)**	Households deposits (r = **3.9 %**) 3) + $1,000 billion **(+39)** 4) + $200 billion **(+7.8)** 7) –$150 billion **(-5.85)**
~~Currency (r = 0 %)~~ ~~6) + $150 billion~~ ~~7) – $150 billion~~	
Required reserves (r = 0 %) 8) + $34 billion	
Interest expense **$40.95 billion**	**Interest income** **$81.95 billion**

Enterprises

~~Deposits with commercial banks (r = 4 %)~~ ~~1) + $1,000 billion~~ ~~3) – $1,000 billion~~	Loans from commercial banks (r = **8.1 %**) 1) + $1,000 billion **(+81)**
Real assets 3) $1,000 billion	
Interest expense **$81billion**	

Example 5.8 Continuation

Government	
~~Deposits with commercial banks (r = 4 %)~~ ~~2) + $200 billion~~ ~~4) – $200 billion~~	Securities sold (issued) (r = 6 %) 2) + $200 billion **(+12)**
4) Expense of transferring government deposits with to households $200 billion **Interest expense $12 billion**	

Households	
~~Real assets~~ ~~$1,000 billion~~ ~~3) – $1,000 billion~~	Equity $1,000 billion
Deposits with commercial banks (r= **3.9 %**) 3) + $1,000 billion **(+39)** 4) + $200 billion **(+7.8)**	
Currency (r = 0 %) 7) + $150 billion	
	4) Income from transferring government deposits with to households $200 billion **Interest income $40.95 billion**

Central bank	
Treasury bonds purchased (r = 6 %) 5) + $200 billion **(+12)**	Deposits from commercial banks (r = 6 %) 5) + $200 billion **(+12)** 6) – $150 billion **(-9)** 8) – $34 billion **(-2.05)**
	Currency (r = 0 %) 6) + $150 billion
	Required reserves (r = 0 %) 8) + $34 billion
Interest expense $0.95 billion	**Interest income $12 billion**

In reality commercial banks usually transfer the lowered profit on their clients by widening the credit spread between interest paid on deposits and interest charged on loans. Until now, we have supposed the credit spread of 4 % (8 % – 4 %). However, if profits of commercial banks are to remain unaffected by the implementation of reserve requirements, interest charged on loans would have to rise and interests paid on deposits would have to fall. In Examples 5.7 and 5.8 interest rates would have to change (both increase and decrease) by **0.1 %** [= $2.05 billion / ($1,000 billion + $1,050 billion)]. Credit spread would have to increase from 4 % to 4.2 % (8.1 % – 3.9 %).

How do the sectors look like **one year later** (Example 5.8)? Comparing Examples 5.8 and 5.6 we find that commercial banks' interest expense decreased from $42 billion to $40.95 billion and that their interest income decreased from $83 billion to $81.95 billion. The net income remained unchanged on level of $41 billion. Entrepreneurial interest expense increased by **$1 billion** (from $80 billion to $81 billion). Government interest expense remained unchanged on level of $12 billion. Interest income of households decreased by **$1.05 billion** (from $42 billion to $40.95 billion). Central bank's interest expense decreased by **$2.05 billion** (from $3 billion to $0.95 billion) and its interest income remained unaffected on level of $12 billion. **The sum of incomes and expenses in the whole economy is, naturally, zero as the interest income of one sector represent interest expense of other sectors.**

Implementation of zero-interest-bearing reserve requirements represents:

- **Taxation imposed on households.** In our example it is $1 billion; and
- **Taxation imposed on enterprises.** In our example it is $1.05 billion.

Who has paid for the central bank's additional net income (and thus for the increased income of the government budget) resulting from implementation of the zero-interest-bearing reserve requirements? **The additional profit of central bank is balanced by additional loss of enterprises (higher interest expense) and households (lower interest income)**. We have proved that zero-interest-bearing reserve requirements represent **taxation of enterprises and households**.

To summarize, zero-interest-bearing reserve requirements (or reserve requirements bearing interest rate lower than the interbank interest rate) impact income statement in a similar way as an issue of currency. Taxation though currency is paid directly by currency holders (i.e. particularly households and enterprises) but taxation through zero-interest-bearing reserve requirements is paid by commercial banks. Commercial banks naturally seek ways how to transfer this taxation on their clients. One way is by higher interest on loans and lower interest on deposits.

6 Financial statements of central banks

Financial statements should inform their users (investors, creditors, regulators and other stakeholders) about the financial condition and results of operations of an entity. However, such statements cannot provide all the information needed for economic decision-making by users because, among other things, they are based solely on the former events and usually do not include non-financial performance indicators. In addition, financial statements in many countries are used primarily to determine the tax base which is a different purpose yielding a different result than the reporting of economic performance.

6.1 The basics of financial statements

We will briefly introduce generally accepted accounting principles of the United States (US GAAP), international financial reporting standards (IFRS) and corresponding legislation of the European Union. We will also present the role of financial statements in financial regulation. Significant differences in national accounting standards make comparisons between companies in the same industry in different countries difficult. There is strong pressure for harmonization of accounting standards in the world. Investors need comparable information.

6.1.1 US generally accepted accounting principles

The legal authority over financial reporting for publicly traded companies in the US is the Securities and Exchange Commission or SEC (established by the Securities Exchange Act of 1934). However, over the years, the SEC has relied heavily on the private sector for the establishment of US GAAP. For the past few decades, the body responsible for establishing accounting standards in the United States has been the Financial Accounting Standards Board (FASB) located in Norwalk, Connecticut. The FASB consists of five independent experts with diverse backgrounds supported by a large staff developing standards based on research and public deliberation with full due process to get the input of all user groups. Newly adopted standards attempt to balance economic benefits with implementation and other costs.

With the tremendous growth in cross border investment and the resulting demand for a common language of financial reporting throughout the world, the FASB and International Accounting Standards Committee (IASC) headquartered in London reached an agreement in September 2002 to work towards the convergence of US and international accounting standards and the joint development of future standards. As a result, all major projects for the development of new standards and amendments of standards are currently carried out jointly by the two standard setting bodies.

Both US GAAP and International financial reporting standards are based on similar general principles but US GAAP covers more detailed rules about how to apply and implement standards. The reason for this is the influence of the powerful SEC which is concerned about diminishing the possibility of evading general principles as well as the desire by some auditors and companies for exact rules which can be used as a defence against potential lawsuits. As a result, US GAAP generally contains few alternatives which, somebody can argue, assure higher comparability of reported data.

6.1.2 International Financial Reporting Standards

International financial reporting standards (IFRS) are being developed by the International Accounting Standards Board (IASB) which is an independent, privately-funded accounting standard-setter based in London. There are 14 members of IASB, each with one vote.

The International Accounting Standards Committee Foundation (IASCF) Constitution provides that "The Trustees shall select members of the IASB, consistently with the Criteria for IASB Members set out in the Annex to the Constitution, so that it will comprise a group of people representing, within that group, the best available combination of technical expertise and diversity of international business and market experience in order to contribute to the development of high quality, global accounting standards. The members of the IASB shall be required to commit themselves formally to acting in the public interest in all matters."

The objective of the IASCF is to develop, in the public interest, a single set of high quality, understandable and enforceable global accounting standards that require high quality, transparent and comparable information in financial statements and other financial reporting to help participants in the world's capital markets and other users make economic decisions;

The IASB establish and maintain liaison with national standard-setters and other official bodies concerned with standard-setting in order to promote the convergence of national accounting standards and IFRS. It has a specific and ambitious program of convergence with the FASB as mentioned above.

More than 100 countries either require or permit the use of IFRS for publicly traded companies. Some other jurisdictions base their national practices on

IFRS. In 2004 IASB and the Accounting Standards Board of Japan agreed to initiate discussions about a joint project to minimize differences between IFRS and Japanese accounting standards towards a final goal of convergence of their standards. It is suggested that mandatory adoption of IFRS in Japan will take place in 2016.

6.1.3 EU directives and regulations

Financial reporting in European Union is subject to the following directives (for all enterprises):

- *Fourth Council Directive 78/660/EEC of 25 July 1978 based on article 54(3)(g) of the Treaty on the annual accounts of certain types of companies,*

- *Seventh Council Directive 83/349/EEC of 13 June 1983 based on article 54(3)(g) of the Treaty on consolidated accounts.*

In addition, the financial reporting of banks and other financial institutions is subject to:

- *Council Directive 86/635/EEC of 8 December 1986 on the annual accounts and consolidated accounts of banks and other financial institutions.*

In reaction to the concept of fair value in IAS 39, EU have adopted directive updating the three directives mentioned above:

- *Directive 2001/65/EC of the European Parliament and of the Council of 27 September 2001 amending Directive 78/660/EEC, 83/349/EEC and 86/635/EEC as regards the valuation rules for the annual and consolidated accounts of certain types of companies as well as of banks and other financial institutions.*

The directive contains the concept of fair value. Some assets as well as some liabilities should be first recorded and later measured at fair value. Implementation of fair value was mainly the response to the use of derivatives by some enterprises.

In order to meet the needs of insurance undertakings, EU has published special directive:

- *Council Directive of 19 December 1991 on the annual accounts and consolidated accounts of insurance undertakings (91/674/EEC).*

The key step in reporting was made in 2002 when EU adopted regulation:

- *Regulation (EC) No 1606/2002 of the European Parliament and of the Council f 19 July 2002 on the application of international accounting standards.*

According to this regulation, **starting on 1 January 2005 all companies (including banks and insurance companises) shall prepare their consolidated financial accounts in strict accordance with IFRS if their securities are admitted to trading on a regulated market of any member state.** National legislations can extend the application of IFRS to solo financial accounts of these companies as well as to financial accounts (both solo and consolidated) of any other entities.

6.1.4 The role of accounting in regulation of financial institutions

Any regulation of financial institution is concerned about the accounting principles raising the transparency of financial transactions and supporting the proper risk management. It is a key instrument for stability of banks and other financial institutions. Accounting serves as a basis for regulation, mainly for capital adequacy. Regulators assist in improvement of accounting practices. Bank regulators focus their attention on financial instruments, including loan allowances. Loan allowances are the key item in any bank income statement. The international agreement about this topic has not been reached yet.

Accounting measures assets, liabilities, equity, expenses and income. It also helps to increase the market discipline by means of transparent reporting. Market discipline is the third pillar of capital adequacy. It requires reliable and timely information about the accounting methods including measurement methods of asset and liabilities, risk management, risk portfolio and equity composition. This information is important to the public. Reliable risk measurement starts with financial reporting data.

From the regulatory point of view the accounting standards must fulfil the following criteria:

- To contribute to the risk management;
- To maintain the market discipline through transparent financial statements and information about accounting methods;
- To facilitate supervision of regulated institutions;

- To provide reliable information about the financial situation of regulated institutions; and
- Not enable alternative treatments (if it does, it must be published).

For capital adequacy purposes regulators sometimes make correction of the accounting data.

6.2 Role of central bank

In order to understand clearly the balance sheet and income statement of central bank one first has to be acquainted with its role. Later we will examine three structures of the central bank's balance sheet, examples of the central bank's financial statements, administration of foreign exchange reserves and seigniorage.

Central banks were evolving gradually over the whole 20th century. Central bank represents public sector agency to which the treasury department of the government delegated some of its powers. **The difference between central bank and other public sector agencies consists in the two tasks that central bank should fulfil independently on the government:**

- **Monetary policy,** and
- **Granting loans to the government (if any).**

In all its remaining tasks, central bank can remain dependent on the government.

The central bank's profit is generally transferred into central government budget. On the other hand, in most cases, the central bank's loss is not explicit part of the central government budget, and it is implicit part of the central government budget. Then there is no money transfer from central government to central bank. If it is explicit part of the central government budget a loss is covered by taxes or the issue of treasury bonds. But in most countries it is politically unacceptable. In some cases the money transfer from the central government budget to central bank is delayed.

One should take into account that at he end central bank's economic results contribute in any case to the of government budget. Hence, we can assert that **any of central bank's income or expense is actually central government budget income or expense.** Central government budget thus benefits from the central bank's profits, and it pays (with some delay) for its losses. From the point of view of the tax system, taxation of central bank is 100 %. Under such circumstances **central bank's equity has no special importance.** Central bank (as well as any other bank) can operate with any (or even with negative) equity without any impact on its operations.

Central bank has usually the authority to perform the following roles:

- Monetary policy;
- Central payment system and the administration of the commercial banks' current accounts (clearing accounts);
- Banking supervision;
- Issue of the currency;
- Administration of foreign exchange reserves and foreign exchange interventions;
- Administration of government accounts;
- Administration of treasury securities auctions;
- Granting loans to government (if any);
- Concern over government budget;
- Financial statistics for local, state and federal authorities; and
- Lender of the last resort.

Central bank exist in almost any country (sometimes it is called monetary authority). Central bank is not the only institution capable to perform these functions. Any other central institution could perform it as well. The absolute majority of central banks are in charge of monetary policy. Nowadays, almost all central banks have the monopoly to issue banknotes. However, there are certain exceptions to this rule, namely in Hong Kong and Scotland where commercial banks issue banknotes under the supervision of central banks. Other tasks (e.g. central payment system, banking supervision, administration of foreign exchange reserves, realization of foreign exchange interventions and administration of the treasury securities auctions) remain under the treasury department or other government agency in some cases.

6.2.1 Monetary policy

Monetary policy will be discussed in the following chapters of this book. It is considered to be a key role of any central bank.

6.2.2 Central payment system and the administration of banks' current accounts

Central payment system will be discussed in the last chapter of this book.

6.2.3 Banking supervision

The task of banking supervision is to avoid bank bankruptcies and thus it protects clients' deposits. In some countries, the bank supervision is not carried out by central bank but by special government agency.

6.2.4 Issue of currency

The issue of currency (banknotes and coins) is central bank's duty in most countries. The banknotes are almost in any country issued by central bank. In some countries, however, central bank issues banknotes, and the treasury department issues coins (e.g. in the United States). Commercial banks pay for currency from their clearing accounts with central bank. Commercial banks do not need the currency for themselves but for their clients. To issue currency central bank must draft the graphical design of banknotes and coins and it prints (stamps) them. It also has to dispose the used banknotes and coins.

6.2.5 Foreign exchange reserves administration and interventions

In this part we deal with foreign exchange reserves administration. Foreign exchange intervention is the topic of one of the following chapters.

According to International Monetary Fund (IMF), **foreign** a country's **foreign exchange (international) reserves** refer to those external assets that are readily available to and controlled by monetary authorities for direct financing of payments imbalances, for indirectly regulating the magnitudes of such imbalances through intervention in exchange markets to affect the currency exchange rate, and/or for other purposes. Foreign exchange reserves cover foreign exchange assets, gold, special drawing rights (SDRs), reserve position in the IMF and other claims. Foreign exchange assets consists of foreign currencies (deposits with foreign banks) and foreign currency deposits and debt and equity securities. They are denominated in reserve currencies, mainly in US dollar, euro, UK pound, and Japanese yen. In majority countries foreign exchange assets are managed by central banks.

As from 2002 till the first half of 2009, the world international reserves increased from $2,104 billion to $8,465 billion. At the first half of 2009, eastern

Asia countries held more than a half of this amount. Mainland China was the country with the highest amount of international reserves ($2,132 billion). Japan held international reserves amounting $2,023 billion. Also the Eurozone ($685 billion), Russia ($401 billion), Saudi Arabia ($395 billion), Taiwan ($321 billion) and India ($271 billion) have reached their records. These countries have accumulated huge international reserves to maintain weak domestic currencies to help their exports, which is needed to save and create jobs, thereby absorbing abundant labour in traditional sectors.

The most part of foreign exchange reserves takes form of U.S. securities, which play an important role in financing of U.S. trade deficit. Therefore foreign entities invest their dollars back to the USA. If Asian banks are not holding these amounts of reserves, the exchange rate of dollar would be much lower. Some Asian countries accumulate international reserves since they still remember impacts of the Asian currency crisis at the end of nineties. This crisis withdrew international reserves in the majority of affected countries. Nowadays, international reserves of many Asian coutries have already exceeded the gross domestic product. By maintaining their exchange rates weak, central banks seek to support domestic exporters. Southern Korean Won, Thai Baht or Singapore dollar are not as strong as the surplus of their trade balance would suggest. In average, Asian currencies (excluding Japanese Yen) are undervaluated by more than 20 %. Their international reserves consist mainly of U.S. dollars. As the value of U.S. dollar is falling, value of these reserves is falling too. Some central banks have, therefore, started to rearrange their reserves into Euro. This fact can also explain partly the strength of Euro.

Foreign exchange reserves depend strongly on currency crises. International reserves of Southern Korea, for instance, were equal $19 billion in 1997, and in time of crisis reserves fell to a mere $6 billion. Weakening Won have strongly supported the export, and international reserves have fast started to grow again. Southern Korean reserves amounted to $66 billion in August 1999, and the amount of reserves has even reached $123 billion in February 2003. On the contrary, crisis in Hong Kong has caused falling exports and increasing unemployment. Brazil has experienced crisis a bit later – in a first quarter of 1998. Foreign exchange reserves of Hungarian central bank exceeded the level of €14 billion in January 2003, although at the end of December 2002 it was only €10 billion. At that time, speculators were trying to force exchange rate of Forint/Euro to break the upper bound of the 30 % fluctuation interval.

There are not many ways how central banks can diversify their assets. They are usually not allowed to purchase corporate bonds and shares. **U.S. dollar is the world predominant reserve currency.** Central banks hold dollars, even though they find it risky. Approcimately, one half of the world trade is carried out in dollars. The whole Asia, for example, represents de facto dollar zone. To see why the U.S. dollar has become so attractive, notice, for instance, that prices of main commodities, like oil, copper, steel, wheat and others, are denominated in U.S. dollars. Another reason is the liquidity and size of the U.S. financial market. U.S. dollar also represents approximately 40 % of the world foreign-exchange transactions. U.S. dollar plays very important role in countries frequently jeopardized by high inflation or political instability.

Despite its predominant position, U.S. dollar faces difficulties nowadays. Among the most serious problem is enormous trade deficit of the United States. U.S. economy has experienced increasing inflow of foreign investments. In recent years, foreign investors have started, for the first time within more than hundred years, to earn in the United States more than their U.S. partners abroad. According to some analyses, trade deficit was the key factor causing the rapid fall of U.S. dollar to Japanese yen and German mark in 1995 and to euro during 2003 and 2004.

Since the launch of European currency in 1999, euro is gradually increasing its share in the world foreign exchange reserves. After the World War I, U.S. dollar needed several decades to replace British pound and Swiss frank in such a manner. The gold is also maintaining its attractiveness, and it represents the second most used reserve asset worldwide.

Higher international reserves can help central bank defend better its currency against sudden attacks of speculators. They avoid the undesirable high volatility of exchange rate. Historically, IMF has suggested that countries should hold foreign exchange reserves equal to the three-month's import of goods and services. The United States holds a reserve not exceeding its one-month's import. To strengthen their reserves, some countries need to employ foreign loans.

International reserves increase when the central bank:

- Intervenes against appreciating home currency;
- Collects interest on international reserves; and
- Accepts foreign currency payments on the account of its clients.

Conversely, international reserves decrease when the central bank:

- Intervenes against depreciating home currency; and
- When its clients ask for foreign currency payments from their accounts.

Foreign reserves do not change when central bank's clients exchange foreign currency for domestic currency or vice versa.

Foreign exchange interventions depend on the currency regime and balance of payments. In the case of the fixed exchange rate regime, interventions are more frequent, and the amount of reserves corresponds exactly to the balance of payments. If there is neither surplus nor deficit, international reserves do not change. In the case of surplus (deficit), reserves increase (decrease). Under the floating exchange rate regime FX interventions do not exist, and international reserves do not follow the evolution of balance of payments.

6.2.6 Administration of government accounts

Government disposes of enormous budget. In modern economies, government redistributes frequently from 30 to 60 % of the gross domestic product. Central bank usually administers the government current accounts. Any government revenues and expenditures run through this account. The majority of these income and expenses change commercial banks reserves with central bank by the amount of a payment. On the other hand, transactions between government and other clients of central bank and transactions between government and central bank itself do not affect bank reserves.

6.2.7 Administration of treasury securities auctions

Since the government budget is almost never balanced or even in surplus, governments often needs to borrow money from commercial banks or from public (i.e. from enterprises and households). In certain countries, government even borrows from its central bank (this issue will be discussed in the next subsection). To finance its deficits, government usually issues treasury securities (T-bills, T-notes and T-bonds). However, borrowing money is hardly the way to solve fiscal problems in a long-term because in most cases the government starts not to control its expenditures.

When granting a loan, commercial bank looks primarily at the return on this loan. Banks, therefore, do not grant loan to eighty years old individual for his repayment capacity is minimal. Contrariwise, the state never dies. Its repayment capacity does not diminish with age, and if the economy grows, debts do not represent serious danger. Many governments pull their debts onwards as huge snowballs. The debt increases with further deficits. The question is how huge the ball could be to allow government repaying it. Central government debts in countries like the USA or EU amounts around 70 % of the gross domestic product without causing serious troubles. On the contrary, Argentina was unable to manage the public debt amounting only to 55 % of GDP. The answer depends on numerous factors. The most important one is the overall economic development. Systematic accumulation of deficits necessarily results in currency devaluation. Anyway, present debt of any government represents higher future taxation.

The Maastricht Treaty (1991) has imposed the upper limit of yearly budget deficit of EU states on level of 3 % of GDP. Member state that fails to meet Maastricht criteria can be penalized by the amount of up to 0.5 % of GDP, and it can be forced to reduce its deficit under the required level within the next twelve months. Theoretically, several budgetary cuts would suffice to meet criteria again. However, electorate does not like economy measures. Social expenditures (e.g. education) represent the major part of the government budget and, therefore, financial trap to any democracy. The first EU country that failed to meet budgetary criteria was Portugal whose deficit amounted to 4.1 % of GDP in 2001. Another important budgetary item is the debt service. Cuts in this field are out of question. Debt service represents a heavy burden reminding that debts are not for free. The debt service in Portugal, for instance, amounts to one third of the government budget.

Some issues of treasury securities and subsequent government spending affect monetary aggregates. Example 6.1 shows how government that issues securities by selling it to non-bank entity uses the raised funds for social transfer to households. Example 6.2 shows government that issues securities by selling it to commercial bank and that uses the raised fund for social transfer to households.

It is obvious that in the first case (treasury securities are bought by non-bank entity – household or enterprise) **monetary aggregates do not change** since the money are eventually transferred from the client X's current account (buyer of treasury securities) to the client Y's current account (recipient of social transfer). On the whole, both transactions in Example 6.1 represent the transfer of money from one non-bank entity to another non-bank entity (similar to Example 2.1).

Conversely, there is an **increase of monetary aggregates** in the second case. The purchase of the treasury securities by commercial bank does not affect monetary aggregates. Nevertheless, the consequent government spending in the form of social transfer increases the recipient's current account balance. T means that monetary aggregates increase. On the whole, both transactions in Example 6.2 are similar to the granting a loan by bank to its client (similar to Example 2.2).

Example 6.1 Issue of treasury securities, their purchase by non-bank entity, and subsequent social transfer

1) Client X of bank A pays $400 to government for treasury securities
2) Government transfers $400 to client Y of bank B (social transfer)

Bank A

Clearing account with central bank

Initial balance	1) $400

Client X's current account

1) $400	Initial balance

Central bank

Clearing account of bank A

1) $400	Initial balance

Clearing account of bank B

	2) $400

Government's current account

2) $400	1) $400

Client X

Current account with bank A

Initial balance	1) $400

Treasury securities

1) $400	

Example 6.1 Continuation

Bank B

Clearing account with central bank	
2) $400	

Client Y's current account	
	2) $400

Client Y

Current account with bank B	
2) $400	

Income	
	2) $400

Government

Current account with central bank	
1) $400	2) $400

Treasury securities issued	
	1) $400

Expenses	
2) $400	

Example 6.2 Issue of treasury securities, their purchase by bank and subsequent social transfer

1) Bank A pays $400 to government for treasury securities
2) Government transfers $400 to client Y of bank B (social transfer)

Bank A

Clearing account with central bank

Initial balance	1) $400

T-bonds

1) $400	

Central bank

Clearing account of bank A

1) $400	Initial balance

Clearing account of bank B

	2) $400

Government's current account

2) $400	1) $400

Bank B

Clearing account with central bank

2) $400	

Client Y's current account

	2) $400

Client Y

Current account with bank B

2) $400	

Income

	2) $400

Example 6.2 Continuation

Government			
Current account with central bank		Treasury securities issued	
1) $400	2) $400		1) $400
Expenses			
2) $400			

We can summarize that **issue of treasury bonds with subsequent government spending:**

- **Does not change monetary aggregates if non-bank entities buy the treasury securities (even if there is no change of monetary aggregates, the operation has positive impact on inflation because the money change hands from non-spending entities to spending entities);** and
- **Changes monetary aggregates if commercial banks buy the treasury securities (the operation has positive impact on inflation because spending entities receive money).**

The government usually spends the raised funds very soon, and thus in both cases the issue of treasury securities stimulates inflationary pressures.

There are three possible ways how treasury securities are issued:

- Auction treasury securities issue;
- Permanent treasury securities issue; and
- Issue by selling treasury securities to the limited number of interested parties.

The administrator of treasury securities issue can be central bank.

In the case of the **auction treasury securities issue** administrator announces the day when it means to sell an amount of treasury securities. It also announces the period for bids. Consequently, it distributes treasury securities to bidders starting with the highest bids (lowest yield to maturity). If the bidders' demand outstrips the available amount of securities, government meets only the highest bids. Successful bidders purchase treasury securities for prices that they have bid (English auction, American auction) or for the price of the last settled bid (Dutch auction, uniform price auction). English auction allows government to sell the specific amount of treasury securities for the highest revenue possible but the issue price of treasury securities is not homogeneous (taxation of such bonds could bring other difficulties). Contrariwise, Dutch auction does not bring such kind of problems but it does not allow government to get the highest revenue possible.

The auction treasury securities issue is widely used as the main kind of treasury securities issue. It assures that government raises approximately funds that it needs. However, there remains certain uncertainty about the exact price of treasury securities and about the interest rate that the government will have to pay. Sometimes, government announces the minimum price acceptable.

In the case of the **permanent treasury securities issue** administrator offers treasury securities for the announced price (or alternatively for the announced yield to maturity). If the treasury securities are not sold out on the issue day, government usually starts selling them in smaller lots. Government has to decide for what yield to maturity to sell it. If it chooses yield too low, there is a risk of selling only a small amount of securities. Government would be, therefore, forced to change the sale conditions. It the yield chosen were too high, government would sell the whole amount of securities but the costs would be unnecessarily high. In such a case, it would burden future generations with high interest.

The method of **issue by selling treasury securities to the limited number of interested parties** lies somewhere between the auction and permanent treasury securities issue. It requires the existence of institutions that underwrite (and charge for it the fee) the whole amount of unsold treasury securities. These institutions are usually investment banks. However, the number of such institutions is limited even in the developed countries. The only exception is Japan whose banks have almost the exclusive right (and obligation) to buy any amount of treasury securities. In exchange for this obligation, Japanese banks get certain tax and interest benefits.

6.2.8 Granting loans to government

Central bank should not directly grant loans to central government or to any state or local governments. In many countries, direct granting of loans is strictly forbidden. In the rest of countries, government has imposed less strict rules i.e., quantitative limits to both direct and indirect granting of loans. Such rules contribute to fiscal discipline. However, these rules are not systematic.

The direct granting of loans (including the purchase of treasury securities on primary market, i.e. directly from the treasury department) by central bank is called **monetization**[10]**.** Government usually spends the raised funds very soon. At this step **monetary aggregates rises** which stimulates inflationary pressures. The degree of inflationary pressures depends on the size of monetization measured as a ratio of the amount of loans and volume of monetary aggregates. Example 6.3 introduces monetization and subsequent social transfer of raised funds. Both operations rise monetary aggregates. The monetization has the same impact as purchase of treasury securities by commercial banks in Example 6.2.

We can summarize that monetization is special case of government securities issue, i.e. when securities are bought by the central bank. In accordance with the summary in previous subsection we can summarize that **monetization with subsequent government spending:**

- **Change monetary aggregates (the operation has positive impact on inflation because spending entities receive money).**

Central bank can also **purchase treasury securities on the secondary market** whereby it meets government expenditures indirectly. It thus grants indirect loan to the government. If central bank purchases treasury bonds from commercial bank, monetary **aggregates remain unchanged**. If central bank purchases treasury bonds from non-bank entities (households and enterprises), **monetary aggregates increase**. The government usually spends the raised funds very soon, and thus monetization stimulates inflationary pressures.

We can summarize that **purchase of treasury bonds by central bank on the secondardy market:**

- **Does not change monetary aggregates if securities are purchased from commercial banks (the operation has no impact on inflation because the money dose not change hands);** and

- **Changes monetary aggregates if securities are purchased from non-bank entities like households and enteprises (the operation has positive impact on inflation because spending entities receive money).**

---

10 Sometimes the term "monetization" is used in a wider sense both for direct and indirect loans by central bank to government. In some cases the term "monetization" is used in even more wider sense for any purchase of assets, e.g. purchase of commercial banks' shares by central bank (like in Japan).

Example 6.3 Monetization and subsequent social transfer

1) Central bank grants loan of $400 to the government
2) Government transfers of $400 to client of commercial bank (social transfer)

Central bank

Loans granted	
1) $400	

Clearing account of bank A	
	2) $400

Government's current account	
2) $400	1) $400

Bank A

Clearing account with central bank	
2) $400	

Client's current account	
	2) $400

Client

Current account with bank A	
2) $400	

Income	
	2) $400

Government

Current account with central bank	
1) $400	2) $400

Treasury securities issued	
	1) $400

Expenses	
2) $400	

Price deregulations provoked monetary turbulences in almost all post-communist countries in the nineties of the 20th century. While the small and medium private enterprises have found themselves with plenty of new opportunities, large enterprises have started to face serious problems. Many of the state-owned enterprises were unable to adapt themselves to the new market conditions. During the nineties, many of Central and Eastern European (CEE) central banks were forced to grant loans to the industrial and agricultural sector. As a result of these activities, many of CEE countries soon observed increasing inflation. Commercial banks in Russia, Byelorussia, Ukraine, Romania, Slovakia and Hungary were often asked to grant bad loans to preferred sectors as well. In Slovenia, it was the case of small farmers and in Lithuania case of big farmers. Other countries were trying to support and maintain their state-owned enterprises and exporters. Each of these prestigious groups was granted with "special" (i.e. subsidised) interest rates. Wide-ranging monetization always causes high inflation and sometimes even hyperinflation. Central banks are unwilling to control the growth of monetary aggregates.

Monetization is forbidden in some countries. Central bank's independence is supposed to be the necessary condition of price stability. Central bank that does not have to fear of the incoming elections is concerned with the short-term monetary expansion. Governments would often like to borrow (expand) money from central bank in order to speed up (temporarily) the economic activity.

Direct borrowing from central bank can take the form loans, purchase of treasury securities on primary market, and overdrafts. These forrovings seem very attractive for government and their use must be, therefore, strictly controlled. There should be legal limits on central bank's loans to government. Limits are usually imposed yearly e.g., the yearly amount of loan granted to government cannot exceed a specific percentage of the government revenues. Such limits are usually constant over the whole fiscal period. However, countries where the fiscal deficit shows seasonal variations can impose additional seasonal limits.

It is hard to implement restrictive measures in countries where the financial markets are week and inefficient or where the securities market does not exists at all. If this is the case, direct granting of loans (if any) should obey following rules:

- The amount of loans granted to government should be subject to some binding limits that can be changed only by legal amendment;
- All loans should bear the market interest rate or the law should, at least, impose the central bank's responsibility for setting the interest rate;

- All loans should be collaterised, i.e. it should be secured by securities; and
- Central bank should prefer **short-term securities** in order to minimize the interest rate risk. Long-term securities should bear the variable interest rates.

6.2.9 Concern over government budget

Central bank usually takes care about the government budget. **This activity can be more deserving than central bank's monetary policy since the government interventions, expenditures and revenues can affect inflation more than changes of interest rates.**

6.2.10 Financial statistics for local, state and federal authorities

Central banks usually deliver information about the development of the financial market (e.g. banking sector statistics and balance of payments). This field is also the one where central banks employ the most of their staff.

6.2.11 Lender of last resort

Textbooks on economics often consider central bank to be the lender of last resort, i.e. to be always ready to grant loans to any commercial bank that would find itself in bank reserves trouble. For example the commercial bank may be threaten a run, i.e. unexpected withdrawals of banking deposits caused by the growing concerns about the bank's financial health. Central banks were really working as lenders of last resort in the past.

But nowadays i**f the central bank intends to help the commercial bank in bank reserves trouble, it grants it the so-called lombard loan, i.e. the collaterised loan. Central bank does generally not grant bank reserves without the eligible collateral. If the central bank grants the uncollaterised bank reserves, it could soon be found itself with the impaired receivable. Losses resulting from such bad loans would have to be paid by government, i.e. by taxpayers**.

If clients of commercial bank are gradually withdrawing their deposits, the bank usually starts selling its liquid assets (including assets eligible as collateral in lombard loans) to other commercial banks or to other commercial banks' clients. Depletion of liquid assets can result in the bankruptcy. Lombard loan cannot be granted to such commercial bank since the bank has already sold eligible assets. Hence, most central banks do not perform the role of a lender of last resort anymore.

6.3 Three structures of the central bank's balance sheet

The balance sheet of central bank contains two items that cannot be found in the balance sheet of any other entity:

- Currency (excluding the vault cash in central bank) on a liability side of balance sheet. Currency in circulation (i.e. monetary aggregate M0) consists of currency held by the public and government, and it is currency minus the vault cash in commercial banks and central bank. The amount of currency slightly exceeds the amount currency in circulation; and

- Commercial banks' clearing accounts on a liability side of balance sheet. We call these balances "bank reserves" or "liquidity of commercial banks held with central bank". This item does not make part of any monetary aggregate, i.e. bank reserves are not money.

The amount of currency is out of central bank's control, and it depends entirely on the willingness of household, enterprises, government and commercial banks to hold currency instead of bank deposits, i.e. on the willingness of these entities to change bank deposits for currency. If the commercial bank needs banknotes or coins for its clients, it simply exchanges it with central banks for the part of its clearing account balance. The amount of currency does not depend on central bank's activities. Rationally thinking entities seek to minimize their holdings of currency for it doesn't bear interest.

Examples 5.5 and 5.6 clearly demonstrate that **every increase of the amount of currency represents the additional profit to central bank and losses to commercial banks, households and enterprises.** In these examples the currency of the amount $150 billion have caused central bank's profit of $9 billion, commercial banks' loss of $3 billion and loss of households of $6 billion.

Lower interest rates diminish loss of currency holding, and thus there is an increase holding of currency at the expense of bank deposits. The amount of currency also depends on stability of the banking sector and on the size of shadow economy.

In terms of bank reserves, we distinguish between three different structures of central bank's balance sheet:

- Central bank providing bank reserves through loans and deposits which are on assets side of the central bank's balance sheet (Figure 6.1);

- Central bank absorbing bank reserves through loans and deposits which are on liabilities side of the central bank's balance sheet (Figure 6.2); and

Figure 6.1 Banking system with central bank providing bank reserves

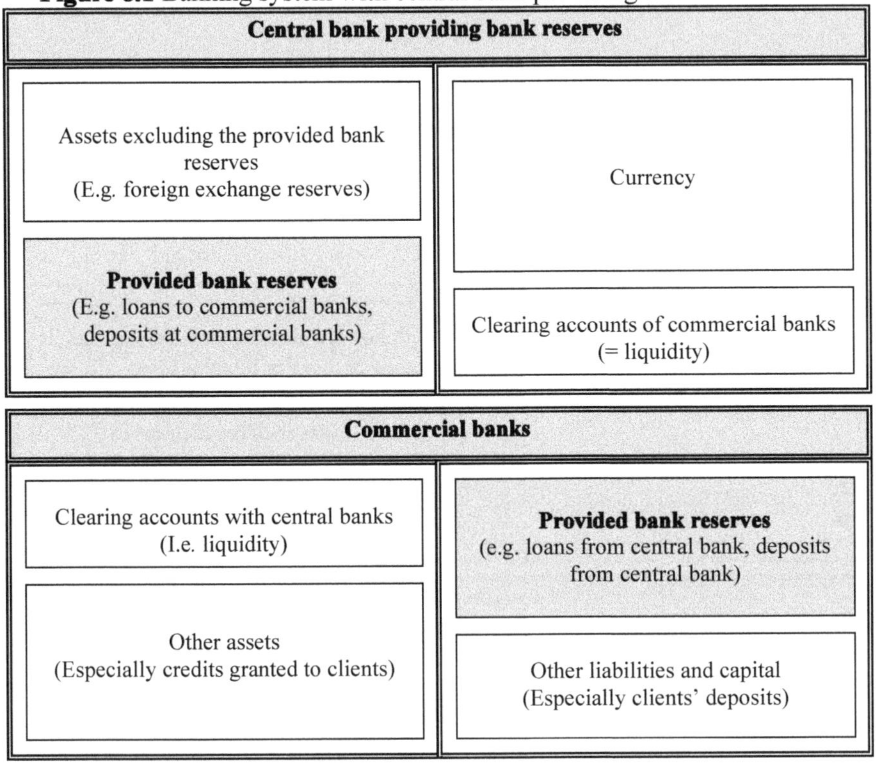

- Central bank providing and absorbing bank reserves (mixed structure) through loans and deposits which are on both the assets side and liabilities side of the central bank's balance sheet. During the year there are some operations providing bank reserves and some operations absorbing bank reserves.

Whether the central bank follows the first, the second or the third structure depends in particular on the volume of central bank's assets (excluding provided bank reserves) and the volume of currency and required bank reserves. In some countries central bank's assets (excluding the provided bank reserves) predominantly consist of foreign reserves (in some countries, foreign exchange reserves are being managed by the treasury department). In such countries **the amount of bank reserves (provided or absorbed) depends mainly on the central bank's**

Figure 6.2 Banking system with central bank absorbing bank reserves

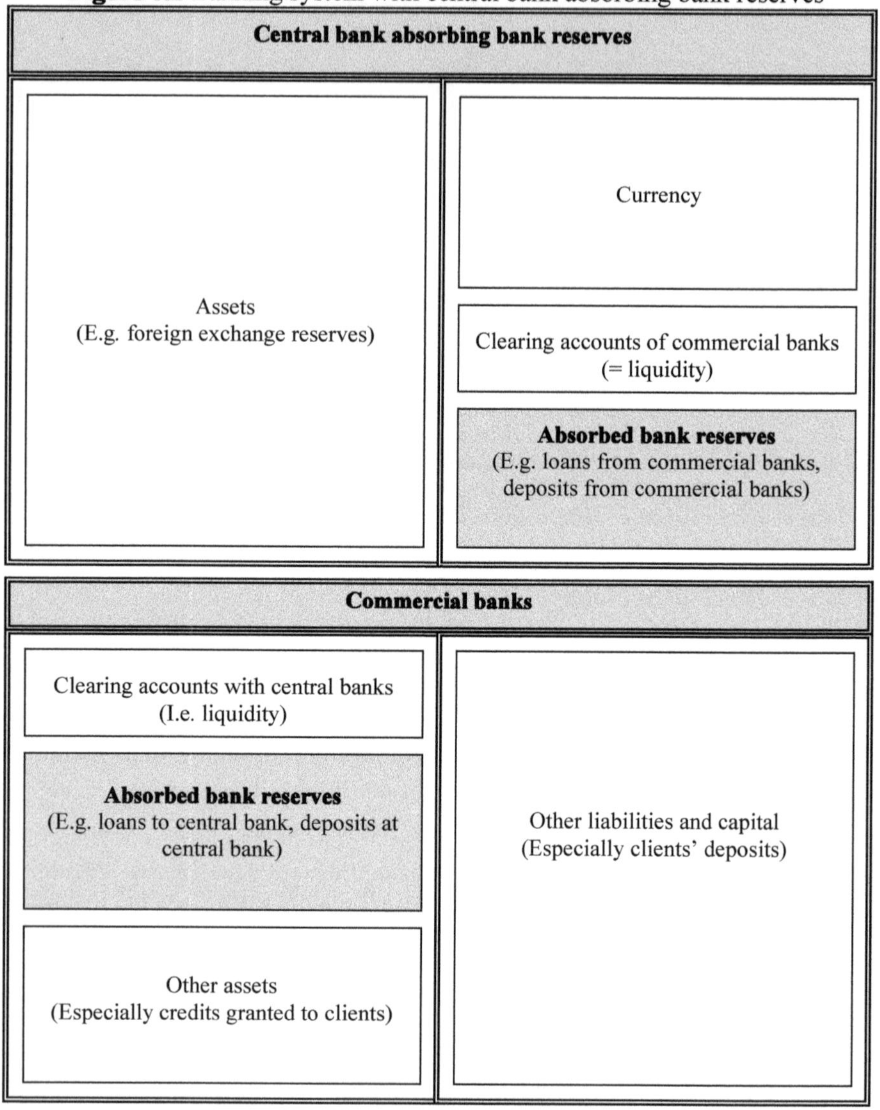

exchange rate policy, i.e. on its foreign exchange reserves. In some countries central bank's assets (excluding provided bank reserves) consist primarily of government securities (the United States, Japan etc.).

Figure 6.3 Banking system with central bank providing bank reserves facing deep conversions of deposit into currency

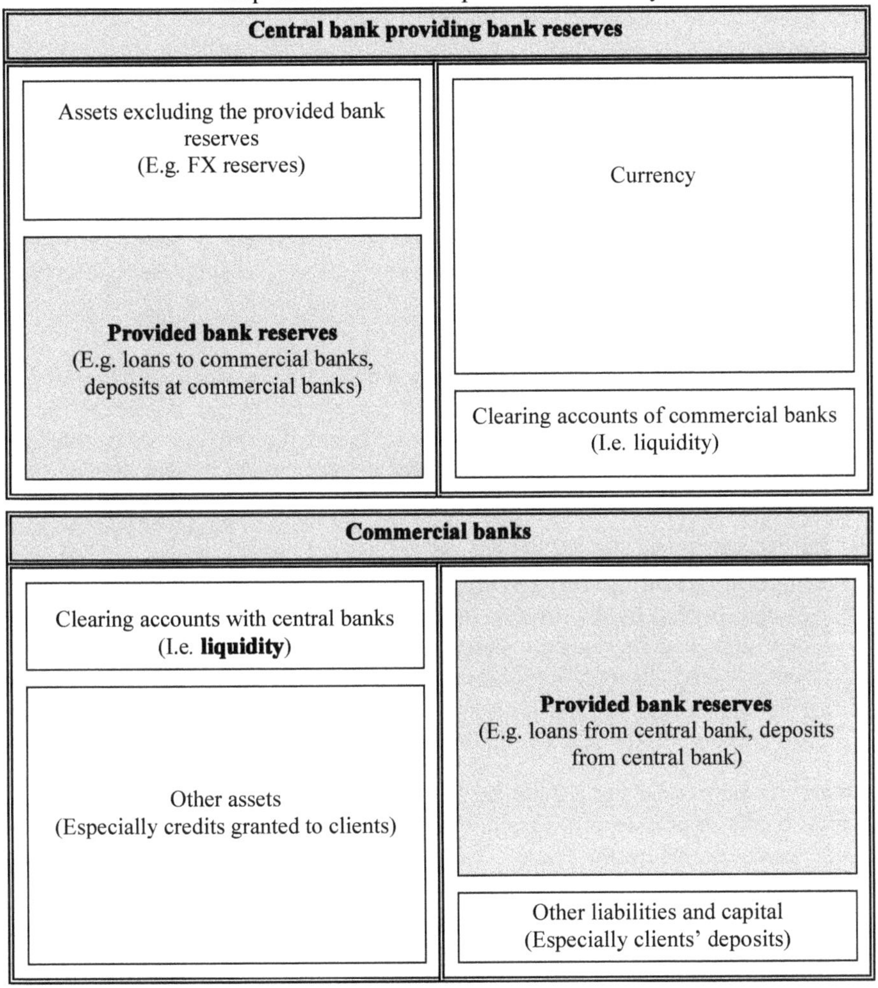

According to section 4.1 **the central bank regulates the overall amount of bank reserves in such a way that commercial banks as a whole are able to meet reserve requirements. If there is a lack of bank reserves then central bank provides bank reserves (Figure 6.1). If there is an excess of bank reserves then central bank absorbs bank reserves (Figure 6.2).**

The provided of absorbed bank reserves can take different legal forms, for instance of loans, deposits or debt securities. The majority of the central banks have traditionally operated in the regime of delivering bank reserves (the Eurozone, the United Kingdom etc.) or in the regime of mixed model (the United States, Japan etc.). The regime of absorbing bank reserves is used only in a small number of countries. The absorption of bank reserves is mainly the result of central bank accumulation of huge amount of foreign exchange reserves.

What can happen if clients start to withdraw massively their deposits from commercial banks, i.e. **if they start converting massively deposits into currency?** Let's suppose, for example, that central bank is absorbing bank reserves.

Then:

- Conversion of deposits into currency reduces the amount of bank reserves to absorb. The balance sheet total of commercial banks decreases (bank reserves and client's deposits decrease), and the balance sheet total of central bank remains unchanged (currency replaces bank reserves); and

- Let the conversion of deposits into currency reaches the level that there is no need for the absorption of bank reserves. Further conversion compels the central bank to start providing bank reserves. The balance sheet total of commercial banks remains unchanged (bank reserves replaces client's deposits), and the balance sheet total of central bank starts rising (bank reserves and currency increase). Figure 6.3 shows the situation with deep conversion deposits into currency. In an extreme case, client's deposits with commercial banks completely disappear.

If the conversion of client's deposits into currency is distributed between commercial banks in proportion to client's deposits, there is **no danger of collapse of any commercial bank.** There is only a certain redistribution of interest expense and interest income among central bank, commercial banks, household, enterprises and government. Central bank's profit increases (its interest expenses diminish) at the expense of currency holders, i.e. households, enterprises and government (their interest income decreases) and at the expense of commercial banks (their interest expense rises). In commercial banks the higher-interest-bearing bank reserves are replaced by low-interest-bearing deposits of clients.

6.4 Examples of the central bank's financial statements

The careful study of any central bank's financial statements provides useful insight view on the central bank. Central bank usually pursues fewer transactions than ordinary commercial bank. In addition, these transactions are easy to operate, and central bank needs, therefore, only a relatively limited number of dealers. In this subsection, we will introduce the balance sheets and income statements of the Fed, the European Central bank, the Bank of Japan and the Bank of England. Unfortunately the items in balance sheets and income statements are not harmonised between central banks and thus items are not comparable.

6.4.1 Balance sheet and income statement of the Fed

The Fed[11] publishes financial statements of:

- Board of Governors; and
- Twelve Federal Reserve Banks.

Balance sheet total of Board of Governors is negligible. Its balance sheet total was only $217 millions as at 31 December 2008.

Table 6.1 and 6.2 shows the consolidated balance sheet and consolidated income statement of the twelve Federal Reserve Banks as at 31 December 2007 and 2008. Federal Reserve Banks do not use the U.S. generally accepted accounting principles (US GAAP) but specialized accounting principles developed by the Board of Governors.

The consolidated balance sheet of the twelve Federal Reserve Banks at the end of **2007** was relatively simple (similar balance sheets were for former years). The assets side consisted mainly of U.S. Treasury securities ($746 billion) as there were no federal agency and government-sponsored enterperise securities at that time, collateralized loans to depository institutions ($49 billion) and securities purchased under agreements to resell ($47 billion). Any of these items delivers bank reserves. In the United States, foreign exchange reserves are administered partly by Fed and partly by the U.S. Department of the Treasury (Treasury's Exchange Stabilization Fund).

Liabilities and equity side consisted mainly of banknotes ($792 billion) as coins are issued by the U.S. Department of the Treasury and distributed by the Fed, securities sold under agreements to repurchase ($44 billion) and deposits of depository institutions ($21 billion).

---

11 The Fed (the Federal Reserve System) consists of:
- Board of Governors;
- Twelve regional privately-owned Federal Reserve Banks;
- The Federal Open market Committee;
- Private members banks; and
- Various advisory councils.

Table 6.1 Consolidated balance sheet of the twelve Federal Reserve Banks as at 31 December 2007 and 2008 in millions of U.S. dollars

Assets	**2008**	**2007**
Gold certificates	11,037	11,037
Special drawing rights certificates	2,200	2,200
Coin	1,688	1,179
Items in process of collection	979	1,804
Loans to depository institutions	544,010	48,636
Other loans	100,082	0
Securities purchased under agreements to resell	80,000	46,500
U.S. government, federal agency and government-sponsored enterprise securities, net	502,189	745,629
Investments denominated in foreign currencies	24,804	22,914
Central bank liquidity swaps	553,728	24,000
Investments held by consolidated variable interest entities (of which	411,996	0
$74,570 is measured at fair value at 31 December 31 2008)	2,572	2,539
Bank premises, equipment and software, net		
Prepaid interest on Federal Reserve notes due from U.S. Treasury	2,425	0
Accrued interest receivable	7,389	6,438
Other assets	629	1,900
Total assets	**2,245,728**	**914,776**

Liabilities and Equity	**2008**	**2007**
Federal Reserve notes outstanding, net	853,168	791,691
Securities sold under agreements to repurchase	88,352	43,985
Beneficial interest in consolidated variable interest entities	2,824	0
Other liabilities to consolidated variable interest entities:	5,813	0
Deposits of depository institutions	860,000	20,767
Deposits of U.S. Treasury, general account	106,123	16,120
Deposits of U.S. Treasury, supplementary financing account	259,325	0
Other deposits	21,671	363
Deferred credit items	2,471	1,811
Interest on Federal Reserve notes due to U.S. Treasury	0	1,532
Interest due to depository institutions	88	0
Accrued benefit costs	3,374	1,281
Other liabilities	367	326
Total liabilities	**2,203,576**	**877,876**
Capital paid-in	21,076	18,450
Surplus (including accumulated other comprehensive loss of $4,683 million and $1,524 million at 31 December 2008 and 2007, respectively)	21,076	18,450
Total equity	**42,152**	**36,900**
Total liabilities and equity	**2,245,728**	**914,776**

Source: http://www.federalreserve.gov

Due to financial crises the consolidated balance sheet of the twelve Federal Reserve Banks at the end of **2008** shows very different position. The assets side consisted mainly of collaterized loans to depository institutions ($544 billion), central bank liquidity swaps[12] ($554 billion), U.S. government, federal agency, government-sponsored enterprise securities ($544 billion) and investments held by consolidated variable interest entities ($412 billion). Any of these items delivers bank reserves. **The balance sheet total was pushed up from $915 billion to $2,246 billion.**

Liabilities and equity side consisted mainly of deposits of depository institutions ($860 billion), banknotes ($853 billion) and deposits on general and supplementary financial accounts of U.S. Treasury ($264 billion).

Total interest income for 2008 amounted to $43 billion mainly due to interest income resulting from holdings of U.S. Treasury securities ($26 billion). Total interest expenses were negligible ($2 million). The net interest income reached $41 billion. Total non-interest income amounted to $2 billion and total operating expense exceeded $4 billion, the main item being salaries and other benefits ($2 billion). The net income prior distribution reached $39 billion. The amount of $32 billion was transferred to U.S. Treasury.

Till the end of 2007 the financial situation of the Federal Reserve Banks was, therefore, very simple: the purchase of U. S. Treasury securities was approximately financed by the issue of dollar banknotes. The Federal Reserve Banks should receive interest resulting from holding of U. S. Treasury securities and the Federal Reserve Banks should pay seigniorage (the so-called payments to U.S. Treasury as interest on Federal Reserve notes) to the U.S. Treasury. These amounts were compensated during the year and only the residual amouta were paid.

Starting 2008 the Federal Reserve Banks have facilitated liquidity problems of some banks. They delivered liquidity to banks with the shortage of liquidity (loans to depository institutions on asset side) and they absorbed liquidity from bank with the excess of liquidity (deposits from depository institutions on liabilites side). That is one reason of the expansion of balance sheet total.

---

12 **Central bank liquidity swap** (central bank liquidity swap lines) represents reciprocal credit line arrangements between two central banks. The first central bank opens credit line in its domestic currency for the second central bank and the second central bank opens credit line in its domestic currency for the first central bank. According to the Table 6.1 and Table 6.2 there was likvidity of $554 million granted by the Federal Reserve Banks granted to other central banks at 31 December 2008. Corresponding interest income was $4 billion for 2008.

Table 6.2 Consolidated income statement of Federal Reserve Banks for years ended 31 December 2007 and 2008 in millions of U.S. dollars

Income and expenses	**2008**	**2007**
Interest income:		
Loans to depository institutions	3,817	71
Other loans	3,348	0
Securities purchased under agreements to resell	1,891	1,591
U.S. government, federal agency and government-sponsored enterprise securities	25,631	38,707
Investments denominated in foreign currencies	623	547
Central bank liquidity swaps	3,606	28
Investments held by consolidated variable interest entities	4,087	0
Total interest income	**43,003**	**40,944**
Interest expense:		
Securities sold under agreements to repurchase	737	1,688
Depository institutions deposits	817	0
Other interest expense	463	0
Total interest expense	**2,017**	**1,688**
Net interest income	**40,986**	**39,256**
Non-interest income (loss):		
U.S. government, federal agency and government-sponsored enterprise securities gains, net	**3,769**	0
Foreign currency gains, net	1,266	1,886
Investments held by consolidated variable interest entities (losses), net	(5,237)	0
Income from services	773	878
Reimbursable services to government agencies	461	458
Other income	899	166
Total non-interest income (loss)	**1,931**	**3,388**
Operating expenses:		
Salaries and other benefits	2,184	2,093
Occupancy expense	275	247
Equipment expense	200	203
Assessments by the Board of Governors	853	872
Professional fees related to consolidated variable interest entities	80	0
Other expenses	662	838
Total operating expense	**4,254**	**4,253**
Net income prior to distribution	**38,663**	**38,391**
Change in funded status of benefit plans	(3,159)	325
Comprehensive income prior to distribution	**35,504**	**38,716**
Distribution of comprehensive income:		
Dividends paid to member banks	1,189	992
Transferred to surplus and change in accumulated other comprehensive loss	2,626	3,126
Payments to U.S. Treasury as interest on Federal Reserve notes	31,689	34,598
Total distribution	**35,504**	**38,716**

Source: http://www.federalreserve.gov

The second reason is the investments of Federal Reserve Banks in consolidated variable interest entities. Such investments included commercial papers, agency and non-agency collateralized mortgage obligations, commercial and residential real mortgage loans, MBS, CDOs, other investment securities and derivatives and associated hedging activities.

6.4.2 Balance sheet and income statement of the European central bank

European central bank publishes financial statements of:

- Financial statements of the European Central Bank; and
- Balance sheet of the Eurosystem.

Tables 6.3 and 6.4 show the balance sheet and income statement of the ECB as at 31 December 2007 and 2008. The ECB does not use the International Financial Reporting Standards but its own accounting principles.

At the end of 2008 the assets side of ECB's balance sheet consisted mainly of claims within the Eurosystem (€295 billion). The increase in this item was due to back-to-back central bank liquidity swaps (central bank liquidity swap lines) conducted with national central banks in connection with providing liquidity in US dollar. On liabilities side the major items were labilities to non-euro areua residents (€254 billion) including liability to the Federal Reserve Banks resulting from central bank liquidity swaps. The ECB made a profit of €1 billion for 2008.

The profit of the ECB shall be transferred in the following order:

- An amount to be determined by the Governing Council, which may not exceed 20% of the net profi t, shall be transferred to the general reserve fund subject to a limit equal to 100% of the capital; and
- The remaining net profi t shall be distributed to the shareholders of the ECB in proportion to their paid-up shares.

The Governing Council decided in 2009 to make no transfer to the general reserve fund and to distribute the remaining balance of €117 million to the euro arean national central banks in proportion to their paid-up capital.

A Table 6.5 introduces the balance sheet of the Eurosystem. The Eurosystem consisted of ECB and 14 national central banks as at 31 December 2007 and ECB and 16 national central banks as at 31 December 2008. It does not publish the income statement. At the end of 2008 the asset side consisted mainly of loans granted to credit institutions in euro area (€860 billion).

Table 6.3 Balance sheet of the ECB as at 31 December 2008 and 2009 in millions of euro

Assets	**2008**	**2007**
Gold and gold receivables	**10,663**	**10,280**
Claims on non-euro area residents in foreign currency	**41,610**	**29,170**
- Receivables form the IMF	346	449
- Balances with banks and security investments, external loans and other external assets	41,264	28,721
Claims on euro area residents in foreign currency	**22,225**	**3,868**
Claims on non-euro area residents in euro	**629**	**0**
Intra-Eurosystem claims	**295,117**	**71,371**
- Claims related to the allocation of euro banknotes within the Eurosystem	61,021	54,130
- Other claims within the Eurosystem (net)	234,095	17,241
Other assets	**13,656**	**11,337**
- Tangible fixed assets	202	188
- Other financial assets	10,351	9,678
- Off-balance-sheet instruments revaluation differences	23	34
- Accruals and prepaid expenses	1,806	1,365
- Sundry	1,272	69
Total assets	**383,903**	**126,028**

Liabilities and Equity	**2008**	**2007**
Banknotes	**61,021**	**54,130**
Liabilities to euro area residents in euro	**1,020**	**1,050**
Liabilities to non-euro area residents in euro	**253,930**	**14,571**
Liabilities to euro area residents in foreign currency	**272**	**0**
Liabilities to non-euro area residents in foreign currency	**1,444**	**667**
Intra-Eurosystem liabilities	**40,149**	**40,041**
Other liabilities	**5,212**	**2,577**
- Off-balance-sheet instruments revaluation differences	1,130	69
- Accruals and income collected in advance	2,284	1,848
- Sundry	1,797	6590
Provisions	**4,038**	**2,693**
Revaluation accounts	**11,352**	**6,169**
Share capital	**4,137**	**4,127**
Profit for the year	**1,322**	**0**
Total liabilities and equity	**383,903**	**126,028**

Source: http://www.ecb.int

Table 6.4 Income statement of the ECB for years ended 31 December 2007 and 2008 in millions of euro

Income and expenses	**2008**	**2007**
Interest income:		
Interest income on foreign reserve assets	997	1,354
Interest income arising from the allocation of euro banknotes within the Eurosystem	2,230	2,004
Other interest income	8,430	4,380
Total interest income	**11,658**	**7,739**
Interest expense:		
Remuneration of NCBs' claims in respect of foreign reserves transferred	(1,400)	(1,356)
Other interest expense	(7,876)	(3,962)
Total interest expense	**(9,277)**	**(5,318)**
Net interest income	**2,381**	**2,420**
Realised gains/losses arising from financial operations	662	778
Write-downs on financial assets and positions	(2)	(2)
Transfer to/from provisions for foreign exchange rate and price risks	(1,339)	(286)
Net result of financial operations, write-downs and risk provisions	**(679)**	**(2,042)**
Net expense from fees and commissions	**0**	**(1)**
Income from equity shares and participating interests	**1**	**1**
Other income	**7**	**6**
Total net income	**1,709**	**385**
Staff costs	(174)	(168)
Administrative expenses	(183)	(184)
Depreciation of tangible fixed assets	(23)	(26)
Banknote production services	(6)	(5)
Profit or loss	**1,322**	**0**

Source: http://www.ecb.int

The major items on liabilities side were banknotes in circulation (€763 billion) and loans accepted from credit institution in euro area (€492 billion). Eurosystem is issuing banknotes since 1 January 2002. Eight percent of banknotes are allocated to the ECB. However the ECB is managing the issue of banknotes. It can also delegate the issue right to euro area member states. The treatment of banknotes is more centralized than the issuing of euro coins as coins are issued by member states.

Table 6.5 Balance sheet of the Eurosystem as at 31 December 2007 and 2008 in millions of euro

Assets	2008	2007
Gold and gold receivables	**217,722**	**201,584**
Claims on non-euro area residents in foreign currency	**160,372**	**139,03**
- Receivables from the IMF	13,192	9,057
- Balances with banks and security investments, external loans and other external assets	147,18	129,973
Claims on euro area residents in foreign currency	**234,293**	**41,975**
Claims on non-euro area residents in euro	**18,651**	**18,822**
- Balances with banks, security investments and loans	18,651	18,822
- Claims arising from the credit facility under ERM II	0	0
Lending to euro area credit institutions related to monetary policy operations in euro	**860,312**	**637,178**
- Main refinancing operations	239,527	368,607
- Longer-term refinancing operations	616,662	268,477
- Fine-tuning reverse operations	0	0
- Structural reverse operations	0	0
- Marginal lending facility	4,057	91
- Credits related to margin calls	66	2
Other claims on euro area credit institutions in euro	**56,988**	**23,798**
Securities of euro area residents in euro	**271,196**	**143,983**
General government debt in euro	**37,438**	**37,062**
Other assets	**218,134**	**264,454**
Total assets	**2,075,107**	**1,507,887**

Liabilities and Equity	2008	2007
Banknotes in circulation	**762,921**	**676,678**
Liabilities to euro area credit institutions related to monetary policy operations in euro	**492,310**	**379,183**
- Current accounts (covering the minimum reserve system)	291,71	267,337
- Deposit facility	200,487	8,831
- Fixed-term deposits	0	101,58
- Fine-tuning reverse operations	0	0
- Deposits related to margin calls	113	1,435
Other liabilities to euro area credit institutions in euro	**328**	**126**
Debt certificates issued	**0**	**0**
Liabilities to other euro area residents in euro	**91,077**	**46,183**
- General government	83,282	38,115
- Other liabilities	7,794	8,069
Liabilities to non-euro area residents in euro	**293,592**	**45,094**
Liabilities to euro area residents in foreign currency	**5,723**	**2,490**
Liabilities to non-euro area residents in foreign currency	**10,258**	**15,553**
- Deposits, balances and other liabilities	10,258	15,553
- Liabilities arising from the credit facility under ERM II	0	0
Counterpart of special drawing rights allocated by the IMF	**5,465**	**5,279**
Other liabilities	**166,5**	**123,076**
Revaluation accounts	**175,735**	**147,123**
Equity and reserves	**71,200**	**67,101**
Total liabilities and equity	**2,075,107**	**1,507,887**

Source: http://www.ecb.int

Loans granted to credit institutions and loans accepted from depository institutions have increased substantially during 2008 as many credit institutions were not willing to loan liquidity each other due to loss of confidence in financial crisis. Consequently some credit institutions lended liquidity to ECB and other credit institutions had to borrow liquidity from the ECB. The same was true in many other central banks in the world.

6.4.3 Balance sheet and income statement of the Bank of Japan

Table 6.6 and 6.7 show the balance sheet and income statement of the Bank of Japan as at 31 March 2007 and 2008. The Bank of Japan does not use the International Financial Reporting Standards but its own accounting principles.

At the end of March 2009 the asset side of the balance sheet consisted mainly of government securities (¥64 trillion) and loans and bills discounted (¥33 trillion). Both items delivered bank reserves. Foreign exchange assets represented only ¥11 trillion. Liabilities side consisted mainly of banknotes (¥77 trillion) and accounts (¥28 trillion). Coins are issued by the government. The equity was approximately ¥3 trillion. The Bank of Japan made a profit of ¥0.4 trillion for a fiscal year ended 31 March 2009. Substantial part of the profit has been transferred to government.

6.4.4 Balance sheet and income statement of the Bank of England

The Bank Charter Act 1844 requires that the banknote issue function be separated from its other activities. Accordingly, for accounting purposes, the Bank of England is divided into Issue Department and Banking Department. The Issue Department is solely concerned with the banknote issue and the assets backing the issue. The Banking Department comprises all other activities of the Bank.

Table 6.8 and 6.9 show the balance sheet and income statement of the **Issue Department** as at 28 February 2008 and 2009. The statements of account are prepared in accordance with the requirements of the Currency and Bank Notes Act 1928 and the National Loans Act 1968. The balance sheet was very simple. At the end of February 2009 the asset side consisted of cecurities of, or guaranteed by, the British Government (£10 billion) and other assets including reverse repos (£39 billion). Liabilities (there is no equity) consisted from banknotes issued (£49 billion). The production and issue of coins throughout the United Kingdom is under the responsibility of the Royal Mint (a government agency). The net income of the Issue Department (£2 billion) is paid over to HMTreasury.

Table 6.6 Balance sheet of the Bank of Japan as at 31 March 2008 and 2009 in billions of yen

Assets	2009	2008
Gold	**441**	**441**
Cash	**246**	**191**
Receivables under resale agreements	**11,952**	**8,767**
Japanese government securities	**64,265**	**67,390**
Commercial papers	**1,556**	**0**
Corporate bonds	**43**	**0**
Pecuniary trusts (stocks held as trust property)	**1,153**	**1,426**
Loans and bills discounted	**32,731**	**29,215**
Foreign currency assets	**10,864**	**5,227**
- Foreign currency deposits	88	61
- Foreign currency securities	4,870	4,994
- Foreign currency mutual funds	36	37
- Foreign currency pecuniary trusts	142	134
- Foreign currency loans	5,726	0
Deposits with agents	**26**	**82**
Other assets	**385**	**464**
- Bills and checks in process of collection	0	48
- Capital subscription to the Deposit Insurance Corp. and the Agricultural and Fishery Cooperative Savings Insurance Corp.	0	0
- Capital subscription to an international financial institution	15	15
- Provision of funds to the Deposit Insurance Corporation's "Jusen account"	100	100
- Provision of funds to the New Financial Stabilization Fund	20	20
- Withdrawn cash to be returned to the government	68	58
- Accrued interest receivable	143	160
- Others	37	61
Tangible fixed assets	**220**	**218**
- Buildings	115	117
- Land	83	83
- Lease assets	6	0
- Construction in progress	2	1
- Other tangible fixed assets	14	16
Intangible fixed assets	**0**	**0**
Total assets	123,888	113,426

Liabilities and Equity	2009	2008
Banknotes	**76,897**	**76,461**
Deposits (excluding those of the government)	**27,922**	**14,276**
- Current deposits	22,148	14,246
- Other deposits	5,773	29
Deposits of the government	**2,374**	**3,505**
- Treasury deposit	149	150

- Domestic designated deposit	1,909	3,057
- Other government deposits	315	298
Payables under repurchase agreements	**10,371**	**12,059**
Other liabilities	**177**	**600**
- Remittances payable	6	72
- Unearned interest and discounts	0	16
- Taxes payable	113	0
- Lease liabilities	6	3
- Others	51	52
Provision for retirement benefits	**190**	**188**
Provision for possible losses on securities transactions	**2,243**	**2,243**
Provision for possible losses on foreign exchange transactions	**794**	**794**
Total liabilities	**120,973**	**110,202**
Capital	**0**	**0**
Legal reserve	**2,614**	**2,582**
Special reserve	**0**	**0**
Profit or loss	**300**	**640**
Total equity	**2,915**	**3,223**
Total liabilities and equity	**123,888**	**113,426**

Source: http://www.boj.or.jp

Table 6.7 Income statement of the Bank of Japan for fiscal years ended 31 March 2008 and 2009 in billions of yen

Income and expenses	**2009**	**2008**
Operating income	**1,274**	**1,618**
Interest on loans and discounts	134	147
Interest on receivables under resale agreements	30	14
Interest and discounts on Japanese government securities	648	682
Interest on commercial papers	2	0
Interest and discounts on corporate bonds	0	0
Gains on sale of Japanese government securities	22	8
Gains on foreign currency assets	376	400
- Gains on foreign currency securities	283	387
- Gains on foreign currency mutual funds	0	2
- Gains on foreign currency pecuniary trusts	10	10
- Interest on foreign currency deposits and loans	82	1
Other operating income	59	364
- Gaings on penuciary trusts (stocks held as trust property)	0	313
- Dividends	1	1
- Fees and commissions	40	40
- Other income	18	10
Operating expenses	**835**	**931**
Interest on payables under repurchase agreements	57	72

Discounts paid on bills sold	1	1
Losses on sale of Japanese government securities	0	0
Losses on foreign currency assets	417	603
- Foreign exchange losses	416	603
- Losses on foreign currency mutual funds	1	0
General and administrative expenses and costs	227	220
- Cost of production of banknotek	52	53
- Administrative expenses for treasury business and Japanese government securities	49	41
- Personnel expense	50	50
- Expenses for transportation and communications	4	5
- Expenses for maintenance and repairs	1	1
- Other general and administrative expenses and costs	45	48
- Taxes excluding corporate income tax, inhabitants taxes and enterprise taxes	3	4
- Depreciation and amortization	18	15
Other general and administrative expense	131	34
- Losses on pecuniary trusts (stocks held as trust property)	17	0
- Fees and commissions paid	0	0
- Other expenses	112	34
Operating profits	**439**	**687**
Special profits	**0**	**1**
Gains on disposal of fixed assets	0	1
Special losses	**1**	**2**
Losses on disposal of fixed assets	1	2
Profit of loss before taxes	**438**	**686**
Provision for corp. income tax, inhabitants taxes and enterprise taxes	**138**	**46**
Net profit or loss	**300**	**640**
Appropriation of net profit or loss:		
Transfer to legal reserve	45	32
ividends, 5 percent of share face value	0	0
Payment to the government	**255**	608
Total appropriation	**300**	**640**

Source: http://www.boj.or.jp

Table 6.10 and 6.11 shows the balance sheet and income statement of the **Banking Department** as at 28 February 2008 and 2009. The financial statements of the Banking Department have been prepared in accordance with the IFRS as adopted by the EU. At the end of February 2009 the asset side of the balance sheet consisted almost exclusively of loans and advances to banks and other financial institutions (£137 billion) through which Bank of England delivered reserves. Liabilities side consisted mainly of deposits from banks and otehr financial institutions (£42 billion), money market instruments issued (£42 billion), deposits from central banks (£24 million) and other deposits (£32 billion). Money market instruments in issue consisted of one-week sterling bills.

Table 6.8 Balance sheet of the Issue Department of the Bank of England as at 28 February 2008 and 2009 in millions of pound

Assets	**2009**	**2008**
Securities of, or guaranteed by, the British Government	9,585	8,168
Other securities and assets including those acquired under reverse re-purchase agreement	39,023	36,810
Total assets	**48,608**	**44,978**
Liabilities	**2009**	**2008**
Notes issued:		
- In circulation	48,608	44,978
Total liabilities	**48,608**	**44,978**

Source: http://www.bankofengland.co.uk

Table 6.9 Income statement of the Issue Department of the Bank of England for fiscal years ended 28 February 2008 and 2009 in millions of pound

Income	**2009**	**2008**
Securities of, or guaranteed by, the British Government	499	735
Other securities and assets	1,768	1,636
Total income	**2,267**	**2,371**
Expenses	**2009**	**2008**
Cost of production of banknotes	48	23
Cost of issue, custody and payment of banknotes	24	17
Other expenses	7	4
Total expenses	**79**	**44**
Profit or loss (payable to the Treasury)	**2,188**	**2,327**

Source: http://www.bankofengland.co.uk

The Bank began issuing sterling bills on 29 September 2008 with the intent to offset the additional reserves. The equity was £3 billion. The Banking Department made a profit of £0.8 billion for a fiscal year ended 28 February 2009. The post-tax profits of Banking Department are effectively shared equally with HM-Treasury unless the Bank and HMTreasury agree otherwise.

Table 6.10 Balance sheet of the Banking Department of the Bank of England as at 28 February 2008 and 2009 in millions of pound

Assets	**2009**	**2008**
Cash and balances with other central banks	1,516	226
Loans and advances to banks and other financial institutions	136,829	62,855
Financial assets designated at fair value through profit or loss	3,334	3,742
Derivative financial instruments	287	122
Other loans and advances	815	4
Available for sale securities	3,937	3,852
Investments in group undertakings	–	–
Intangible assets	17	19
Property, plant and equipment	176	217
Investment properties	26	26
Retirement benefit assets	294	404
Other assets	697	534
Total assets	**147,928**	**72,001**
Liabilities and Equity	**2009**	**2008**
Money market instruments in issue	42,212	–
Deposits from central banks	24,356	18,594
Deposits from banks and other financial institutions	42,186	24,872
Other deposits	31,638	21,297
Financial liabilities designated at fair value through profit or loss	2,965	3,377
Derivative financial instruments	81	727
Current tax liabilities	235	10
Deferred tax liabilities	134	170
Retirement benefit liabilities	178	184
Other liabilities	622	477
Total liabilities	**144,607**	**69,708**
Capital	15	15
Retained earnings	2,748	1,821
Other reserves	558	457
Total equity attributable to shareholder	**3,321**	**2,293**
Total liabilities and equity	**147,928**	**72,001**

Source: http://www.bankofengland.co.uk

In fiscal year ended 28 February 2009 the Bank of England have facilitated liquidity problems of some banks. It delivered liquidity to banks with the shortage of liquidity (loans to depository institutions on asset side) and it absorbed liquidity from bank with the excess of liquidity (deposits from depository institutions on liabilites side). That is the major reason of the expansion of balance sheet total.

Table 6.11 Income statement of the Banking Department of the Bank of England for fiscal years ended 28 February 2008 and 2009 in millions of pound

Income and expenses	2009	2008
Profit before tax	995	197
Corporation tax net of tax relief on payment to HM Treasury	(162)	(36)
Profit for the year attributable to shareholder	**833**	**161**
Other recognised income and expense	199	125
Revaluation of available for sale securities		
Gains transferred to income stat. on disposal of available for sale securities	–	(3)
Revaluation of properties	(43)	(32)
Actuarial (losses)/gains on retirement benefits	(213)	408
Tax credited/(charged) on items directly to equity	5	(145)
Net (expense)/income recognised in equity	**(52)**	**353**
Total recognised income and expense for the period attributable to the shareholder	**781**	**514**

Source: http://www.bankofengland.co.uk

6.5 Seigniorage

We have seen already that the balance sheet of central bank contains two items that cannot be found in the balance sheet of any other entity (excluding the balance sheet of the government if government issues coins), namely currency and bank reserves. The seigniorage relates to the currency. Currency constitutes the zero-interest liability to central bank and the zero-interest asset to its holders. In principle, currency can be considered as zero-interest bonds issued by central bank. It would be technically very difficult to develop method for paying interest to holdings of banknotes and coins, i.e. to estimate holdings of currency of each entity during a year.

The seigniorage is the reduction of the expense of central bank corresponding to the zero-interest cost of currency. The seigniorage results from the central bank's monopoly to issue currency, and it is always positive or zero. In such a way **central bank imposes implicit tax on currency holders** (i.e. on households, enterprises, government and commercial banks). The tax base for seigniorage (i.e. the amount of currency) depends on the demand for currency. The tax rate is relatively low – the main interest rate of central bank. In majority of contries the seigniorage contributes to the government budget. On the other hand, the seigniorage is interest loss of currency holders, since the currency constitutes the zero-interest asset. The seigniorage thus represents benefit of central bank and, consequently, benefit of central government at the expense of currency holders. The term seigniorage is also used for benefits of the treasury department resulting from the circulation of coins issued by treasury.

How to calculate the amount of seigniorage? There are two methods of the calculation. According to the **first method** the seigniorage is income from asset allocated against currency minus cost of currency production, custody and distribution. The seigniorage depends which assets are allocated against currency. In the United Kingdom the seigniorage of the Bank of England for the fiscal year ended 28 February 2009 amounted to £2,188 million, i.e. it is the profit of the Issue Department (Table 6.9). The seigniorage of the Bank of England for the fiscal year ended 28 February 2008 amounted to £2,327 million. These amounts were directly transferred to the Treasury. In the United Kingdom seigniorage is explicit item in financial statements of the Bank of England.

Unfortunately, in the majority of countries the seigniorage is not explicit item in financial statements of central banks, and seigniorage should be calculated by the **second method**. This method compares the current financial statements with the hypothetical financial statements with no currency on liability side with:

- Currency to be replaced by bank reserves provided – when central bank provides bank reserves; or
- Currency to be replaced by bank reserves absorbed – when central bank absorbs bank reserves.

Seigniorage depends on the average holdings of currency by households, enterprises, government and commercial banks during a year and on the average main interest rate of the central bank during the same period (cost of currency production, custody and distribution is usually omitted):

$$\textit{seigniorage} = \textit{currency} \times \textit{average main interest rate of the central bank}$$

In the case of the **Federal Reserve Banks**, the average amount of currency outside the central bank during 2007 (taking the data about currency holding at the beginning and at the end of the year) was $787.5 billion [= (783+792)/2]. The average federal funds rate was 5.05 % (calculated as a weighted average). Therefore, seigniorage for 2007 was $39.8 billion, since:

$$\textit{Seigniorage} = \textit{\$787,5 billion} \times 0.0505 = \textit{\$39.8 billion}$$

During 2007 the Federal Reserve Banks received interests resulting from holding of U. S. Treasury securities and paid seigniorage to the U.S. Treasury. These amounts get weekly compensated and only the resulting amount was paid.

Over the last several decades, the amount of U.S. banknotes held by non-residents has rapidly increased. Estimates show that now about two thirds (from 60 % to 70 %) of dollar banknotes circulate outside the United States. That means that the U.S. government gets every year the indispensable amount of seigniorage from abroad. The outside world's contribution to U.S. federal budget amounted approximately to $26 billion in 2007.

In the case of the **European Central Bank**, the average amount of currency outside the central bank during 2007 (taking the data about currency holding at the beginning and at the end of the year) was €652.5 billion [= (628+677)/2]. The average interest rate of main refinancing operations was 3.92 % (calculated as a weighted average). Therefore, seigniorage for 2007 was €25.6 billion, since:

$$\textbf{\textit{Seigniorage}} = \text{€}652{,}5 \textit{ billion} \times 0.0392 = \text{€}25.6 \textit{ billion}$$

The seigniorage was scattered in the income statement of the European Central Bank and in the income statements of euro area national central banks.

In the case of the **Bank of Japan**, the average currency outside the central banks during fiscal year ended 31 March 2008 (taking the data about currency holding at the beginning and at the end of the year) was ¥76.5 trillion [= (76+77)/2]. The average uncollaterised overnight call rate was 0.50 % (calculated as a weighted average). Therefore, seigniorage for fiscal year ended 31 March 2004 was ¥0.0 trillion, since:

$$\textbf{\textit{Seigniorage}} = ¥76.5 \text{ trillion} \times 0.0050 = ¥0.38 \textit{ billion}$$

Substantial part of the profit (including seigniorage) has been transferred to government.

In the case of the **Bank of England**, the average currency outside the central banks during fiscal year ended 28 February 2008 (taking the data about currency holding at the beginning and at the end of the year) was £41,5 billion [= (38+45)/2]. The average repo rate was 5.54 % (calculated as a weighted average). Therefore, seigniorage for fiscal year ended 28 February 2008 was £2.3 billion, since:

$$\textbf{\textit{Seigniorage}} = £41{,}5 \times 0.0554 = £2.3 \textit{ billion}$$

This amount is almost the same as the seigniorage of £2,327 million using the first method (Table 6.9). The entire seigniorage of £2,327 million was transferred to the Treasury.

Some economists compare the amount of seigniorage to the gross domestic product or to budgetary receipts. In the United States, the ratio of seigniorage to GDP amounted in 2007 to 0.3 % (= $39.8 billion / $13808 billion), and the ratio of seigniorage to U.S. federal budget receipts reached 1.7 % (= $39.8 billion / $2,416 billion). On the other hand, Argentinean seigniorage represented in average 6.2 % of GDP and 46 % of budgetary receipts during the period from 1960 to 1975. High seigniorage usually corresponds to the high inflation.

Part III: Monetary policy

7 Basics of monetary policy

This and the next chapters deal with the basics of monetary policy, monetary policy instruments, operating targets, intermediate targets, ultimate targets, inflation targeting, monetary policy transmission mechanism, monetary policy rules and foreign exchange interventions. The chapters are closed with description of the monetary policy of the Fed, the Eurosystem, the Bank of Japan and the Bank of England.

7.1 Monetary policy framework

Throughout the centuries, the growth of money stock was considered the decisive factor of the overall long-term price trends. Currently, the major part of money in developed countries takes form of clients' deposits at commercial banks, and the governments have transferred responsibility for monetary development into the hands of central banks.

Monetary policy among countries has converged substantially during the last two decades. The differences are negligible when not taking into account the way how central authorities formulate monetary policy. Nowadays, **monetary policy consists in the regulation of the short-term interest rates by the central bank with a view to achieve price stability**. That is the core of monetary policy. Monetary policy exists only in market-oriented countries, for prices in centrally planned economies are subject to direct regulation.

But inflation does not depend solely on interest rates. There are a number of other factors determining inflation as well. However, these factors are out of central bank's control. Taxation and governmental expenditures are considered to represent one of the key factors. Central bank's care for government budget is often more deserving than its monetary policy. **Level of taxation and government expenditures affect inflation more directly and unambiguously than changes of interest rates.**

Monetary policy (Fig. 7.1) is defined as the regulation of the operating target (i.e. the short-term market interest rate) that the central bank accomplishes by means of monetary policy instruments in view to achieve operating target, intermediate target and, subsequently, the ultimate target (usually price stability). This sequence represents the causality chain of monetary policy. Monetary pol-

Figure 7.1 Monetary policy framework and exchange rate policy
(Formerly used instruments and targets are stroked out)

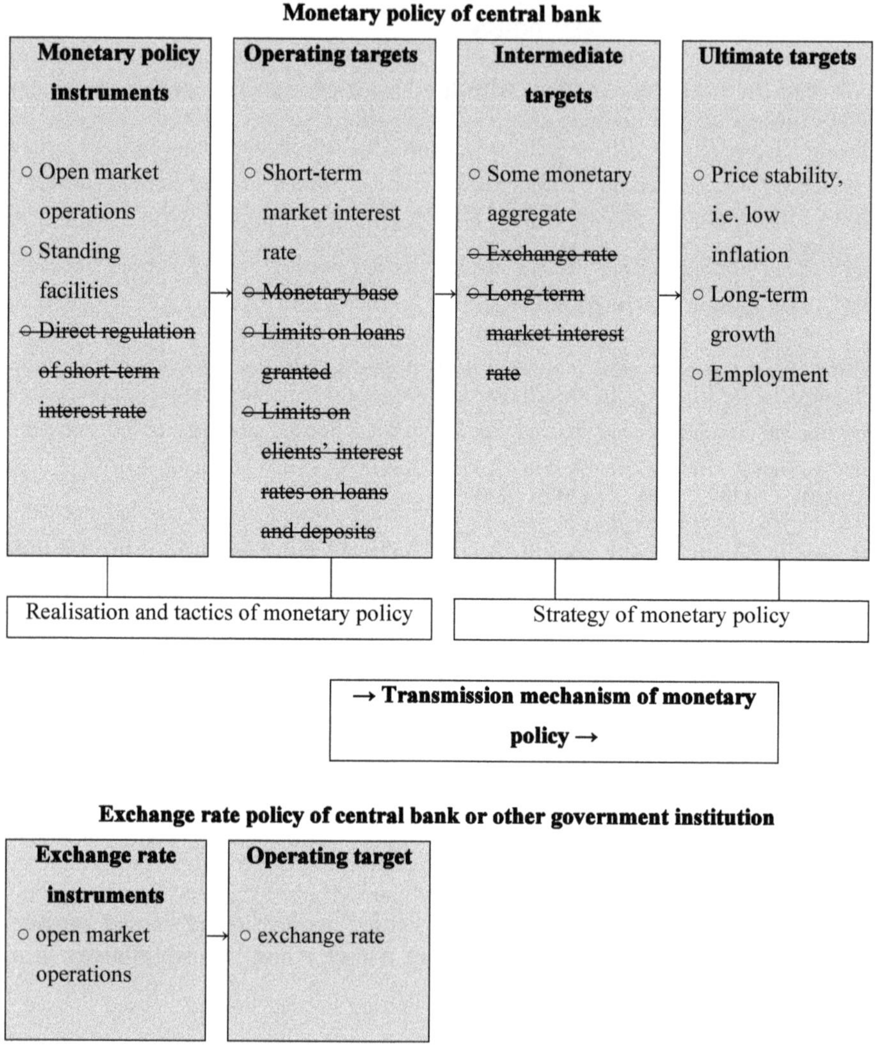

icy instruments constitute the realisation of monetary policy and operating target represents its tactics. Monetary policy instruments and operating target are sometimes called "nuts and bolds" of monetary policy. Intermediate target and ultimate target form the strategy of monetary strategy. Monetary policy transmission mechanism is the way in which the operating target affects the ultimate target. Monetary policy instruments relate to the everyday realisation of monetary policy, while the planning horizon for ultimate target is usually several months or even years.

Although the central bank has some power to influence exchange rates (directly by selling or purchasing foreign currency, or indirectly by changing domestic interest rates), particular value of exchange rate never represents its ultimate monetary target. If the central bank influences exchange rate, it does not do it in the view of price stability. Nowadays, monetary policy denotes exclusively the regulation of interest rate with view to achieve the specific intermediate target and/or ultimate target. Monetary policy has secondary effect on the exchange rate of domestic currency.

Monetary and exchange rate policies shall be regarded primarily as two separate policies even if the regulation of interest rates can affect indirectly the exchange rate as well. Central bank regulates the exchange rate directly by means of foreign exchange interventions and indirectly by interest rate regulation.

We distinguish between two possible settings of the operating target, namely the accommodative and tight monetary policy. Similarly, we can talk about the anti-inflationary (hawks) and pro-growth (doves) policies. **Expansive (accommodative) monetary policy** consists in measures taken to lower the short-term interest rates (i.e. to lower the interest rate paid and charged on the absorbed and provided bank reserves). Central bank lowers thereby all interest rates in the economy. Commercial banks are therefore willing to grant more loans and their clients tend to apply for more loans. In addition, both household and enterprises spend more money, i.e. the velocity of money tends to increase. Accommodative monetary policy is usually employed to stimulate the economy, i.e. when the economy embodies high interest rates, weak growth, unemployment and lower inflation expectation. Once the interest rates fall low enough and the economy gets stimulated, central bank starts to have concern about inflation again, and it passes to the tight monetary policy.

Conversely, the **tight monetary policy** represents series of actions taken to increase the short-term interest rate (i.e. to increase the interest rate paid and charged on the absorbed and provided bank reserves). Central bank increases thereby all remaining interest rates in the economy. Commercial banks are, therefore, willing to grant fewer loans, and their clients tend to ask for fewer loans. In addition, both household and enterprises spend less money, i.e. the velocity of money tends to decrease. Central bank is employing tight monetary policy if there is a danger of increasing inflation, i.e. when the economy embodies low interest rates, when there is overheated economy (situation when there is a strong growth connected with increasing wages and consumer prices), low unemployment and high inflation expectation. Once the interest rates increase high enough, and high inflation expectations disappear, central bank starts to concern about the economic growth again, and it passes to the expansive monetary policy.

Economy development in a small open economy (and especially its inflation) depends much more upon the development in foreign countries than upon domestic interest rates. If, for example, the world oil prices jump to $100 for a barrel, nobody can avoid domestic fuel prices to jump as well. If the economy of its largest business partners faces recession and slowing inflation, small open economy faces slowing inflation (or even deflation) too, for tradable goods often represent more than a half of its consumption basket.

Price level also depends on weather. In the case of good weather, overproduction of food starts pushing the prices down. Moreover, government often regulates prices of some foodstuff, rentals and services. Monetary policy has no means to influence these prices.

Change of interest rate affects prices very slowly. Roughly speaking, the monetary policy operates in a following way. When the interest rates fall, banks get more willing to grant loans and simultaneously start paying lower interests on deposits. Enterprises invest more (and increase thereby their production capacities) and demand for more inputs. Therefore, prices of both inputs and outputs increase. Consumers spend more and consume more. Demand for consumption goods increases causing the consumer prices to increase too. If the economy is open, lower interest rates result in the outflow of capital abroad, and the exchange rate starts to depreciate. Imported goods get more expensive, and hence the prices start rising. All these events occur with a particular delay of one year or more. Meanwhile, changes abroad can affect domestic prices significantly. Inflation regulation resembles shooting on a long-distance moving target.

The proper understanding of monetary policy operational procedure can help to elucidate the real power of monetary policy.

7.2 Monetary policy instruments

Monetary policy instrument is a technique consisting in a permanent maintenance of an operating target, i.e. of the short-term interbank market interest rate. In other words, once the certain interest rate in explicitly agreed, monetary authority must assure that this interest rate is systematically achieved by means of open market operations and automatic facilities. This means that central bank first decides about the explicit short-term interbank market interest rate, and it consequently puts this rate into practice by means of open market operation and automatic facilities. This agreed short-term interbank interest rate influences subsequently all remaining interest rates in the economy. There is no other monetary policy instrument than open market operations and automatic facilities.

In the past some monetary authorities introduced direct regulation of short-term interest rate. For example, regulations can take the form of limits imposed on interest rates that commercial banks can pay and charge on clients' deposits and loans. Another way to influence interest rates is to impose upper limits on the value of loans that commercial banks can grant. Nowadays, such monetary instruments are used only in several less-developed countries. Nevertheless, developed countries were frequently using them before the so-called "deregulation" (from 1975 to 1985). Before deregulation, monetary policy consisted in several open market operations and in direct regulation of financial markets and institutions. Changes of monetary policy were changes of one instrument or changes of the whole bulk of instruments. Sometimes, instruments were combined together with the active exchange rates regulations (daily corrections or administrative settings). Currently, monetary policy is more transparent and easier to elucidate.

7.2.1 Open market operations

Open market operations represent the domestic currency operations (usually between central bank and commercial banks) initiated by central bank with a view to pursue the chosen level of the short-term interbank market interest rate. There is no other objective of the open market operations. Central bank provides or absorbs bank reserves for specific interest rate. **The short-term interbank market interest rate should not be determined by the excess bank reserves but exclusively by the interest rates on provided and absorbed bank reserves.** These provided or absorbed bank reserves and the interest rate paid and charged on them are booked in the commercial bank's balance sheet. Commercial bank consequently adjusts interest rates of other balance sheet items based on this short-term interbank market interest rate, i.e. it adjusts especially the interest rates on accepted deposits and loans granted.

Open market operations change commercial banks' bank reserves held on clearing accounts with central bank. Anyway, open market operations must lead to a certain amount of excess bank reserves. If the amount of bank reserves is lower than the sum of reserve requirements and excess bank reserves, central bank must provide it. Otherwise, commercial banks would get unable to meet reserve requirements and short-term interbank market interest rates would therefore jump over the desired level (perhaps even unlimitedly high). If, on the other hand, the amount of bank reserves exceeds the sum of reserve requirements and excess bank reserves, central bank must absorb it. Otherwise, commercial banks could meet reserve requirements very easily and short-term market interbank interest rates would fall under the desired level (perhaps even to zero).

How central bank manages bank reserves? Operations can take only two forms: either central bank grants or accepts loans or deposits to/from commercial banks or central bank purchases or sales any asset. If the central bank is providing bank reserves (Example 7.1), it is usually:

- Granting loans or deposits to commercial banks for the official interest rate. Loans (deposits) usually take the form of reverse repurchase agreements (in this case, the interest rate is called repo rate). The Fed uses the term "borrowed reserves" for these reserves; or

- Purchasing any asset (e.g. debt securities including its own debt securities) from commercial banks. The Fed uses the term "non-borrowed reserves" for these reserves.

If the central bank is absorbing bank reserves (Example 7.2), it is usually:

- Accepting loans or deposits from commercial banks for the official interest rate. Loans (deposits) usually take the form of repurchase agreements (in this case, the interest rate is called repo rate); or

- Selling any asset (e.g. debt securities including its own debt securities) to commercial banks.

Bank reserves providing operations do not represent stronger control over interest rates than bank reserves absorbing operations. Bank reserves market is the special kind of market. Central bank operates on both demand and supply side of it. It determines the demand by setting reserve requirements and by setting conditions for the interbank clearing system. At the same time it determines supply by means of open market operations. Open market operations are used to achieve the desired level of interest rates.

Example 7.1 Central bank providing bank reserves

1) Central bank grants loan to commercial bank of $1 billion
2) Central bank purchases debt securities not-issued by commercial bank from commercial banks for $2 billion
3) Central bank purchases debt securities issued by commercial bank from this bank for $3 billion
4) Central bank purchases its own debt securities from commercial bank for $4 billion

Central bank providing bank reserves

Loans granted	
1) $1 billion	

Securities	
2) $2 billion 3) $3 billion	

Clearing accounts of commercial	
	1) $1 billion 2) $2 billion 3) $3 billion 4) $4 billion

Securities issued	
4) $4 billion	Initial balance

Commercial banks

Clearing accounts with central bank	
1) $1 billion 2) $2 billion 3) $3 billion 4) $4 billion	

Securities	
Initial balance	2) $2 billion 4) $4 billion

Loans accepted	
	1) $1 billion

Securities issued	
	3) $3 billion

7.2.2 Automatic facilities

We have seen already that open market operations take place on the initiative of central bank. Nevertheless, central bank allows commercial banks acting also on their own initiative. Such operations also change bank reserves, and we call them **automatic (standing) facilities**. We define automatic facilities as domestic currency operations taking place on the initiative of commercial banks so as to

Example 7.2 Central bank absorbing bank reserves

1) Central bank accepts loan from commercial bank of $1 billion
2) Central bank sales debt securities not-issued by commercial bank to commercial banks for $2 billion
3) Central bank sales debt securities issued by commercial bank to commercial bank for $3 billion
4) Central bank issues debt securities for $4 billion for commercial bank

Central bank absorbing bank reserves

Securities

Initial balance	2) $2 billion 3) $3 billion

Clearing accounts of commercial banks

1) $1 billion 2) $2 billion 3) $3 billion 4) $4 billion	Initial balance

Loans accepted

	1) $1 billion

Securities issued

	4) $4 billion

Commercial banks

Clearing accounts with central bank

Initial balance	1) $1 billion 2) $2 billion 3) $3 billion 4) $4 billion

Securities

2) $2 billion 4) $4 billion	

Loans granted

1) $1 billion	

Securities issued

3) $3 billion	Initial balance

increase or decrease their bank reserves. There are two automatic facilities, namely **deposit facility** and **lending facility**. Both facilities are generally with an overnight maturity.

If some commercial bank finds itself with the lack of bank reserves, there is at least one other bank with the excess bank reserves. This bank is ready to lend bank reserves to any bank for the interbank market interest rate. Vice-versa, if some commercial bank finds itself with the excess of bank reserves, there is at least one other bank with the lack of bank reserves. This bank is ready to borrow bank reserves from any bank for the interbank market interest rate.

The interest rate on the central bank's lending facility is always higher than interbank market interest rate (close to the level of the short-term interbank market interest rate). The interest rate on the central bank's deposit facility is always lower than interbank market interest rate. Commercial banks, therefore, always prefer the interbank market instead of deposit or lending facility as the interest rates applied to them are unfavourable when compared with market rates. It means that the use of deposit or lending facility is exceptional. They still play important role in setting short-term interbank market interest rates. Bindsell[13] concludes that "the simplest system for controlling short-term interest rates is that with a symmetric standing facilites corridor around the target rate..."

7.2.3 The Fed

a) Open market operations

The Fed both delivers and absorbs bank reserves held by depository institutions with Federal Reserve banks. Open market operations take place at the Domestic Trading Desk which is situated in Federal Reserve Bank of New York (Desk). These operations follow instructions of the Federal Open Market Committee (FOMC).

Each morning, the staff at the Federal Reserve Bank of New York and at the Board of Governors prepares estimates of factors determining the volume of bank reserves for the next several days and for the two-week period. The manager of the New York group contacts at 11:15 a.m. members of the Board of Governors, who are at the moment members of FOMC. They discuss the recent development of bank reserves, trends on financial markets and the data on monetary and loan aggregates. A special interest is put to conditions at the bank

13 Bindseil, Ulrich: *Monetary Policy Implementation: Theory Past and Present.* Oxford University Press, Oxford 2004.

reserve market, particularly to the level of federal funds rate in relation to the level set by FOMC. Consequently, they set the schedule for open market operations. Then approximately at 11:30 a.m. the FOMC members and FOMC non-members get information about operations that Fed plans to undertake during the day.

As soon as the Fed decides to make certain operations, the Federal Reserve Bank in New York informs dealers trading T-securities and mortgage-backed bonds of federal agencies. All operations are conducted in auctions, with all primary dealers invited to bid. There are approximately fourty dealers with which the Desk transacts (primary dealers), which are especially large banks and securities dealers. Fed also transacts with several other institutions, such as foreign central banks. After the transaction, reserve account of each dealer's bank gets credited or debited and bank reserves of the banking system changes.

Fed uses the following types of open market operations:

- Outright purchases of the Ú.S. treasury securities (T-bills, T-notes and T-bonds) and mortgage-backed bonds issued by U.S. federal agencies (providing bank reserves) or outright sales of the same securities (absorbing bank reserves). These operations represent the so-called Fed's permanent open market operations; and

- Loans granted in the form of reverse repurchase agreements (providing reserves) or accepting loans in form of repurchase agreements (absorbing reserves). These operations represent the so-called Fed's temporary open market operations.

Outright purchases and sales of debt securities take usually the form of auctions. The Desk may not increase Fed's holdings of securities by purchasing new securities when they are first auctioned. The reason is that the Fed has no authority to lend directly to the Department of the Treasury. Therefore, it can make any increase of holdings through purchases from primary dealers in the secondary market or from foreign institutions. When purchasing or selling securities in the secondary market, the Desk receives from primary dealers bids on securities of a particular type. In determining which bids to accept, the Desk considers the bids that represent the highest yield (for purchases) or the lowest yield (for sales).

Temporary open market operations help to offset short-term imbalances between reserve shortage and surplus. The Desk arranges repurchase agreements to add bank reserves and matched sale–purchase transactions to withdraw bank reserves. When the Desk arranges a **repurchase agreement**, it purchases securities from a primary dealer (or his customer), and it agrees to resell the securities to the dealer (or his customer) on a specified future date.

The Desk arranges two types of repurchase agreements: system and customer-related. For both types, the Desk receives offers from primary dealers. The dealers may make offers on their own behalf or on behalf of their customers. The offers announce a rate and an amount of repurchase agreements that the dealer (or its customer) is prepared to transact. The Desk ranks the bids in descending order of rate. It accepts the offer with the highest rate first, and it continues to accept lower rates until the total volume of offers equals the amount of reserves that the Desk wants to inject into the system.

When conducting **system repurchase agreements** the Desk does not announce the intended size of the operation when it announces offers. The dealer (or customer) whose offer is accepted sends securities to the Federal Reserve Bank of New York and the Bank pays for them by increasing balances in the Federal Reserve account of the dealer's (or his customer's) clearing bank. System repurchase agreements are conducted on an overnight or term basis. Term repurchase agreements may last no longer than 15 days, and they may be either withdrawable or fixed term. If the agreement is withdrawable, the dealer has the option to ask, before 10:00 a.m. on any day before the agreement terminates, for the return of its securities. It usually does so if repo rates fall below the rate arranged with the Desk. If the repurchase agreement is fixed term, the dealer may not withdraw its securities before termination.

Customer-related repurchase agreements are a type of transaction arranged by the Desk with primary dealers on behalf of foreign institutions that maintain accounts at the Federal Reserve Bank of New York. These institutions maintain accounts at the New York Reserve Bank to help manage their dollar payments and receipts. The Federal Reserve provides a means by which the cash balances on these accounts can be invested overnight.

Matched sale–purchase transactions (reverse repurchase agreements) are the way by which the Fed decreases bank reserves temporarily. In these transactions, the Fed agrees to sell a Treasury bills at a specified price, and simultaneously it agrees to buy the bills back on a specific date. In a matched sale–purchase transaction, the Desk indicates the bills and the rate at which it will buy the bills. Dealers then submit offers for the amount of the bills they will buy and the rate at which they will resell it to the Desk.

b) Discount window

Discount window is the instrument allowing depository institutions to borrow from the Fed the short-term liquidity, i.e. to accept bank reserves on its account with Fed for the discount rate. The term "discount window" comes from the past when the commercial banks needed bank reserves. All loans of the discount rate are fully collaterised. Nowadays, commercial banks are using discount window loans rarely. Detailed information on discount window can be found at the website (http://www.frbdiscountwindow.org).

There are three kinds of discount window loans:

- **Primary credit** is available to sound depository institutions as a very short-term loan, typically overnight, at a rate above the target rate for federal funds. The Fed expects that institutions will use the discount window as a backup rather than a regular source of funding. Primary credit may be used for any purpose. Reserve Banks do not require depository institutions to provide reasons for requesting this short-term loan. They only provide the minimum information necessary to process a loan (usually the amount and maturity of the loan). This loan may be extended for periods of up to a few weeks. Depository institution should be in sound financial condition, and it is in the position that it cannot obtain temporary funds in the market at reasonable terms. Primary credit is designed to small-sized depository institutions. Large and medium-sized institutions generally do not meet the test;

- **Secondary credit** is available to depository institutions that are not eligible for primary credit. It is short-term loan, typically overnight, at a rate above the primary credit rate. Secondary credit is available as a backup source of liquidity. This credit should help credit institution to overcome troubles, and depository institution should return to a reliance on market sources of liquidity. Secondary credit may not be used to fund an expansion of the depository institution's assets. The secondary credit is associated with a higher level of Reserve Bank administration and oversight than the primary credit. A Reserve Bank must have sufficient information about a depository institution's financial condition and reasons for borrowing to ensure that secondary credit will be consistent with the purpose of the program; and

- **Seasonal credit** is designed to assist small depository institutions in managing seasonal mismatches in their loans and deposits. Seasonal credit is available to depository institutions that can demonstrate a clear pattern of recurring yearly mismatches in funding needs. Eligible institutions are usually located in agricultural or tourist areas. Under the seasonal credit program, depository institutions may obtain longer-term funds during periods of seasonal need so that they can carry fewer liquid assets during the rest of the year. To become eligible for seasonal credit, an institution must obtain a seasonal qualification with its Reserve Bank. Deeply undercapitalized depository institutions are not eligible for seasonal credit.

In unusual and urgent circumstances, the Board of Governors may authorize a Reserve Bank to provide **emergency credit** to individuals, partnerships and corporations that are not depository institutions. Emergency credit may occur only when credit is not available from other sources, and failure to provide credit would adversely affect the economy. Emergency credit has not been made since the mid-1930s till the financial crisis.

Each of this credit bears different discount rate. Therefore, there is not only one interest rate but there are three rates. In December 2009 federal funds rate was of 0 – 0.25 %, interest rate on primary loans was of 0.50 % (i.e. 0.25 – 0.50 % higher than the federal funds rate), interest rate on secondary loans was of 1.00 % (i.e. 0.75 – 1.00 % higher than the federal funds rate), and interest rate on seasonal loans was 0.15 % (i.e. approximately on the level of the federal funds rate). The board of directors of every Federal Reserve Bank shall propose a discount rate every two weeks. This discount rate is subject to the decision of the Board of Governors. Fed makes the changes of discount rate based on its own judgments, not automatically. Their decisions come, therefore, with a certain delay after the change of federal funds rate. It should be pointed out, that changes of discount rate do not affect the market short-term interest rates (they depend mainly on the federal funds rate).

The monetary policy role of discount window has changed substantially since the establishment of the Fed. During the twenties, discount window represented the decisive monetary policy instrument in providing bank reserves to depository institutions. Discount rate was traditionally playing the role of the announcement factor, i.e. it was signalling changes of monetary policy to the market. Higher discount rate was signalling tight monetary policy, and lower discount rate was indicating the accommodative monetary policy. Nowadays, discount rate changes get coordinated with changes of the federal funds rate. U.S. financial markets were gradually developing, and bank reserves provided by means of open market operations became easier and more efficient. Discount window importance has thus slowly decayed.

From the beginning of sixties, **the basic discount rate has been often lower than the federal funds rate.** In order to limit the access to discount window (and thus to limit the frequency and volume of lending), Fed relied on administrative measures. Despite the attractiveness of discount window interest rates, depository institutions used it rarely, and the importance of this instrument has diminished. During nineties, depository institutions had limited the use of discount window. The excessive lending in the 1980s accomplished by several banks in troubles have induced other banks to keep away of it. Depositors would interpret the use of discount window as a sign of potential troubles of a bank.

Prior to adoption of the Depository Institutions Deregulation and Monetary Control Act of 1980, the use of discount window had been restricted to commercial bank that were members of the Federal reserve System. This act extended reserve requirements to non-member depository institutions. Further, it enabled equal access to discount window to all institutions whose deposits are subject to reserve requirements. Since that time, all domestic banks and thrift institutions as well as affiliates of foreign banks have been allowed to use the discount window. Institutions expecting to use the discount window should negotiate a series of legal documents with the Fed.

All discount window credits must be secured to the satisfaction of the lending Reserve Bank by collateral that is acceptable for that purpose. Most performing or investment grade assets held by depository institutions are acceptable as collateral. Assets accepted as collateral are assigned a lendable value (credit value plus market or face value multiplied by a margin). The financial condition of an institution may be also considered when assigning appropriate collateral.

The following assets are most commonly pledged to secure discount window advances:

- Commercial, industrial, or agricultural loans;
- Consumer loans;
- Residential and commercial real estate loans;
- Corporate bonds and money market instruments;
- Securities of U.S. government agencies and government-sponsored enterprises;
- Asset-backed securities;
- Collateralized mortgage obligations;
- U.S. Treasury securities; and
- State or political subdivision securities.

7.2.4 The Eurosystem

The Eurosystem delivers bank reserves (liquidity). The Eurosystem's open market operations can be divided into the following four categories:

- o **Main refinancing operations** are regular liquidity-providing transactions with a weekly frequency and with a maturity of normally one week. These operations are executed by the national central banks on the basis of standard tenders. The main refinancing operations play a decisive role in pursuing the purposes of the Eurosystem's open market operations, and they provide the bulk of liquidity to credit institutions. In December 2009 interest rate of main refinancing operations was 1.00 %;

- o **Longer-term refinancing operations** are liquidity-providing transactions with a monthly frequency and with a maturity of normally three months. These operations are aimed at providing credit institutions with additional longer-term liquidity, and they are executed by the national central banks on the basis of standard tenders. In these operations, the Eurosystem does not intend to send signals to the market, and therefore it normally acts as a rate taker;

- o **Fine-tuning operations** are executed on an ad hoc basis with the aim of managing the liquidity of credit institutions and managing interest rates, in particular in order to smooth the volatility of interest rates caused by unexpected liquidity fluctuations. Fine-tuning operations are normally executed by the national central banks through quick tenders or bilateral procedures. The Governing Council of the ECB can decide whether, under urgent circumstances, fine-tuning bilateral operations may be executed by the ECB itself; and

- o **Structural operations** are carried out whenever the ECB wishes to adjust the structural position of the Eurosystem with the financial sector (on a regular or non-regular basis). Structural operations are carried out by the national central banks through standard tenders.

Standing facilities are aimed at providing and absorbing overnight liquidity. They signal the general stance of monetary policy and are bound overnight market interest rates. Two standing facilities are available to eligible credit institutions on their own initiative, subject to their fulfilment of certain operational access conditions:

- o Credit institutions can use the **marginal lending facility** to obtain overnight liquidity from the national central banks against eligible assets. Under normal circumstances, there are no credit limits or other restrictions on access to the facility apart from the requirement to present sufficient underlying assets. The interest rate on the marginal lending facility normally provides a ceiling for the overnight market interest rate. In December 2009 interest rate on marginal lending facility was 1.75 %; and

- Credit institutions can use the **deposit facility** to make overnight deposits with the national central banks. Under normal circumstances, there are no deposit limits or other restrictions on access to the facility. The interest rate on the deposit facility normally provides a floor for the overnight market interest rate. In December 2009 interest rate on deposit facility was 0.25 %.

Counterparties in open market operations and standing facilities cover institutions subject to minimum reserve requirements, i.e. credit institutions. Their operations are carried out on the basis of standard tenders. The Eurosystem may select a limited number of credit institutions to participate in fine-tuning operations.

All Eurosystem credit operations (i.e. liquidity-providing operations) have to be based on adequate **collateral**. The Eurosystem accepts a wide range of assets underlying its operations. The Eurosystem has developed a single framework for eligible assets common to all Eurosystem credit operations. The single framework comprises two distinct asset classes – marketable assets and non-marketable assets.

As to marketable assets the debt instrument should be with a fixed and unconditional principal amount and with a coupon that cannot result in a negative cash flow. The first requirement does not apply to asset-backed securities. The Eurosystem sets some conditions on asset-backed securities. Two types of non-marketable assets are eligible as collateral in the single framework for eligible assets: credit claims and non-marketable detail mortgage-backed debt instruments.

Eligible assets may be used on a cross-border basis, by means of the correspondent central banking model or through eligible links between EU securities settlement systems, to collateralise all types of Eurosystem credit. All assets eligible for Eurosystem monetary policy operations can also be used as underlying assets for intraday credit.

7.2.5 The Bank of Japan

The Bank of Japan (BOJ) is using its **open market operations** to provide or absorb liquidity of depository institutions and non-depository institutions, such as securities companies, securities finance companies, and tanshi companies (money market brokers). Auctions for transactions to adjust liquidity for the day are offered to participants at 9:20 a.m., and those to adjust liquidity for the following days are offered to participants at designated time between 9:30 a.m. and 12:10 p.m.

BoJ's instruments vary depending on the character of transaction:

- Granting of short-term liquidity:
  - Purchases of Treasury Bills and Financing Bills (TBs/FBs) [14] under repurchase agreements;
  - Outright purchases of TBs/FBs;
  - Borrowing of Japanese Government Bonds (JGB) against cash collateral (JGB repos);
  - Outright purchases of bills;
  - Purchases of commercial papers (CP) under repurchase agreements; and
  - Outright purchases of bills backed by corporate debt obligations;

- Absorption of liquidity over a short-term:
  - Sales of TBs/FBs under repurchase agreements;
  - Outright sales of TBs/FBs; and
  - Outright sales of bills issued by the Bank of Japan;

- Granting of long-term liquidity:
  - Outright purchases of JGBs.

Through **standing facility** the banks may borrow liquidity at their own initiative against collateral. Loans bear interest at the official discount rate. The official discount rate provides a ceiling for the fluctuations in the short-term money-market interest rate, since the banks can always borrow at the central bank.

7.2.6 The Bank of England

The Bank of England uses **open market operations** to deliver and absorb liquidity so that adequate amount of liquidity is available. Till the financial crisis the British banking system was short of liquidity, and the Bank of England provided liquidity via open market operations. The Bank's operations are conducted through a group of counterparties, which include banks, building societies and securities firms.

---

14 TBs (Treasury Bills)/FBs (Financing Bills) are discount debt securities that are issued at a price less than the face value of the debt security.

There are three kinds of open market operation:

- o Weekly;
- o Fine tuning; and
- o Long-term.

The size and direction (to absorb or supply liquidity) of the weekly open market operations reflects expected weekly changes in banknotes in circulation, longer term open market operations and other sterling flows across the Bank's balance sheet.

Fine-tuning open market operations (to absorb or supply liquidity) are normally overnight and are carried out at the end of each reserves maintenance period. They ensure that reserves scheme members can achieve their aggregate reserves targets. The Bank may hold fine-tuning open market operations on days other than the final day of the maintenance period.

Weekly and fine tuning open market operations to supply liquidity are undertaken as repos, whilst operations removing excess reserves are usually conducted by sales of Bank of England's sterling bills. In its repo operations to supply liquidity to market participants, the Bank of England purchases eligible securities from its counterparties, and it agrees to sell back equivalent securities at a predetermined future date, around two weeks later. The interest rate charged on these two-week repos is the official repo rate.

Weekly and fine tuning open market operations are normally held at the official repo rate (set by the Monetary Policy Committee, MPC). They usually take place on Thursdays. On days when there are no scheduled interest rate announcements, the Bank undertakes these operations at 10:00 a.m.. On the days when the MPC makes scheduled interest rate decisions, the Bank undertakes these operations at 12:15 p.m., in order to follow the MPC's noon announcement.

Long-term supply of liquidity is carried out through long-term repo and through gilt purchases to back note issue. In this case, the amount the Bank of England pays for the bills less than are their nominal values. The Bank of England lends at 3, 6, 9 and 12-month maturities. The price of long-term repos are determined in auctions. The securities purchased are required to be of high credit quality, actively traded in a continuous, liquid market, held widely across the financial system and available in adequate supply. The choice of obtaining liquidity by repo or outright purchases of securities and the particular eligible instrument provided as collateral, are normally at the counterparty's discretion, subject to settlement constraints. Long-term repos are normally conducted monthly, usually at 10:00 a.m. on a Tuesday mid-month. Since December 2007 the Bank of England has increased the amount and frequency of its three-month lending, and ithas expanded the range of collateral eligible in those operations.

The Bank of England offers **standing facilities** with the aim to stabilise expectations that overnight market interest rates will be in line with the Bank of Enland's official rate. Through this tool the banks can manage unexpected payments shocks that could otherwise take their reserves accounts either below zero or to a level where they would otherwise be unremunerated. The rates currently paid/charged on the facilities are 0.75% (standint lending facility) and 0.00% (standing deposit facility). The standing deposit facility is uncollateralised. The standing lending facility is overnight reverse repo against eligible collateral. The standing facilities are available all day subject to operational constraints arising from deadlines in payments and securities settlement systems.

8 Operating, intermediate and ultimate targets

8.1 Operating targets

Nowadays, the nominal short-term market interest rate (i.e. not the real interest rate) represents almost exclusively **operating target**. In the past, monetary policy have also used monetary base, limits on loans granted and limits on clients' interest rates on loans and deposits. To achieve the targeted short-term market interest rate, monetary authorities use the open market operations. Hence, central bank does not manage its ultimate target of price stability directly, but indirectly by means of short-term market interest rates. It thus follows that the short-term market interest rate does not come from the market but from the decisions taken by the central bank. **Thus monetary policy has generally only one output: short-term market interest rate and nothing more.**

8.1.1 Operating targets in the history

Let's look on the infamous U.S. history of the **regulation of monetary base**. On Saturday, 6 October 1979, Fed, under the governorship of Paul Volcker, has adopted a modified version of the monetary base targeting using the M1 as an intermediate target. To moderate potential extreme movements of market interest rate, central bank was using the discount window. Previously, the Fed was controlling the level of the Fed funds rate. The method was intended to target non-borrowed reserves. This experiment lasted until September 1982. Volatility of short-term interest rates during this period increased four times, i.e. the monetary base regulation caused the excessive volatility of short-term interest rates. In addition, increased volatility affected both the long-term interest rates and foreign exchange market. The monetary base targeting even caused higher volatility of monetary aggregate M1. Hence, the volatility of the whole financial market increased.

Subsequently, the Fed has implemented, for a short time, targeting of borrowed reserves as its operating target. There is no fundamental difference between these two methods. During the first half of the 1980s, many countries abandoned monetary targeting. The stable connection between intermediate monetary target and ultimate monetary target in the form of inflation or nominal GDP had broken (if it ever existed). History of unstable relationships between monetary aggregates and nominal GDP has hampered the effort to consider monetary aggregates as intermediate target. Instead of this, central banks have started changing interest rates following inflation and foreign exchange rates.

In the former times, central banks were also using **limits (ceilings) on loans granted**. The whole limit was usually distributed among individual banks. This method was widely used especially in European countries in the 1970s and it still makes basis of monetary policy in many developing countries, particularly in Africa. However, the definition of institution subjects to these ceiling was allowing many ways to avoid it. Efficiency of ceiling was thereby substantially limited. Ceilings were also hardly affecting competitiveness by penalizing dynamic institutions. Once the bank has reached the ceiling, there was no further stimulus to compete regardless the profitability of investment opportunities. There were several suggestions about how to restore competitiveness, e.g. to allow trading with quotas. However, these suggestions were never introduced into practice.

Countries, where the loan ceiling method was abandoned in favour of indirect monetary policy instruments, usually find themselves unable to control monetary and loan aggregates as precisely as before. Monetary aggregates in the United Kingdom in the 1970s, for instance, expanded rapidly after the central bank has abandoned these ceilings. Neither loans nor money have embodied stable relation with nominal GDP and inflation. Developing countries that have recently abandoned loan ceilings are loosing control over monetary aggregates as well. Some countries have also imposed **limits on clients' interest rates on loans and deposits.** However, this method was already almost abandoned for similar reasons.

8.1.2 Current operating targets

Fed announces only one interest rate, namely the intended federal funds rate. This rate represents the rate that the Fed member banks use for their over-night interbank loans and deposits. Originally, Fed was not announcing this rate, and analysts were deriving it from the Fed's open market operations. In December 2009 the intended federal funds rate was **0 – 0.25 %.**

Eurosystem declares three interest rates, namely the interest rate of one-week main refinancing operations, the interest rate of deposit facility and the interest rate of loan facility. The market one-week Euribor is lower than the interest rate of main refinancing operations. For example in December 2009 the interest rate of main refinancing operations was **1.00 %** while the one-week Euribor was on the level of 0.4 %. At the same time interest rate of deposit facility was 0.25 %, and interest rate of loan facility was 1.75 %.

Bank of Japan announces the uncollaterised overnight call rate. From October 2001 this rate was set at historical low level 0,001 %. Subsequently in 2006 this rate has been step-by-step increased up to 0.5 % in 2007. Then official interest has been gradually lowered to **0.1 %** in December 2009.

Bank of England sets out official bank rate of the two-week repo operations delivering liquidity. The market two-week sterling Libor is approximately the same level. For example in December 2009 the official bank rate was **0.50 %.**

8.2 Intermediate targets

As **intermediate target** monetary authorities usually use one of monetary aggregates, exchange rate or the long-term market interest rate. Further, they can use the total amount of loans granted, assets prices and other fundamental indicators. Sometimes, we could also observe other than monetary indicators serving as intermediate target. At the same time, there needs to be a relatively stable and easily predictable relation between this indicator and ultimate target. These aspects differ in individual countries substantially. Financial variables are hardly observable by public, and the frequency of their measurement is generally longer than one month. In order to achieve the ultimate target, central authority sets the operating target based on current observations of the intermediate target. Roughly speaking, the choice of a specific monetary aggregate results from the observation that every creation of money can increase future inflation. This attitude is common especially to monetarists.

8.2.1 Monetary aggregates targeting

According to many economists, the price level depends on monetary aggregates. They think that the total amount money determines the price level. History of this attitude is very long dated. Among many authors, we can mention Irving Fisher who has defined the formal identity of quantity theory of money, John Maynard Keynes who was strictly opposing it, and Milton Friedman thanks to whom this theory was revived.

The comeback of quantity theory of money was made possible also because of the inflationary development during the 1970s and the beginning of the 1980s. That was a period when central authorities of many countries were forced to redefine their monetary policies. As the monetary anchor in the form of the fixed exchange rate disappeared with the end of Bretton-Woods system, central banks had no way to stop the excessive monetary expansion. In order to reverse such development, some developed countries started to rely upon the money stock as a monetary conditions indicator or even as intermediate target. Money stock was supposed to be a good leading indicator of inflationary development, i.e. the control over money stock was supposed to help stabilize inflation.

According to Goodhart[15] however, by the end of the 1970s, "...the crucial long-term relationships, i.e. the relationships between the money stock and nominal incomes (velocity), and between prices in two countries and their nominal exchange rate (purchasing power parity), appeared far more fragile than expected." Goodhart noticed some other economists[16].

Money stock targeting stems from findings suggesting that in a long-run, the development of money stock is said to determine the price level. Monetary policy of money stock targeting thus concentrates on the maintaining the adequate growth rate of a chosen monetary aggregate. According to the quantity theory, this variable has relation to the growth rate of nominal GDP. This regime can take a variety of forms concerning the choice of monetary aggregate, size of a targeted growth rate and manner of targeting.

Important question arises about **which monetary aggregate to choose,** i.e. what aggregate shows the econometrically documented stable relationship with the price development, or with the development of nominal GDP. The problem can be that central bank could not be ready to manage such monetary aggregate. Experience shows, that excessive changes of monetary growth affect inflation with a long lag. Thus central banks have to react in advance.

Central banks construct, therefore, diverse definitions of money, from narrow money in form of currency and deposits on current accounts to broader money including mid-term and long-term deposits, mortgage backed securities and so forth. The choice of individual central bank does not follow some uniform rule. Experience shows that the broader the aggregate, stronger is its relation to inflation, and it is harder controlled by central bank.

---

15 Goodhart, Charles: The Conduct of Monetary Policy, The Economic Journal, 1989, 99(396), 293-346.

16 Goodhart, Charles: The Conduct of Monetary Policy, The Economic Journal, 1989, 99(396), 293-346. According to Goodhart: "Yet a large wing of mainstream (mostly US) macro-theoretical economists appear to have taken little notice of such historical experience in recent years, driving ever deeper into an artificial (Arrow/Debreu) world of perfectly clearing (complete) markets, in which money and finance do not matter, and business cycles are caused by real phenomena, e.g. Kydland and Prescott (1982), Long and Plosser (1983), King and Plosser (1984). Moreover, in a number of analytical studies of this kind, e.g. Lucas (1972), Sargent and Wallace (1975), the only reason why monetary policy may affect real variables is owing to an informational imperfection, which would seem simple and worthwhile to overcome. This leaves something of a gap between state-of-the-art macro-theory and practical policy analysis, see Laidler (1988 a, b)."

The targeted growth of monetary aggregate usually does not comprise one number but rather the band specifying the desired value of monetary aggregate by the end of the year or corridor for the desired development of monetary aggregate during the whole year. More and more central banks cease using the one-year's growth rate target but rather prefer the band for several years. Overheated economy could result in a growth of money stock. Central bank is, therefore, increasing interest rates in order to reduce the inflationary pressures. Conversely, weakening economy usually produces slowing growth of money stock. In such a case, central bank usually cuts interest rates, and hence it boosts the consumer demand and inflation.

If there is the precise causality between money growth and inflation, the money stock targeting would be suitable, especially in countries, where the relationship between the targeted monetary aggregate and inflation is stable and predictable. **To manage monetary aggregates efficiently, central bank needs a functional credit channel, where the loan activity reacts to changes of interest rates.** Nevertheless, current practice teaches us about other factors determining the price level. Discussions on monetary policy often concentrate on topics such as which factors determine the relation between money and prices. Analytic approaches often use the definition of Granger causality. They search especially for the time structure of lags of prices behind money and other macroeconomic indicators. Analysts also search for reverse causality, especially how current prices depend on future money, and how prices affect GDP.

By the end of the 1980s, the most of central banks have abandoned, formally or informally, monetary aggregates targeting in favour of methods allowing them working with diverse economic indicators. They have also implemented more flexible monetary instrument regimes allowing for influencing monetary conditions faster and with changing emphasis. These changes of monetary policy were caused primarily by the increasing instability of monetary aggregates and disappearing correlation of these aggregates with inflation. Since there was no suitable intermediate target, many central banks have chosen monetary policy concentrating directly on ultimate monetary target, i.e. on inflation (inflation targeting).

However, this does not mean that money stock has lost its information importance. It just does not represent the whole transmission mechanism, and it cannot serve, therefore, as an intermediate target. It maintains the role of information variable. The monetary policy decision-making is always based on imperfect information about the future economic development of which the monetary aggregates represent a part.

8.2.2 The use of monetary aggregates

In former times, many central banks were considering monetary aggregates highly important monetary policy intermediate targets. However, experiences from central banks vary substantially. In the United States, Canada and the United Kingdom, results of this method were hardly satisfactory. On the other hand, this regime was relatively successful in countries like Germany and Switzerland.

Estimates show that the lag of inflation behind monetary aggregate in **EU member states** before the adoption of euro was about six to nine months. Some countries were showing lags of even more than one year. Countries where the growth of monetary aggregate was more moderate were observing weaker correlation between money and inflation, since there were also other factors determining inflation. These relations are very hard to model and estimate even ex post. Ex ante forecasts, therefore, can hardly provide reliable data for monetary policy decision-making.

In the **USA** the role of monetary aggregates in monetary policy has changed with their reliability. During much of the post-World War II period, M1 had the stable relationship to aggregate spending. Full Employment and Balanced Growth Act of 1978 (the Humphrey-Hawkins Act) introduced the obligation of Fed to specify limits for the desired growth of money stock. The Fed had to publicly announce its monetary growth target in every February and to review and possibly redefine it every six months. The Fed set target growth rate ranges for all three aggregates. This measure supposed relatively stable relationship between money growth and monetary policy targets, i.e. that this relationship can be used to achieve the monetary policy targets. It was supposed, that money stock can fix the price level.[17]

This act was also taking into account possible revision of monetary policy if the relationship between money and loan aggregates and economy (e.g. velocity of money[18]) become unpredictable. Under such circumstances, it would become

---

17 The golden standard was supposed formerly to determine it as well.

18 Velocity of money is a key term in the quantity theory of money, which centres on the "equation of exchange":

$$M^* V = P^* Q$$

Where: M some monetary aggregate (M0, M1, M2 etc.);
V velocity of money;
P price level; and
Q production of the economy measured through GDP.

economically undesirable to rely on monetary aggregates. Fed thus does not have to keep its announced targets concerning money or loan growth. In such case, however, it has to explain reasons to the Congress and to the public. Consequently, analysts started examining carefully the reports about movements of money stock (especially the movements of M1). If, for example, Fed reported faster growth than expected, analysts started expecting Fed to raise the federal funds rate in order to decelerate it.

Thus before the financial markets deregulation in the 1980s, monetary aggregates in the United States represented reliable inflationary indicator. In addition, Fed could relatively simply manage it. That is why Fed was paying special interest on monetary growth in the 1970s and at the beginning of the 1980s. From 1979 to 1982 the Fed was explicitly targeting money stock. However, the relatively stable relationship between monetary aggregates and inflation started to slowly disappear during the late of the 1970s as there were new financial products (NOW and Super NOW accounts) introduced, and as the economic agents became more willing to hold the narrow (M1) money. Before deregulation, banks were not allowed to pay interest on M1 deposits, and individuals were, therefore, holding only the most necessary amounts of money to arrange their current expenditures. The amount of M1 deposits was thus closely correlated with expenditures.

At the beginning of eighties, U.S. banks were allowed to pay interests on checking accounts. The subsequent introduction of NOW accounts (negotiable order of withdrawal) in 1981 and Super NOW accounts in 1983 resulted in massive transfers of money from saving accounts (part of M2) to the new ones which make part of M1. NOW and Super NOW accounts offered the mix of transaction properties of demand deposits with interest properties of term deposits. New financial products thus resulted in overshooting the target zone for M1 regardless the slowdown of U.S. economy.

Once the banks were allowed to pay explicit interest on checkable deposits (NOW and Super NOW accounts), M1 did not reflect reliably expenditures since people started to keep their money deposited on these accounts, i.e. balances of these accounts started to exceed the amounts necessary for their transactions. In addition, financial markets started providing new instruments substituting M1 deposits, and many people transferred their deposits in favour of these instruments. Relationship between M1 and expenditures was, therefore, further weakened. Among these newly instruments, we can mention the introduction of sweep accounts in 1994 that substantially diminished M1 aggregate without changing the M2 aggregate. M1 aggregate also become more sensible to changes of short-term interest rates. Since the M1 aggregate was bearing low and relatively stable interests, the change of market interest rate was causing remarkable changes of M1 money. The relationship between M2 and M3 aggregate and inflation weakened too.

Until 1987, Fed was examining particularly the development of monetary aggregate M1. The relationship between this aggregate and nominal GDP slowly diminished during the 1970s and 1980s. Fed therefore shifted its attention to the monetary aggregate M2 in 1987 for the correlation between this aggregate and nominal GDP was substantially stronger.

Another argument against the use of monetary aggregates highlights unstable velocity of money. The velocity of M2 aggregate remained relatively stable for the long period of time (even though it was changing slightly with changes of interest rate). However, at the beginning of the 1990s, the velocity of M2 abandoned its historical behaviour. It increased remarkably. This velocity increased when the market interest rate decreased. This fluctuation caused the worsening predictability of the velocity of money and problems with achieving the overall economic objectives.

During the 1990s, the stable relationship between M2 and aggregate spending also broke down. Beginning in July 2000, the Fed discontinued setting monitoring ranges for M2 and M3. M3 was never strongly related to aggregate spending. The Fed then proclaimed that the money stock does not represent the accurate measure for monetary policy, and that it will further use it only as one of indicators Thus, the United States now has two definitions of money (M1 and M2 as publication of the monetary aggregate M3 discontinued in March 2006) that appear to provide little information about the monetary policy.

Since that time, Fed monitors a wide range of indicators of future development of GDP, employment and inflation. Among others we can mention different monetary aggregates, growth of real and nominal GDP, commodity prices, exchange rates, inflation expectations and different credit spreads and current yield curve. Relationships between these variables and effects on monetary policy help throw more light on models. Monetary policy decision makers thus rely rather on their own judgments. Sometimes they differ in attitude towards a specific indicator in relation with another indicator. It is not surprising because these indicators are hardly interpretable or sometimes even supporting different measures.

Alternative indicators have thus begun to play more important role in U.S. monetary policy. In Canada, evolution of financial innovations was very similar, and Bank of Canada has left, therefore, M1 as intermediate target, and it started to use the whole set of other economic indicators. This policy is often denoted multi-criteria or "looking at everything". This approach has consequently transformed into the so-called inflation targeting. Monetary policy based on monetary aggregates used during the monetarist era of the 1970s and 1980s has been replaced by the monetary policy based on inflation targeting.

8.2.3 Exchange rate targeting

Under this regime, central bank uses interest rates changes and direct foreign exchange interventions in order to secure the stabilized nominal exchange rate. **It usually seeks to import low inflation from another country.** To fulfil this objective, central bank needs some prerequisites. Above all, there must be a low inflationary differential between these to countries, sufficient foreign exchange reserves, sustainable competitiveness and credibility of country employing this way of targeting including its legislative, institutional and political stability. When the domestic currency depreciates, central bank increases interest rates and vice versa. Fixed rate regime can also support the economic and political integration. This was the case of the European Exchange Rate Mechanism (ERM) that anticipated the launch of euro.

The fixed exchange rate of domestic currency to one or several foreign currencies represents the basic regime of exchange rate targeting. Inflation of the "anchor" country is generally very low, and this country has usually considerable share in mutual trade. There are other regimes based on exchange rate targeting. Central bank can, for instance, set a corridor within which the exchange rate can fluctuate. If there is a danger of exchange rate breaking this limit, central bank intervenes. This regime is usually chosen in order to increase the foreign exchange risk which helps reduce the speculative flows of capital. Exchange rate targeting can also take the form of crawling peg. Under such regime central bank sometimes change the corridor (central bank usually devaluates home currency). This devaluation is usually less than the inflationary differential. This regime helps prevent inappropriate appreciation of domestic currency that could endanger competitiveness of domestic producers. In extreme cases, central banks can choose the currency board regime. This regime features higher credibility and resistance against speculative attacks.

Among the major **disadvantages** of the exchange rate targeting is the weakening autonomy of monetary policy, since the domestic interest rates must follow interest rates of the anchor country (in the environment of liberalized capital flows). The number and efficiency of measures the central bank can use to react in the case of the demand or supply shocks are also limited. Conversely, shocks affecting the anchor country are easily imported through monetary policy into the domestic economy. There is also an increased risk of speculative attacks on domestic currency (with the exception of currency board regime). This risk increases even more when the domestic exchange rate is overvalued for a long time, and the price competitiveness of domestic producers, therefore, erodes. The probability of monetary instability increases, and it pushes interest rates upwards. Such a development can have negative impacts on domestic economy. Furthermore, this policy is very expensive. If the economy is slowing down, and if central bank raises interest rates, the economic weakness intensifies.

The results of this policy also depend on market expectations about the attainability of exchange rate target. Foreign investors could find higher interest rates temporary. Tightening of monetary policy would thus have only limited impact. To achieve its original objective central bank would have to raise interest rates more dramatically, which would damage economy even more.

The exchange rate targeting regime is suitable for small open economies where the exchange rate substantially determines the domestic price level. Exchange rate also provides relatively stable anchor to regulate capital flows. Reduced capital flows help eliminate the risk of exchange rates speculation. Conversely, it delays the identification of potential economic problems. Increased liberalization of capital flows and financial markets globalization have forced many central banks to abandon this regime.

8.3 Ultimate targets

The **ultimate target** of monetary policy is the price stability (i.e. low inflation) or alternatively the long-term economic growth and the full employment. Within the last years, central banks got increasingly concentrated on the main target, which is the price stability, i.e. on stabilization of the purchasing power of money unit (low inflation). In some cases, there were a particular percentage points actually imposed by law. It is supposed that the ultimate target can be only the price stability and not the GDP growth, since central bank can influence GDP only in short terms. Price stability helps maintain the stable environment for business activity. It is, therefore, indirectly expressing the central bank's responsibility for the sustainable economic growth. However, the central bank's activity itself can not assure price stability, for there are a number of other inflationary factors which are out of the central bank's control.

8.3.1 Price stability

At the beginning of the 1960s, economists were confident that central banks could simultaneously achieve the low inflation, strong economic growth, high employment, stable exchange rate, low interest rates and even balance of the current account. However, central banks cannot provide society with a cheap "medicine" against all of its economic troubles. Nowadays, economists agree that central banks should concentrate primarily on **price stability**, which makes part of monetary stability (monetary stability contains exchange rate stability as well). Experience shows that the **price stability boosts the economic growth and employment**. Low inflation does not distort prices of goods and services. Stable prices also encourage savings and capital accumulation, since assets values do not erode by the unpredictable inflation. Price stability thus represents the ultimate long-term objective. Short-term inflationary fluctuations are inevitable, and central bank seeks to smooth them. As the monetary policy influences the economy with the substantial and unpredictable lag, central banks cannot influence prices in a short term.

Stable low-inflationary environment makes the macroeconomic conditions easier to predict. Such environment also allows households and enterprises make their economic decisions based on information that is more reliable, since they can distinguish more easily changes of relative prices from the overall trends. Both of these aspects make the resource allocation more efficient. That is the key factor of a long-term economic prosperity. Enterprises can make their long-term investments without being afraid of future price swings making their today's decisions wrong. Similarly, households can make their consumption and savings plans without facing the risk of future shifts of real and financial assets values. This also allows financial markets to fulfil efficiently their basic function of optimal resource allocation.

The effort taken to maintain the price stability reflects the historical experience demonstrating that high inflation damages economy. **High and unstable inflation affects badly the economic growth**. Empirical evidences demonstrate unambiguously that the economic growth in countries with lower inflation exceeds the growth of countries with higher and unstable inflation. In the United States, the average real GDP growth during the low-inflation period (i.e. from 1952 to 1965) was of 3.3 %. During the higher-inflation period (from 1967 to 1980), the average real GDP growth fell to 2.7 %. This figure is substantially lower despite the stimulus provided by the Vietnam War. The disinflation (slowing inflation) leading to price stability often brings short-tem costs consisting in a lower economic growth and lower employment. However, the long-term growth effects more than balance these costs.

Other negative impacts of higher inflation are:

- High inflation causes direct redistribution effects, for inflation liquidates real value of money. **High inflation redistributes wealth from lenders**

to borrowers, while small inflation and deflation redistributes wealth from borrowers to lenders This redistribution represents a latent burden to people who save, and it cannot secure purchasing power of their incomes and savings. During the 1970s and 1980s, those who were able to borrow money to finance holdings of assets whose value was rising gained, since the inflation has diminished real value of their debts. Those who were able to adapt their tax and other affairs in the way to benefit from inflation have gained too. Inflation expectations motivate people to seek to minimize the impact of inflation or to take advantage of it;

- High inflation redistributes wealth through the income taxes. Income taxes do not take into account inflation. The whole amount of interests received, therefore, constitutes the basis for taxation even though a part of these interests represent compensation for inflation. Similarly, the whole amount of interests paid by enterprises represents costs, and reduces, therefore, the tax burden even if a part of these interests represents a compensation for inflation. This means that in the case of high inflation, tax system taxes interest incomes more and interest expenses less. Borrowers therefore benefits at the expense of lenders;

- High inflation represents the source of uncertainty that makes the economic decisions more difficult. High inflation periods are usually periods of the increased volatility of inflation. Prices and wages change increasingly. If there is a high and volatile inflation, people cannot estimate correctly, how fast the overall price level would increase, and what is the right price of individual goods and services. This makes the price system less efficient in allocation of resources. The uncertainty about the future relative prices as well as about the overall price level pushes debt markets to require higher risk premium to compensate it;

- In the case of high and volatile inflation, investors tend to concentrate more on the short-term financial investments and on hedging against inflation and less on investment projects with longer-term returns. The economic growth is based primarily on long-term investments;

- In times of high inflation, people and enterprises spend more time thinking about how to hedge against inflation, and they concentrate less on productive activities, i.e. the production of goods and services. They also spend additional costs of monitoring economic development and actions taken by central bank;

- High inflation often means higher interest rates that attract short-term speculative capital. This can lead to fluctuations of exchange rate; and

- If the higher inflation lasts for a longer period, economic entities implement higher inflation expectations into their decision-making processes.

On the other hand, there are a number of arguments for **evading the zero inflation targets**. First, the economy is subject to the so-called downward nominal rigidities. That means that prices and wages usually do not fall even if the market equilibrium would require it. If there is a low inflation, prices and wages can fall relatively. Low inflation can make the price system more efficient. Second, statistical observation can overestimate inflation. This would be the case when it does not take into account increasing quality of goods and services. Central bank can consequently take false steps and it can target lower inflation compared with the situation if these observations are correct. These argument help justify the general approach of targeting low positive inflation. Many central banks target inflation close to 2 %.

When achieving the price stability, central bank has to take into account many long-term and short-term accompanying effects. In a long-term, price stability contributes to GDP growth and employment. However, in a short-term, it can cause certain pressures between efforts for the price stability on one hand and GDP growth and employment on the other hand. It might be the case in times when the economy faces supply side shocks such as poor harvest of agricultural products or increased oil prices pushing prices upwards and causing economic slowdown and increasing unemployment. Under such conditions, central bank has to decide whether and how much it will seek to stop inflation or whether and how it will strive to support economic growth and employment. Public can also incorporate higher inflation expectations into its decision-making about prices and salaries, i.e. these expectations become the self-fulfilling prophecy, and they cause the temporary fall of GDP and employment. Central bank must, therefore, use a tighter monetary policy, which can bring certain risk of short-term falls in GDP and employment. However, such costs are usually justifiable, since the costs of higher inflation expectations would be much higher.

Central bank achieves its targets more efficiently if the public understands well these targets, and if it is convinced that central bank will do its best to achieve it. For instance, a credible anti-inflationary policy realized by means of reducing the growth of aggregate demand can reduce the public's inflation expectations, which can help reduce inflation. Employees will not require higher growth of their wages, and enterprises will be raising their prices more slowly. Inflation will consequently decrease proportionally to the fall of aggregate demand whilst the slowdown of the resources markets will be lower than if the higher inflation expectations persist.

8.3.2 Definition of Inflation

Inflation is the rise of prices in a specific economy. The real value of currency in relation to consumer goods and services decreases. If there is inflation, consumer needs to purchase the same basket of goods and services for more and more units of currency. In practice, we measure inflation by means of the so-called consumer price index (CPI), GDP deflator and producer price index. The double-digit inflation accompanied by the stagnation of economic growth is called **stagflation.** The fall of prices in an economy is called **deflation**. The process of the inflation slowdown is called **disinflation**.

According to International Financial Reporting Standards (IFRS) **hyperinflation** means the loss of purchasing power of a currency in such an extent that a price comparison of transactions taking place at different moments gets misleading. Hyperinflation features the following characteristics:

- The general population prefers keeping its wealth in the form of non-monetary assets or in form of a relatively stable foreign currency;
- The general population considers money amounts denominated in domestic currency as being denominated in a relatively stable foreign currency;
- Sales and purchases on credit take place at prices that compensate for the expected loss of purchasing power during the credit period;
- Interest rates, wages and prices are linked to price index; and
- The cumulative rate of inflation over three years is approaching, or exceeds, 100 %.

As a deterring example, we could mention the Weimar Republic of Germany hyperinflation during 1921–1923 caused by monetizing the government debt[19] as the German government did not have funds to pay workers. Some people argue that Germany had to inflate its currency to pay the war reparations required under the Treaty of Versailles. This hyperinflation resulted in a dangerous rise of political extremism, and likely it has contributed to the Nazi takeover of Germany.

---

19 Any government finances its deficit by issuing new bonds and selling them to commercial banks and to the public. In such a way government acquires funds to pay for its spending. Exceptionally these bonds can be purchased by the central bank through its open market operations. This process of financing government spending is called **monetizing the government debt.**

Consumer price index (CPI) refers to the inflation in relation to the consumption basket only. CPI is measure of inflation from the point of view of consumer. However, there are several technical problems. The determination of consumer basket, for instance, depends on consumption of all households and on the choice of particular goods and services reflecting increasing quality of goods and services.

To calculate the consumer price index, Laspeyres index I is generally used:

$$I = \sum p_n q_0 / \sum p_0 q_0$$

Where: p_n prices of goods (services) in the current period,
p_0 prices of goods (services) in the base period,
q_0 fixed weights of goods (services)

The weights q_0 remain constant for several years, since the structure of households expenditures does not change too much. This figure measures the so-called "net price changes", i.e. price changes not influenced by changes of the consumption basket structure.

In the **United States**, there are two consumer price indexes. The Consumer Price Index for All Urban Consumers (**CPI-U**) is based on all-urban consumer population which consists of all urban households in the so-called Metropolitan Statistical Areas and in urban places of 2 500 inhabitants or more. The index was introduced in 1978, and it is representative of the consumer habits of approximately 80 % of the population of the U.S., compared with 32 % represented in the CPI-W. Financial markets focus very carefully on it.

The Consumer Price Index for Urban Wage Earners and Clerical Workers (**CPI-W**) is based on urban wage earner and clerical worker population which consists of consumer units with clerical workers, sales workers, craft workers, operative, service workers or laborers. Excluded are professional, managerial and technical workers, the self-employed, short-term workers, the unemployed, retirees and others not in the labor force. The index is a continuation of the historical index that was introduced after World War I for use in wage negotiation.

Both indexes are published by the U.S. Department of Labour, Bureau of Labour Statistics at the website http://stats.bls.gov (or http://www.dol.gov) monthly, two or three weeks after the end of a month. These indexes measure prices of a fixed consumption basket of goods and services.

The **Eurozone** uses the Harmonized Index of Consumer Prices (HICP) which is publsihed by Eurostat. The HICP differs from the CPI-U mainly in two aspects. First, the HICP attempts to incorporate rural consumers into the sample while the CPI-U maintains a survey strictly based on the urban population. Second, the HICP excludes owner-occupied housing from its scope. The CPI-U calculates "rental-equivalent" costs in the case of owner-occupied housing while the HICP excludes it.

In **Japan** Consumer Price Index (CPI) is compiled by the Statistics Bureau, Ministry of Public Management, Home Affairs, Posts and Telecommunications adopting the Laspeyres formula. Currently, the base year of the CPI is 2005, and it is revised every five years. The items and weights for the CPI are reviewed together with this base revision. The number of CPI items in 2005 base was 584. They are selected according to the relative importance of each item in total living expenditures.

In the **United Kingdom,** Office for National Statistics publishes monthly Retail Price Index (RPI). It is used by the government as a base for various purposes. Monetary policy in the United Kingdom had been based on Retail Price Index Excluding Mortgage Payments (RPIX) till December 2003 when RPIX was replaced by CPI (UK HICP). But the RPIX continues to be published each month by the Office for National Statistics.

Producer price index (PPI) measures the inflation of domestic producers' prices. PPI measures inflation from the point of view of sellers. The U.S. Department of Labour publishes PPI at the same web site as it publishes the CPI.

GDP deflator measures inflation concerning the whole GDP and not only the consumption basket. Unlike price indexes, the GDP deflator is not based on a fixed basket of goods and services. The GDP deflator reacts automatically to changes of consumer preferences, i.e. it takes into account new goods and services, and it excludes the non-attractive ones. The basket changes with people's consumption and investment patterns. In practice, the difference between the GDP deflator and a price index is often relatively small.

8.3.3 Real and nominal interest rates

Real interest rate denotes the nominal interest rate deducted by the depreciation of real value (i.e. purchasing power) of money during some period. This depreciation is measured by inflation. The real interest rate is, therefore, the nominal interest rate deducted by inflation. If we calculate the real interest rate at the end of period, we talk about the ex post approach. In such a case, we use the already measured inflation, and we get the ex post real interest rate. If we calculate the real interest rate before the end of period, we talk about the ex ante approach. In such a case, we use the expected inflation, and we get the ex ante real interest rate. One nominal interest rate can correspond to a number of ex ante real interest rates, since economists can expect different inflation. The relation between nominal interest rate r, real interest rate R and inflation i during the period t (in a number of days) is (we use the annualized values of r, R and i):

$$\left(1+r\frac{t}{360}\right)=\left(1+R\frac{t}{360}\right)\cdot\left(1+i\frac{t}{360}\right)$$

whence:

$$R=\left(\frac{1+r\frac{t}{360}}{1+i\frac{t}{360}}-1\right)\cdot\frac{360}{t}$$

In the case of time period of one year, i.e. $t = 360$ days, the former relation is simplified as:

$$R=\frac{1+r}{1+i}-1$$

Provided that both nominal interest rates and inflation (either actual or expected) are low, we can use the approximation consisting in deduction of inflation from the nominal interest rate:

$$R\approx r-i$$

Let's take an example of the higher inflation environment. Suppose that the nominal interest rate is 8 %, and the expected inflation equals 10 % (annualised values). Then the real interest is:

$$R=\frac{1+0.08}{1+0.10}-1=-0.0182$$

I.e. $\boldsymbol{R}$ **= –1.82 %**

Using the approximate formula, we would get the real interest rate $R \approx -2.00$ %. The real interest rates in a high inflationary environment are usually (not necessarily) negative.

Our next example relates to a deflationary environment. Let the nominal interest rate is 2 %, and the expected deflation equal 1% (annualised values). Then the real interest is:

$$R = \frac{1+0.02}{1-0.01} - 1 = +0.0303$$

I.e. $\boldsymbol{R} = \mathbf{+3.03\ \%}$

Using the approximate formula, we would get the real interest rate equal to $R \approx$ +3.00 %. The real interest rates in a deflationary environment are usually (not necessarily) positive.

The demand for goods and services does not depend on nominal interest rates. It is a function of real interest rates. Real interest rates influence entities (households and enterprises) in their decisions about expenses. In 1975 the U.S. federal funds rate amounted to 6 %. However, the inflation reached 10 %. The real interest rate was –4.0 %. Monetary policy was thus stimulating the demand. Conversely, in 1998, the nominal interest rate amounted to 5.5 % while the inflation was low on a level of 1.4 %. The real interest rate amounted to + 4.1 %. Monetary policy was thus tightening the demand. It follows that the nominal interest rate of 6 % in 1975 was more stimulating demand than the nominal interest rate of 5.5 % in 1998.

Average long-term real interest rates were positive in the USA, the Euro-zone, Japan and the United Kingdom as is shown in Table 8.1.

Table 8.1 Long-term real interest rates in some countries (in percent per annum)

Country	Period	Average official interest rate		Average inflation	Average real interest rate
United States	1960–2008	Federal funds rate	6.0	4.2	**1.8**
Eurozone	1999–2008	Main refinancing operations interest rate	3.0	2.2	**0.8**
Japan	1970–2008	Uncollaterised overnight call rate	4.2	3.2	**1.0**
United Kingdom	1970–2008	Repo rate	8.4	6.7	**1.7**

8.3.4 Deflation

Deflation is the fall of prices in an economy. Deflation can be (but not necessarily) accompanied by the economic slowdown, rising unemployment, rise of real interest rates, serious troubles of banks and enterprises and general uncertainty. Many economists consider deflation more dangerous than modest inflation. It seems that deflation represents a very serious problem.

a) Historical evidence

Deflation was a common phenomenon in the **19th century and the first fourty years of 20th centrury** (Figure 8.1 for the USA and the United Kingdom). It was a period of deflationary economic growth. The growth in the USA in the 19th century was especially due to the expansion of the railroads. The deflation periods were broken by wars when the inflation rose steeply.

In the United States, there were three high inflation periods connected with wars:

- The War of 1812;
- American Civil War (1861–1865); and
- World War I (1914–1918).

Within the last 35 years of 19th century (reconstruction and the rise of industrialization) prices in the USA fell by 50 % while the economy was growing. However, during the World War I and soon after it, the United States has experienced high inflation as many other countries. But thus inflationary period did not last for a long time. Period from 1920 to the beginning of World War II was again deflationary. From **1929 to 1933**, the price level of the world largest economies fell sharply (in the USA by 25 %). This deflation was accompanied by the comparable fall of production, chain of bankruptcies and the highest unemployment of modern times.

By contrast, after the World War II, world has experienced a long period of inflation. In the United States, prices have increased by 1,250 % from 1800 to 2008. In the United Kingdom, prices have increased during the same period by 5,740 %. Within **the last seventy years**, the world was afraid almost exclusively of inflation and not of deflation. According to Figure 8.2, inflation in developed countries was gradually increasing since the 1950s. It has reached its peak in the 1970s and since that time, it is gradually decreasing.

Figure 8.1 CPI and RPI development in the United States and the United Kingdom respectively (charts differ only in scales of their vertical axes) according to Rogoff[20]

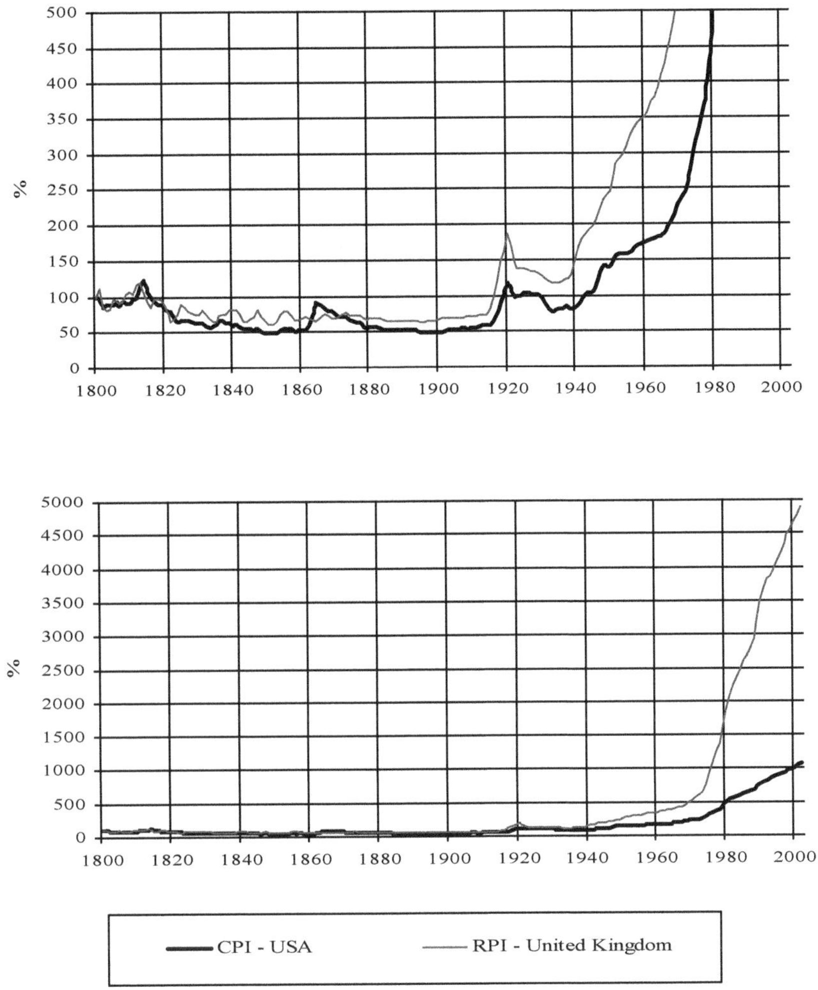

20 Rogoff, Kenneth: *Deflation: Determinants, Risks, and Policy Options — Findings of an Interdepartmental Task Force.* IMF, Washington 2003.

Figure 8.2 The average yearly change of the CPI in developed countries according to Rogoff

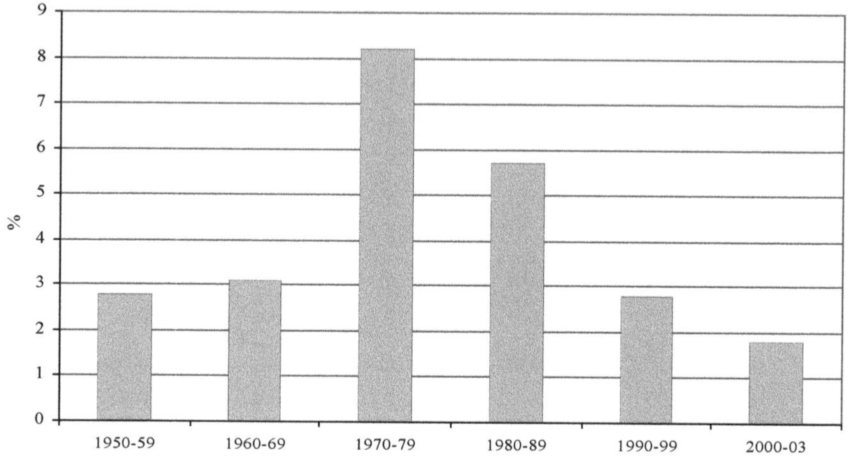

In the 1990s, the world has experienced global disinflation. Commodity prices decreased substantially because of falling demand of Eastern-Asia countries, particularly of Japan. As a result, producers' prices in the Europe and in the United States were falling. Since more than two thirds of the GDP in developed countries consists of services, deflation did not expand. However, the beginning of new century was characterized by deflation in only one major country (Japan).

b) Causes of deflation

Economists usually mention the following main causes of deflation:

- Fall of the share prices;
- Fall of real estate prices;
- Industrial overcapacities, i.e. excess supply of goods and services;
- Increasing households preferences to save instead of spending, i.e. falling demand;
- Sudden fall of key commodities prices;
- Deflationary development in countries of major business partners;

- Rapid liberalization of labour or of a financial market;
- Appreciation of domestic currency; and
- Rigidity of nominal wages and salaries.

Causes of deflation usually consist in a foregoing speculative bubble at markets of certain assets when the non-realistic expectations of investors drive prices too high. Naturally, this cannot last eternally, and these markets eventually collapse. This is usually the case of shares and real estate. Deflation in 1929 started after the collapse on stock exchange. This crash has provoked numerous bankruptcies, falling prices and finally the Great Depression. The deflation in Japan at the end of the 1990s started after the fall of the stock and real estate market. Both deflations represented the epiphenomenon of economic crisis.

a) Effects of deflation

During deflation, both prices and wages are falling. The purchasing power of money is increasing, and the real interest rates are increasing as well (nominal interest rates are converging to zero, and prices are falling). Lenders and people who save and live from capital benefit from such situation. **Deflation redistributes significantly the wealth from borrowers to lenders**, for prices are falling more rapidly that wage contracts. Deflation increases the real value of receivables. Lenders are getting richer, and borrowers are becoming poorer. Real wages are rising which affects negatively enterprises that are paying wages. Under falling prices the real value of money rises. Such situation motivates people to save and it postpones their consumption, since "prices will be lower in few weeks". Nominal interest rate of 1 % represents under the deflation of 2 % the real yield of 3 %.

Enterprises find themselves under the double pressure. Both real repayments of their debts and real labour costs are rising. At the same time, however, the demand for their products is decreasing. To overcome these difficulties for a short term at least, they lower prices, which makes deflation even worse. Falling demand results in falling income and profit. Since the growth of real wages cannot be maintained in a long term, enterprises will have to, sooner or later, decrease nominal wages and reduce staff. Once this happens, households reassess their expectations and reduce their demand. This produces further deflationary pressures. Enterprises produce goods that cannot be sold. Consequently, **they try to repay their debts as much as possible.** Some enterprises become unable to repay their debts. They would be able to repay it only if interest rates were falling too. However, this is not possible, since interest rates cannot fall below zero. Some enterprises thus turn bankrupt, and banks soon follow them.

Households face serious problems as well. Their wages are under the permanent pressure. Either they will accept reduced social benefits and frozen or lower wages or they will be dismissed, and maybe they will be hired later for lower wages and social benefits. Decreasing prices force enterprises to cut their margins, production and investments. Households consequently reduce their consumption, which is, however, the main factor of economic growth.

Banks suffer serious losses since loans are more impaired (repayment of loans rapidly worsens), and the value of collateral falls. Credit crunch starts. Banks want to lend money but nobody wants it even interest rate is extremely low. The demand for loans falls to zero. Financial flows slow down. "Old" borrowers turn bankrupt, since repayments of loans ruin them. Borrowers' crisis becomes banking crisis. If the deflation lasts for several years, enterprises reduce investments, and households reduce consumption.

Both enterprises and banks do not profit, and they reduce their economic activity. This can open the deflationary trap and spiral of decreasing prices, GDP, profits and employment. The output gap gets larger. These hardly predictable process results in further instability of the economy, public looses confidence in banking sector, corporate bankruptcies, high unemployment and enormous costs of renewing integrity of the economy. Price development thus gets its own dynamics exceeding the original impulse.

Is the deflation good or bad? The answer is hardly unambiguous. If the deflation is of structural character (e.g. the Great Depression in the 1930s or Japanese crisis in the 1990s), then it is unquestionably bad, for such deflation is usually bound up with high unemployment and economic crisis. On the other hand, if the falling prices follow from implementation of new technologies and increasing productivity, there is nothing bad about it, since real incomes, demand and production further grow. Before the World War I, a decline in the average price level was quite common during periods of rapid technological change, such as the late of 19th century. Yet these were also periods of strong growth. Nowadays productivity in come countries is growing thanks to the globalization and implementation of information technology. However, decreasing prices still raise a lot of fears.

b) Monetary policy in the case of deflation

Central bank can fight against deflation only by lowering interest rates. There is no other vehicle. However, once central bank lowers interest rates to zero, and deflation continues, it can not do anything more than to hold interest rates at zero (it is impossible to go below zero) and to wait until the deflation stops itself. **Once there are zero interest rates, central bank gets out of operation.** Deflation is like a black hole. Once the monetary policy falls into it, it looses all its powers. Such a situation is sometimes called Keynesian liquidity trap.

In the situation of zero interest rates some central banks argue that they have other instruments of monetary policy. They mention **quantitative easing.** It is questionable weather it is still instrument of monetary policy even if extreme form of monetary policy instrument. Under quantitative easing central bank stimulates an economy by purchasing financial assets, including government bonds and corporate bonds from financial institutions (mainly from banks). Afterwards the banks can purchase other government bonds and corporate bonds, and thus they create new money. Quantitative easing can lead to hyperinflation. The colloquial expression for the term "quantitative easing" is "printing money". This policy was used by the Bank of Japan in the early 2000s and by the Fed, the Bank of England and the European Central Bank during financial crisis in 2008 and 2009.

c) Deflation in Japan from the end of the 1990s

Japan represents a classic example of a country which faced deflation. Prices in Japan were falling since the end of the 1990s. But deflation was moderate. The CPI index declined from 104.0 in October 1998 to 100.5 in September 2002. Japan had adopted an almost-zero interest rate policy (0.5 % for the call rate) in September 1995 and a zero interest rate policy since February 1999. It was strategy which the Bank of Japan hoped would be successful in lifting the economy out of the bottleneck. Even if the Japanese economy in the 1990s did not resemble the United States during the Great Depression of the 1930s, unemployment in Japan increased and in September 2002 reached 5,4 %. The share prices declined substantially as the index of Nikkei 225 lowered from a high of 20,833 in April 2000 to 7,608 in April 2003.

It is supposed that the Japanese deflation started in reaction to the end of bubble of the real estate market. Prices of real estate have fallen rapidly, which lowered the value of collaterals of the bank loans. Subsequent problems of banking sector have affected the whole economy. Interest rates have fallen to zero. Falling prices further negatively affected consumption expenditures. **The indebtedness of enterprises had fallen,** i.e. enterprises repaid more debts than they established new ones. Lower demand reduced corporate profits, banks were seriously hit, and GDP of the world second largest economy decreased. Japan spent over a lot of money on public works and other government projects in order to encourage private sector. However, results of this enormous spending were hardly observable. The public debt reached almost 165 % of GDP by the end of 2004 which was by far the highest ratio among the developed countries. The period of the 1990s is sometimes called “lost decade”. But according to Koo[21] “lost decade” was far from being lost. The Japanese economy would be much worse without government spending and without favourable export conditions.

---

21 Koo, Richard C.: *The Holy Grail of Macroeconomics: Lessons form Japan's Great Recession*. John Wiley & Sons, Singapore 2008.

9 Inflation targeting

Inflation targeting is the monetary policy regime when the central bank tries to achieve its ultimate target (price stability) directly by means of operating target and not through the intermediate targets. Central bank publicly announces an explicit inflation target for a time horizon and it consequently regulates short-term interest rates (i.e. the operating target) so that the inflation will reach the desired level. To set the short-term interest rate, central needs to know first the difference between the expected and targeted inflation. At the same time, central bank must take other intermediate variables of non-target character into account. Another important feature of this strategy is its mid-term character. Central bank seeks to create transparent system. Monetary decision-making in this system is subject to clear rules and procedures. System should allow central bank to follow its long-term price stability target while pursuing the active anti-cyclical monetary policy.

9.1 History of inflation targeting

In the 1990s, many central banks decided to use explicit monetary policy targets (e.g. inflation target, money stock target, exchange rate target or the combination of these). Most of central banks chose to target inflation or to target inflation together with other economic variables. This tendency was common to both developed and developing countries. According to Bank of England, number of countries targeting exchange rate has increased during the 1990s from 30 to 47. Number of countries targeting money stock has increased form 18 to 19 and the number of countries targeting inflation has increased from 8 to 54. Thirteen of those countries were using inflation as their only monetary target. At the beginning of the 1990s only New Zealand used inflation as its main target.

On the other hand, during the 1990s 17 countries abandoned some form of target or changed the explicit monetary policy target. Ten of these countries have abandoned the exchange rate target (e.g. the United Kingdom, Finland, Croatia, Czech Republic, Sweden) mostly in reaction to exchange rate crisis. No country abandoned inflation targeting.

The inflation targeting "takes everything into account". However, large number of information contains contradictory signals. Information needs to be, therefore, classified. That is why central banks are trying to work out lists of suitable indicators. One of these indicators is the output gap. Another one is the deviation of expected inflation from inflation target. None of these indicators is faultless, and monetary policy thus follows a relatively large number of variables.

Inflation targeting represents a relatively general monetary policy containing other monetary policy regimes as special cases. Let's compare the inflation targeting regime with the money stock targeting regime. Both contain inflation (explicitly or implicitly) as its ultimate target. Taking into account the transmission lags of monetary policy; both of these regimes use the same operating target, i.e. the short-term market interest rates. The difference between these two regimes consists in weights assigned to informational variables. Inflation targeting regime employs the broadest set of information to which it assigns different weights. Conversely, money stock targeting regime considers only money stock, and it ignores information of non-monetary substance. From this point of view, money stock targeting represents a limit case of inflation targeting where the weight assigned to money equals one, and the weights assigned to other factors are zero.

Inflation targeting does not represent a new mode of monetary policy. Knut Wicksell, Irving Fisher and John Maynard Keynes were advising targeting of price indexes already at the beginning of 20th century. Sweden implemented the price target already in the 1930s in order to avoid depression resulting from collapse of golden standard. Explicit inflation targets were implemented for the first time in New Zealand (in March 1990). This measure was followed by other fundamental changes of economic policy including the statute of central bank. New Zealand was followed by Canada in February 1991. The United Kingdom has implemented inflation targeting after leaving the Exchange Rate Mechanism in September 1992. Sweden has launched inflation targeting in February 1993, Finland in March 1993, and Australia implemented this regime in April 1993. Central banks of these countries are publicly announcing their inflation targets. None of these banks specified rules to achieve these targets. The Eurozone did not implement the pure inflation targeting system yet.

In Table 9.1 Mervyn King from the Bank of England shows the average inflation of six countries targeting inflation before and after the implementation of this regime. Almost all countries succeeded in significantly lowering their inflation. Lower inflation did cause neither economic slowdown nor increasing variability of GDP growth. The question arises as whether this was really caused only by inflation targeting or by some other factors (inflation in these countries started to lower already before the launch of inflation targeting). On the other hand, it is evident that all of these countries have experienced an essential economic recovery.

Inflation targeting brought certain rules and discipline into the central bank's decision-making process. As a result, to predict central bank's reactions to economic development has become easier. Hence, not only particular decisions of central bank represent relevant information to financial markets but also the published statistical data serve so. Roughly speaking, inflation targeting is a successful monetary policy since it has helped stabilize low inflation (even if sometimes out of targeted corridors).

Table 9.1 Average inflation and GDP growth in countries targeting and not targeting inflation according to King[22]

	Countries not targeting inflation							
	Average Inflation				**Average growth of GDP**			
	1980s		**1990s**		**1980s**		**1990s**	
	Inflation	**Variability**	**Inflation**	**Variability**	**Inflation**	**Variability**	**Inflation**	**Variability**
France	7.4	18.86	2.3	0.56	2.3	1.95	1.4	2.33
Italy	11.3	35.85	5.2	0.94	2.4	2.52	1.2	2.11
Japan	2.5	5.14	1.4	1.67	3.8	1.49	2.2	3.79
Germany	2.9	4.69	3.1	2.01	1.8	3.18	2.1	4.67
USA	5.6	12.52	3.4	1.13	2.8	6.91	2.1	2.30
Average	5.9	15.40	3.1	1.30	2.6	3.20	1.8	3.00
	Countries targeting inflation							
	Average Inflation				**Average growth of GDP**			
	1980s		**1990s**		**1980s**		**1990s**	
	Inflation	**Variability**	**Inflation**	**Variability**	**Inflation**	**Variability**	**Inflation**	**Variability**
Australia	6.2	8.41	2.7	1.71	3.2	10.18	4.2	0.96
Finland	5.2	3.37	1.1	0.51	1.4	17.33	3.2	6.49
Canada	5.8	7.90	2.0	2.51	2.8	9.99	1.9	3.09
New Zeal.	11.6	25.70	2.5	2.70	1.8	6.95	2.4	7.78
Sweden	6.6	6.65	2.3	2.29	1.6	4.73	1.9	5.09
UK	5.2	2.21	2.8	0.09	2.4	5.76	3.0	1.04
Average	6.8	9.00	2.2	1.60	2.2	9.20	2.8	4.10

There have been a range of recent contributions evaluating the success of inflation targeting, for example, Bernanke and Woodford[23] and Levin, Natalucci and Piger[24]. Woodford's textbook[25] is an excellent treatise on matters of transparency and accountability, as well as implementation.

22 King, Mervyn Allister: The inflation target five years on. *Bank of England Quarterly Bulletin*, 1997, November, 434-42.

23 Bernanke, Ben S. and Michael Woodford (eds): *The Inflation Targeting Debate*. The University of Chicago Press, Chicago 2005.

24 Levin, Andrew T., Fabio M. Natalucci and Jeremy M. Piger: The Macroeconomic Effects of Inflation Targeting. *Federal Reserve Bank of St. Louis Review*, 86(4), 51-80.

25 Woodford, Michael: *Interest and Prices: Foundations of a Theory of Monetary Policy*. Princeton University Press, Princeton 2003.

There have been, however, also cogent arguments against inflation targeting. Many economists believe that a simple announcement of inflation target cannot reduce inflation. No country has reduced the inflation by a "divining rod". Some central banks have proclaimed that they do care only about inflation ("inflation nutter"), and they were keeping a distant attitude toward any strictly specified inflation targets since it was clear that monetary policy cannot adjust inflation in short-term, and that there are short-term impacts on real economy. There exists a possible trade-off between the volatility of inflation and volatility of GDP. Inflation targeting represents a mid-term policy. Central authorities hence announce rather the desired inflation and factors supposed to affect it. Some of these factors can represent a significant source of inflationary pressures (e.g. wages, public finances, foreign trade) while being out of central bank's control. Central bank thus needs a precise knowledge of both past and current development, premeditation of its actions and cooperation with other central authorities such as treasury department.

This monetary policy trend requires the three following prerequisites:

- Guarantee that the price stability represents the main target of monetary policy; that is what differs central bank from other central institutions;
- Guarantee that other public authorities (particularly government) will cooperate on the declared policy as well; and
- Central bank puts the announced monetary target into practice based on its own judgments on situation.

Inflation targeting is based on two main pillars:

- Explicit inflation target; and
- High transparency and accountability of central bank.

9.2 Explicit inflation target

Among the main features of inflation targeting belongs the public announcement of the explicit inflation target or of a series of targets by central bank (often in cooperation with treasury department or other central authorities). Central bank communicates thereby its target towards public. Such a target helps create environment suitable for much more intensive manipulation of inflation expectations. Inflation target should be higher than zero in order to avoid deflation. De-

---

Woodford, Michael: *Central Bank Communications and Policy Effectiveness.* Paper. Columbia University, New York 2005.

veloped countries usually use target varying from 2 to 3 %. Inflation targets take usually form of intervals declaring where the inflation should be on a certain moment (e.g. by the end of the year) or of continuous decreasing or horizontal bands. This policy thus represents an active and direct determination of inflation expectations. Inflation band should be publicly announced and subsequently compared with current inflation.

Inflation targeting also reduces uncertainty. Both household and enterprises know that if the inflation exceeds bounds of the interval, central bank will intervene to reduce it. Inflation target does not represent a fixed band within which the inflation should be at any time. These bounds do not represent the electric fence. Central banks cannot influence all items of consumer price index. Some central banks target, therefore, rather an index excluding prices out of central banks' control. These indexes are called **core inflation** and **net inflation**.

There is no monetary aggregate or exchange rate used explicitly as an intermediate target. There are also other factors determining inflation. The absence of monetary intermediate target thus does not represent the absence of the main target. Among these other factors, we should mention particularly labour market variables, import prices, producers prices, output gap, real and nominal interest rates, real and nominal exchange rate and public finances. This regime accounts for these variables as being predictable and useful for managing inflation.

Some of these factors can be influenced by interest rates, i.e. by central bank. Other factors such as wages, public finances and foreign trade are always out of the central bank's control. This regime thus relies more on the elaborate procedures and decision-making than on mechanical actions taken based on some fixed rules.

The Bank of Canada is cooperating on setting of the inflation target with the government. The same holds for the Bank of England. Central bank should be independent in activities designed to help it achieve its target, but the setting of targets should be subject to discussion with other institutions. It is important especially in a long term. Once the government agrees to cooperate in maintaining stable inflation, it cannot conduct too expansive fiscal policy since otherwise it would contradict its own objective.

If the prognosis shows that inflation will exceed the target, monetary policy should take measures that are more restrictive, i.e. central bank should increase the short-term market interest rate. However, the deviation of prognosis from target can result from exceptional circumstances, and shocks whose inflationary symptoms can abate soon. In such a case, monetary measure could superfluously damage the economy. Such circumstances make usually part of the official list of **exceptions,** and central bank does not react to them.

9.3 Transparency and accountability of central bank

Inflation targeting does not represent a radical shift in monetary policy regime. **The most important feature of this regime is the accent on transparency and responsibility of central bank.** Transparency plays a very important role since:

- It reduces uncertainty about the status of monetary policy;
- It helps change the behaviour of public so that it supports monetary policy targets; and
- It increases discipline of central bank over its market operations, and it makes itself more responsible for success of these operations.

Operations of central bank should not be confidential. Behaviour based on rules represents one of the monetary policy privileges. Central bank introduces thereby predictability, and it assures markets that expectations correspond to the target of stable prices. Predictable monetary policy (not in terms of stable interest rates but in terms of predictable reactions to changes of the economic development) reduces disturbances produced normally by monetary policy itself. Monetary policy should avoid GDP and employment fluctuations caused by uncertainty.

Transparent monetary policy means that the **announced changes of the official interest rate do not represent surprise to market**. Economic news should not seek to estimate decisions of body responsible for short-term interest rates but to provide business statistics. Based on these statistics, market shall be ready to forecast central bank decisions. Contradictory monetary policy means that decisions of central banks are unpredictable, and monetary policy does not conform to the economic development. In the extreme case, when the decisions of central bank are fully accidental, business news have no impact on market short-term interest rates, and all market players concentrate rather on decisions of central bank. Transparency means that monetary policy is easily predictable.

According to King[26] the **accountability** of central bank represents the answer to questions "to whom" and "for what". Bank of England is accountable to the Chancellor of the Exchequer for implementing his inflation target, to Parliament

26 King, Mervyn Allister: The Inflation Target Five Years on. *Bank of England Quarterly Bulletin*, 1997, November, 434-42.

through the Treasury Select Committee (TSC), to the Court of Directors of the Bank of England for the proper conduct of the Monetary Policy Committee (MPC) and, more widely, to the public at large. Currently, there are five ways of Bank of England responsibility:

- The decisions of the MPC are announced immediately following the monthly meeting at 12 noon on a Thursday. The minutes of those meetings are usually published 13 days late after the MPC meeting. These minutes contain not only an account of the discussion of the MPC and the issues that it thought important for its decisions, but also a record of the voting of each MPC member;

- The Inflation Report represents the basis for accountability to Parliament. The original objective of the Report was to act as a disciplining device on Government. The Report would set out views of the likely implications for inflation of decisions taken (or not taken) by the Chancellor. After the responsibility has been delegated to the MPC, the Report plays a rather different role. It is now an instrument of accountability. It is one of the principal ways in which the explanations of the MPC can be assessed and subjected to scrutiny by outside commentators;

- MPC members respond to the TSC. They are asked to appear before the TSC following each Inflation Report;

- The MPC is required to send an open letter to the Chancellors if inflation is more than 1 % on either side of the target of 2.0 %. It is important to stress that avoiding the need to write such letters is not the objective of monetary policy. The inflation target is not a range of 1.0 % to 3.0 %, it is a target of 2.0 % on average. Indeed, one of the main purposes of the open letters is to explain why, in some circumstances, it would be wrong to try to bring inflation back to target too quickly. In other words, the MPC will be forced to reveal in public its proposed reaction to large shocks; and

- Finally, the MPC is accountable to the Court of Directors of the Bank of England for the procedures it adopts and for the proper conduct of its business. The 16 non-executive members of the Court report annually to Parliament on the conduct of the Committee, and the Annual Report is debated in Parliament.

King follows with the answer to the question of accountability "for what". Bank of England is accountable for reaching the inflation target of 2.0 %. However, unpredictable shocks can deviate inflation from this target. In addition, long lags between changes of interest rates and impacts on inflation mean that to compensate shocks will take some time. This also means that MPC cannot always maintain the inflation at 2.0 % level. If, in addition, these shocks come from the supply side, which increases inflation even if the GDP is currently decreasing, maintaining of inflation at 2.0 % would be hardly desirable.

To test whether the monetary policy works well we need to use the average inflation for several years and compare it with the desired level of 2.0 %. Regarding the uncertainties and lags, it is quite impossible to answer unambiguously the question whether a certain decision was right or not. Accountability thus does not comprise simple comparison of inflation with target. MPC must clearly explain all its actions. All its members were elected to reach the explicit inflation target of 2.0 %.

9.4 The role of inflation forecasts

As the lags between changes of monetary policy and their impacts on inflation are long and variable, monetary policy must be based upon forecasts. Inflation targeting does not mean that monetary policy acts in reaction to current inflation but it reacts to changes of the expected inflation. The rise of interest rates afterwards the inflation has already speeded up is a too late measure that can hardly avoid further rise of inflation and instability of inflation and GDP.

On the other hand, inflation forecasts can easily discredit central bank since it is very difficult to estimate inflation for the period of more than one year. Monetary policy thus needs to rely upon its intermediate targets having a closer relation to inflation. To put it another way, intermediate targets must provide a good estimate of inflation. It is more convenient to express explicitly the forecast not by means of a single number but by means of a stochastic prediction. To increase the credibility of such forecasts, central banks publish fan charts of inflation prognosis including probabilities of reaching some areas of the fan. Inflation reports prepared by Bank of England, for instance, include charts depicting probabilities of individual results over the next two years. The central area represents the most likely result (probability of 90 %), following are a bit less likely result (80 %) and so forth. Like in other fields of business, decision-makings must be based on probabilities. Inflation reports contain charts representing data available to MPC.

When deciding about interest rates central bank faces two problems. First, the adequate reaction to supply shocks is to turn inflation back to the target. How long will it take depends upon the character of a shock, two years or a bit more seem adequate. If the inflation during that time rises or decreases then the optimal interest rate depends on period when inflations should be back to the target.

Second, if there is an uncertainty about the impacts of interest rates changes on economy, central bank should change slowly interest rate until it reaches the desired level rather than make a radical shift that would cause increased volatility of the economy. In practice, central banks really change interest rates very sensitively. We should notice that even if forecasts represent the basis for decision-making, nobody should use it automatically. In other words, **the optimal reaction of monetary policy cannot be derived solely from the expected inflation, and central bank should take into account shocks in economy that follow monetary policy reaction.**

10 Monetary policy transmission mechanism

The maintenance of low inflation does not represent a simple task. We know about this problem relatively little. **Transmission mechanism of monetary policy** is the chain of economic relations allowing central bank to influence inflation (eventually also GDP and employment) by means of a change of the operating target, i.e. the market short-term interest rate. The transmission mechanism begins with changes of operating target. This change leads to the changes of the "intermediary" variables. This subsequently results in the change in the "target" market whose price development the central bank seeks to influence. Transmission mechanism works through several parallel channels. The regulation of interest rates is sometimes called accelerator and brake pedal. However, this comparison rather fits to the extremely active monetary policy.

10.1 Monetary policy channels

Figure 10.1 shows the scheme of monetary policy transmission mechanism, i.e. how the monetary policy really operates. There are four channels: the credit channel, entrepreneurial channel, expenditures channel and exchange rate channel. First three channels (i.e. credit, entrepreneurial and expenditures channels) influence the domestic demand for domestic goods and services. First channel and entrepreneurial channel (partly) operate indirectly through the money stock. Expenditures channel and entrepreneurial channel (partly) operate directly.

Plus and minus signs indicate the direction of transmission in the case of step reduction of short-term interest rates provided that the expected inflation remains unchanged, i.e. in the case of step reduction of the nominal short-term interest rate (and also the real short-term interest rate). If the central bank raises nominal interest rates, transmission operates in the opposite direction. This illustration deals with the impact of short-term interest rates reduction, provided that other things remain unchanged. We suppose further that fiscal policy remains unchanged too.

Credit channel is the channel of loan supply on the part of banks and demand for loans on the part of their clients (household and enterprises). Households make decisions about whether to apply for consumer loan, mortgage loan and other loans. Enterprises make decisions about applying for loans for their businesses. Banks evaluate applications for loans, and finally they decide on the of anticipated client's capacity to repay the loan. To evaluate it correctly, bank must take into account number of factors such as the expected economic development, prospects of a business sector and the like. Through this channel the system determines the amount of loans, i.e. the money stock. Money stock has

Figure 10.1 Transmission mechanism of monetary policy
(White areas represent the effects of prices of foreign goods and services)

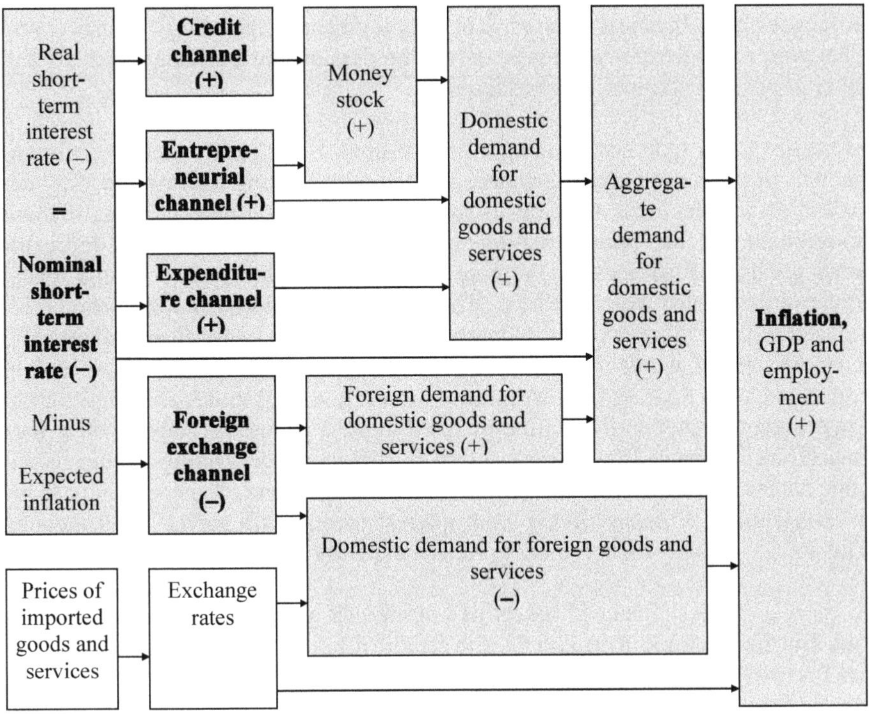

impact on inflation. It can happen, that even if money stock increases the prices fall, e.g. in Japan at the end of the 1990s and at the beginning of the 2000s.

The lower short-term interest rate causes the increased demand for loans both on the part of households and enterprises, which increases the money stock, and it thereby increases the domestic demand for domestic products, the inflation, the GDP and the employment. Lenders are less prudent to grant loans when the interest rates are lower. The increased amount of loans serves partly to finance the additional consumption.

Households increase especially the demand for real estate, cars and other durable goods. Lower interest rates reduce interest costs of borrowers and incentives to save. To households, purchases of houses or apartments represent the major investments. Lower interest rates motivate households to apply for mortgage loans. The number of new houses increases. The increased housing construction influences also business sectors. The employment in building industry rises. Changing number of new houses affects the demand for building materials and other goods and services for households.

Mortgage loans represent the major part of households' debts, and the substantial part of these mortgage loans is connected with floating interest rate. Any decrease of interest rates thus raises the remaining disposable income of these households, i.e. the same gross income allows households to spend more for other goods and services. In the case of unsecured loans (e.g. consume loans) lower interest rates work similarly. The current level of consumption can be increased without further debts. Households, therefore, expand their demand and expenditures for goods and services. Remaining mortgage loans, which are not connected with floating interest rates, do not allow households to benefits from lower interest rates until the time of fixed interest payments elapses. New borrowers are influenced by lower interest rates from the beginning of their mortgage contracts till the new fixing of interest rate. However, this does not hold for all households. A person living from interest income will suffer lower income. This lower income will force her to reduce expenditures.

In most countries, financial assets of households exceed their financial liabilities. But for example in Australia, the sector of households is, in aggregate, the net borrower and therefore the net payer of interests. Roughly speaking, young people borrow the most, especially to finance the purchases of houses. Consequently, they start to repay these debts, and they gradually become net owners of financial assets. At first sight changes of interest expenses and interest income with the change of interest rate of these groups get roughly balanced, i.e. the lower interest rate decreases cash outflow of borrowers and it simultaneously decreases cash inflow to lenders. However, the interest rates elasticity of these two groups of households often differs. Therefore, there is certain impact of interest rates changes on aggregate expenditures of households.

It is supposed, that borrowers are more sensible to changes of interest rates than lenders since they do not possess enough financial assets to maintain their expenditures when their incomes get changed. If that is so, decrease of interest rates will increase expenditures of borrowers more than decrease expenditures of lenders. The net impact will, therefore, represent the net increase of aggregate households' spending. Conversely, the increased interest rates will change aggregate expenditures in the opposite direction.

The expected increase of future demand motivates **enterprises** to increase their demand for investment goods. The decreased interest rates further cause that more investments generates the higher income. New investment projects get therefore realized. In practice, however, it is hard to observe these movements, since there are a number of other factors determining investments. Investments depend primarily upon the business cycle that affects demand for goods and services and cash available for investments. Employment tends to increase.

The most of enterprises represent the net borrowers. Interest expenses usually amount to 25 % of corporate income. Changes of interest rates affect, therefore, substantially their aggregate expenses. By the end of the 1980s, for instance, when the amount of debts and the level of interest rates were relatively high, interest expenses were often amounting to nearly 40 % of corporate income. These extremely high expenses have probably caused the subsequent decline of business activity. Many enterprises are dependent upon short-term loans and therefore very sensible to changes of short-term interest rates. Lower interest rates improve the financial standing of these enterprises and, conversely, higher interest rates damage it. This means that the probability of new investments increases when the interest rates fall. Changes of financial standing motivate enterprises to re-evaluate their investment and employment plans. Lower interest rates thus support activity, and higher interest rates cause postponement of investments and reduction of inventories. Lower interest rates do no affect all enterprises in the same way. Enterprises that hold deposits get lower interest income.

Entrepreneurial channel is the channel of business activity. Business activity affects domestic demand both directly and indirectly through money stock. **The lower short-term interest rate boosts business activity that directly or indirectly increases the domestic demand for domestic goods and services, inflation, the GDP and the employment.**

Expenditure channel is the channel of expenditure preferences or savings preferences of households and enterprises. Thriftiness does not affect monetary aggregates but only the velocity of money. Provided that the money stock remains constant, increased spending of households and enterprises increases the velocity of money. If the aggregate production increases in the same extent, the price level remains unchanged. If the aggregate production grows slower than velocity, price level starts increasing. Household and enterprises are still making decisions about what part of their wealth to hold in form of money and what part in the form of other assets. If they decide to hold less money, they increase expenditures.

The lower interest rate makes economic agents prefer expenditures instead of savings. That boosts directly the domestic demand for domestic goods and services, and hence it increases inflation, GDP and employment. When people are not afraid of loosing their jobs, they spend more. Households spend more on consumption and enterprises on investments. Reduced savings mean that people do not postpone their consumption. Every economy depends primarily on consumption expenditures.

Expenditures are also affected by the **wealth effect,** i.e. by **assets prices**. Roughly speaking, lower interest rates increase the value of assets, and the increased wealth boosts expenditures. The market value of debt securities changes reciprocally to interest rates, i.e. lower interest rates increase the value of debt securities and vice versa according to exact mathematical equations. Ceteris paribus, lower interest rates also induce higher share prices (however, not according to the precise mathematical relations). It follows from the fact that future cash flows are discounted using lower discount factors which means that the present value of any future cash flows increases. In addition, shares can become more attractive than debt securities. Share prices thus tend to rise. Higher share prices motivate enterprises to issue more shares.

Real estates represent the decisive part of households' wealth. Lower interest rates make generally mortgage loans cheaper. Therefore, demand for real estate grows. Higher demand increases prices of real estate. Changing values of houses influence households' expenditures in the same way as changes of financial wealth. Households feel wealthier when the value of real estate in their possession rises. Houses can be also used as collaterals, and households can, therefore, borrow more money. In the United Kingdom, for instance, increasing prices of real estate by the end of the 1980s boosted consumption. Conversely, lower prices of real estate at the beginning of the 1990s have reduced consumption.

However, changes of assets prices do not follow mechanically the changes of interest rate. Asset prices depend on a variety of other factors such as changes of expectations and business cycle trends. The role of wealth effect in transmission mechanism cannot be exaggerated.

In respect of the **exchange rate channel,** changes of short-term interest rates affect immediately the exchange rate through the flows of capital (within the scope of the balance of payments' financial account) in reaction to changes of the difference between domestic and foreign interest rates. The lower interest rates provoke the immediate outflow of speculative capital (domestic currency becomes less attractive) that results under the floating exchange rate regime in **depreciation of domestic currency.**

Foreign demand for domestic goods and services and foreign supply of goods and services gradually change. There is an immediate increase of prices of imported goods and services for domestic households and enterprises, and there is an immediate decrease of price of exported goods and services for foreign households and enterprises. The prices of domestic exports fall and prices of imports rise. Foreign demand for domestic production grows, and domestic demand for foreign production decreases. Export grows, and import falls. **The lower domestic short-term interest rate depreciates domestic currency, and it increases, therefore, foreign demand for domestic goods and services, and it decreases domestic demand for foreign goods and services. Hence, the inflation, GDP and employment start growing.**

Conversely, the appreciation of domestic currency affects adversely many domestic producers. Producers have many fixed expenses denominated in local currency but they face competition from foreign producers whose expenses are fixed in other currencies. Appreciation of local currency worsens the competitive position of the producers for their profits are lower due to reduced sales. There are a number of sectors affected, such as agriculture, manufacturing, hotels and other sectors dependent on tourism and financial and consulting services. By making imports cheaper, appreciation of domestic currency affects adversely domestic demand for domestic goods and services. Domestic economy thus faces serious losses and contraction.

White areas of Figure 10.1 also show that besides transmission mechanism of monetary policy there are other factors affecting the inflation, GDP and employment. Two of such factors are:

- The prices of imported goods and services expressed in foreign currencies; and
- Changes of exchange rate caused by factors distinct from the short-term interest rate change. Depreciated domestic currency immediately lowers the prices of domestic exports, and it increases prices of imports. **Depreciated domestic currency increases foreign demand for domestic production, and it decreases domestic demand for foreign production. Hence, the inflation, GDP and employment grow.**

All of these four channels affect inflation, GDP and employment through its impacts on demand for domestic goods and services in the same direction. The economists' attitudes towards the importance of individual channels differ. It is also hard to estimate time lags between impulses and reactions. Time lags and feedbacks make the mapping of all these processes very difficult. In addition, there is never a 100 % correlation between the individual channels and the ultimate target of monetary policy, i.e. inflation.

If the demand for domestic goods and services rises, economy starts facing inflationary pressures. The relation between demand and domestic capacities (including labour market) represents the key factor determining domestic inflation pressures. If the demand for labour rises, increasing wages soon affect domestic price level. Strong demand for labour enables employees to ask higher wages. These impacts on wages and prices are closely related to each other. Increased prices boost demand for higher salaries, and higher wages soon increase other expenses. Higher expenses soon force producers to increase prices. Once the wages start to rise, it becomes very hard to slow it down.

The large number of inflation models shows that there still exist many doubts about the correct understanding of monetary policy transmission mechanism. Some models stress the role of money, others the role of other factors. Hence, none of these models can provide complex solution.

Besides interest rates, **moral suasion** and **negotiations with government and unions** can also have certain impact on inflation. In respect to government, central banks usually talk about budget deficit. In the case of unions, negotiations concern with future wage demand. Moral suasion and negotiations represent a very powerful instrument. In the extreme case, central bank can also impose the limits on the amount of loans granted by commercial banks.

10.2 Transfer to other market interest rates

Changes of the short-term interest rate (e.g. of maturity of one day or one week) transfers immediately to other short-term and long-term interest rates of the interbank market. Once the central fixes a new "short end" of yield curve, in most cases the whole yield curve shifts since banks immediately correct their interbank interest rates.

Modification of one short-term interest rate by some value (e.g. by 0.25 %) does not mean that all remaining interest rates change by the same value. Actually, the change of other rates can even be in the opposite direction. The reasons for such development are as follows:

- If the market expects central bank to cut short-term interest rates, the medium-term and long-term market interest rates lower before the central bank action, i.e. yield curve shifts down itself. Hence, the action of central bank means a much more moderate shift of the "long end" of the yield curve;
- Long-term interest rates depend also upon the expectations about the future development of short-term interest rates. The strongly upward slop-

ing yield curve (i.e. long-term interest rates are much higher than short-term interest rates) can signal that monetary policy have become too expansive. Market expects that the current level of short-term interest rates will be followed by future increase of short-term interest rates. Conversely, downward sloping yield curve (short-term interest rates are higher than long-term interest rates) can signal that monetary policy have become too restrictive. Market expects that the current level of short-term interest rates will be followed by future cut of short-term interest rates. This means that the impact on long-term interest rates also depends on changes of inflation expectations; and

- Long-term interest rates also depend on a variety of other factors, such as uncertainty about future interest rates. The upward sloping yield curve does not have to signal necessarily that monetary policy became too expansive but also that market became more uncertain about the future development of interest rates. In other words, liquidity premium that make part of long-term interest rates has increased.

Within a few days after the change of short-term interest rates commercial banks change interest rates to their clients, especially in the case of new deposits and loans and in the case of new bonds. The interest rates spread between interest-bearing assets (especially of loans granted) and liabilities (especially deposits) remain approximately constant. The credit spread can change in the course of time because of a change of market environment. The credit spread usually does not change in reaction to changes of short-term market interest rate. Within a few months, interest rates of credit and deposit instruments bearing the floating interest rates change as well. Floating interest rates of mortgage loans change usually even later.

10.3 Effects of inflation expectations

Central bank can influence inflation to a certain degree by changing public expectations about the future inflation. According to Figure 10.1 hypothetical step increase (decrease) of the expected inflation can have the same impact on inflation (and on GDP and employment) as the step decrease (increase) of the nominal short-term interest rate. Such a situation is hypothetical case as in practice the expected inflation changes gradually and not in the discrete steps.

Inflation expectations became important part on central bank monetary policy. Many analysts study the impact of inflation expectation on inflation. Central bank, therefore, should contribute to the formation of low-inflation expectations. If it succeeds, inflation gets really lowered. The confidence of public represents the essential condition for this success. When people do not trust the official rhetoric about lower inflation, and they expect the increase of inflation, then the prices and wages rise.

World economists study how to achieve favourable inflation expectations. Part of the answer to this question lies in the construction of the monetary policy system. A system that clearly sets the inflation target and markedly seeks to achieve it can help public to concentrate on inflation expectations. These activities represent one important part of inflation targeting in many contries. Central institutions also have to demonstrate it clearly by means of the practical monetary policy. Monetary policy must be consistent with its targets if central bank wants to succeed.

10.4 Persistence of prices and wages

To assure functionality of transmission mechanism described above, central bank needs that the role of unions in wages negotiations were relatively small. There are deviations from the mechanism in countries, where unions play a significant role.

Production of goods and services reacts to actions of central bank first. Prices and wages react with a certain delay. There exists a substantial persistence of prices and wages. The economy consists of both formal and informal contracts that limit changes of prices and wages in a short-term. The inflation expectations that affect contract negotiations adapt very slowly. In other words, prices and wages do not adapt immediately to changes of the aggregate demand. Sales and production are slower than aggregate demand. With the next period, inflation expectation start adapting, new contracts are negotiated, and other corrections take place. As a result, prices and wages get corrected slower with changes of the aggregate demand.

The increase of wages over the labour productivity reflects the combined impact of the positive inflation expectations and of the positive or negative element resulting from the demand for labour. The increase of wages, that does not exceed the growth of labour productivity, does not increase the expenses of production and therefore does not affect prices of outputs. However, the increase of wages caused by inflation expectations or the increased demand for labour increases unit labour expenses, and many enterprises tend to change their prices. Therefore, even if there is not the excess demand for labour, unit expenses rise above the expected inflation since both enterprises and labourers thing in real terms. This increase of unit labour expenses affects more or less prices of goods and services.

10.5 Monetary policy lags

Monetary policy operates with lags, since today's actions affect inflation, GDP and employment not sooner than within one or two years. Management of inflation thus cannot rely on the current inflation. To stop the current inflation that was caused by circumstances occurring one or two years earlier, central bank should have to employ extremely tight monetary policy that could cause recession. These lags thus explain why the central bank pays so much attention to business forecasts, especially to estimates of future inflation trends. Some central banks use public forecasts as a key feature of its policy targets formulations.

We have already mentioned that a change of monetary policy governs immediately the market short-term interest rates. The impact on clients' interest rates of banks is usually slower. Changes of mortgage loan interest rates can occur even after several months. It takes even longer time before the changed mortgage repayments affect other consumption expenditures. Unexpected changes of consumption expenditures affect consumption inventories and purchase orders of enterprises. Changes of purchase orders affect producers' inventories, and they cause changes of production which results in changes of employment and households' incomes. These changes further affect households' expenditures. But all of these sequential processes take some time.

Why is it difficult to predict the length of these lags? Since the monetary policy concentrates on affecting the demand of public, it has to estimate reactions of people. But everybody knows how difficult it is to estimate even reactions of one person. The impact of monetary policy actions on economy depends, for example, on people's opinion about impacts of these actions on inflations. If people think that the tight monetary policy means that central bank seeks to keep inflation under its control, they will change immediately its inflation expectations downwards. In future, they will require more moderate increase of wages and prices, and, therefore, monetary policy will achieve its target. Conversely, if people are not confident about the central bank ability to keep the inflation low, they will require in future higher wages, and prices and monetary policy will, therefore, fail. In such a case, a central bank will have to tighten its monetary policy to such an extent that employment and GDP substantially fall.

Experience shows that in developed countries **it takes one year approximately before the monetary policy actions affect the demand, and that it takes another year before the changed demand affects inflation.** However, the uncertainty about the length of these lags is still substantial. There are many factors influencing inflation, such as the overall economic conditions, consumer confidence, world economic development, future inflation expectations and others.

These factors are out of central bank control but their influence over the length of lags is substantial. These corrections influence lags in decision-making about expenditures and lags in renegotiating wages and prices.

To illustrate how do central banks forecast impacts of their actions on inflation and real GDP, we will refer to a macromodel designed by the Bank if England (Figure 10.2 and 10.3). This simulation does not provide probabilities of results. Shaded areas correspond to the two alternative simulations based on different assumptions about the monetary and fiscal policy functions. The upper limits of the bands in both Figures were derived for monetary policy assuming inflation target and constant government consumption in money terms. The lower limits were derived assuming monetary policy based on the output gap, inflation target and government consumption proportionate to GDP. The both Figures show the response of real GDP and inflation (relative to a base projection) to an unexpected 1 % rise of the short-term interest rate that lasts for one year.

In both paths real GDP starts to fall rapidly after the monetary policy action. It reaches a minimum of between –0.2 % and –0.35 % below its original level after five quarters. Afterwards real GDP returns to its original level as a result both of the equilibrating forces and of the reversal of the short-term interest rate. The inflation changes a little during the first year in both paths. But during the second year inflation falls sharply, and it reaches the minimum after nine quarters. In the first case, inflation fell by 0.2 % and in the second case by 0.4 %.

In both cases, the impact on inflation then starts to diminish, but it has not returned to the original level three years after the change of short-term interest rate, even though short-term interest rate was reversed after one year. We have to point out that these simulations are only illustrative. The Figures cannot be used to infer how much interest rates should be lowered to achieve some reduction in inflation. Simulations prove that short-term interest rate changes affect real GDP and inflation with some lags. This model generates the simulations which are symmetric, i.e. rises and falls in the official rate of equal size have effects of similar magnitude but of opposite sign.

10.6 Monetary policy, GDP and employment

It follows from the monetary policy transmission mechanism that the change of market short-term interest rate does not affect only inflation but also GDP and employment. The decrease of interest rates stimulates, with a certain lag, growth of GDP and employment. Conversely, the increase of interest rates causes, with a certain lag, slower growth of GDP and lower employment. Nevertheless, the Figure 10.2 shows that these changes are of a temporary character, since GDP growth and employment return back to its original level within two years.

Figure 10.2 Effect on real GDP, relative to base, of 1 % increase in the official rate maintained for one year according to the Bank of England[27]

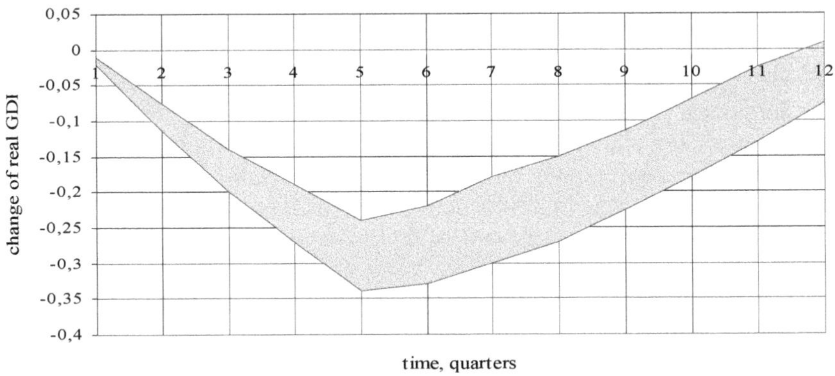

Figure 10.3 Effect on inflation rate, relative to base, of 1 % increase in the official rate maintained for one year according to the Bank of England

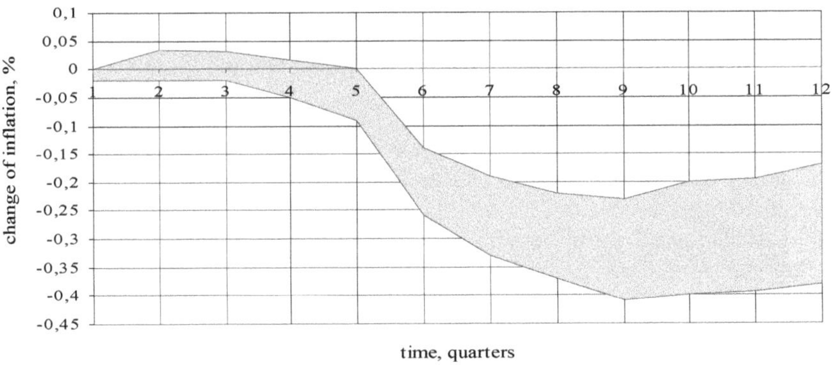

Monetary policy affects the GDP and employment only in a short-term and the inflation in a long-term. In a long-term the target of monetary policy can be only inflation and not GDP. The U.S. experience has also shown that the effects of "pumping economy up" were only short-term. Central bank cannot have these two targets at the same time: long-term price stability and long-term GDP and employment.

27 *The transmission mechanism of monetary policy.* Bank of England, London 1999.

Central bank is able to boost or weaken economic growth and employment but it cannot do it continuously. The continuous effort to expand economy above its long-term potential can cause only the higher and higher inflation. In other words, the continuous accommodative monetary policy cannot generate a long-term benefit but a higher inflation.

The long-term price stability does not necessarily represent the only monetary policy target. Low volatility of GDP and employment are also valuable. Central bank therefore concentrates on the short-term economic performance as well. However, this target is in contradiction with long-term price stability. Central bank thus has to decide which one of these targets is currently more important. Imagine than the economy is facing recession, and that the central bank seeks the higher employment through the expansive monetary policy. A short-term success can result in a long-term trouble since the expansive monetary policy increases inflation. Central bank thus has to balance short-term economic stabilization and long-term price stability.

Monetary policy thus has two major targets:

- To achieve a desired rate of inflation in a mid-term and in a long-term; and

- To avoid fluctuations of GDP and employment, i.e. to avoid the so-called "boom and bust syndromes".

There is a certain level of GDP when enterprises employ exactly their current capacities without being forced to change production or prices faster than expected changes of the price level. This level of GDP is called potential GDP level. If the actual GDP equals the potential GDP, production does not cause inflationary pressures, and enterprises do not face pressures towards changes of labour expenses. There is a balance between domestic supply and demand.

The difference between the actual GDP and its potential GDP is called **output gap**. If the output gap is positive, high demand is pushing production above its potential level, and enterprises are operating over their normal capacities. The excessive demand can cause a trade deficit but it will cause primarily inflationary pressures. Production costs of many enterprises are rising as they operate over the level of efficient production. Other enterprises start demanding more labour to increase their production. The additional demand for labour subsequently causes rise of wages and prices. Some enterprises take advantage of this development and raise their profit margins by increasing prices more than costs. If the output gap is negative, opposite movements take place. When the economy grows above its potential level the inflation increases and vice versa.

However, the output gap is very hard to estimate. Structural changes (e.g. development of technology or labour market) can shift the potential output in an unknown direction. Economy consists of many heterogeneous sectors. In addition, business cycles differ from each other. Some sectors can expand while others face recession. Finally, the growth of labour productivity changes with time as well. The output gap approach cannot, therefore, show a precise numerical relation to inflationary pressures. On the other hand, it is a helpful indicator, since to control inflation central bank needs to estimate the level of business activity.

Provided that there are no external shocks, the maintaining of real GDP at its potential level would represent the sufficient condition for stable inflation only if the targeted inflation equals to the expected inflation. **The zero output gap corresponds to any rate of inflation expected by economic agents.** These expectations make already part of wages and hence part of prices of goods and services. Potential GDP thus corresponds to both high stable inflation and low stable inflation. The inflation rate depends on monetary policy actions and public confidence.

Central banks in some countries (e.g. Australia) consider a short-term trade off between inflation and business activity. The inflation target must be fulfilled in average for the whole business cycle period. That means that in a short-term, monetary policy can seek to achieve the antagonistic targets – faster economic growth and low inflation. Let's imagine that central bank considers inflation too high. Higher interest rates can help lower inflation but at the same time, we can expect that the economic growth will slow down. Whether and how to increase interest rates depends on the actual economic conditions. When the economy operates slightly above its potential, central bank can use **a fast increase of interest rates**. On the other hand, if there are substantial overcapacities, central bank should rather choose to **raise interest gradually**.

In a long-term, GDP and employment depend upon other factors than monetary policy that the central bank cannot control. These factors represent the production capacity of an economy consisting in a technical progress, quantity and quality of labour and others. Some government policies can influence these supply side factors but the monetary policy cannot. Monetary policy cannot increase the long-term economic growth.

Economy operates in cycles. GDP and employment are often bellow and above their long-term potential. Although the monetary policy cannot influence these aggregates in a long-term, it can do so in a short-term. In the case of falling demand and recession, central bank can temporarily stimulate economy and can push it back to its potential level by cutting interest rate. Central bank therefore concentrates also on a short-term stabilization, i.e. on smoothing GDP and employment on their potential level. Sometimes, we could observe that some states or regions are in recession while the national economy goes well. Central bank has no instrument against such development.

10.7 Monetary policy rules

The task of monetary policy is to make the economy richer and not to leave the card room with money of its partners. In practice, however, monetary policy is changing interest rate and the public can sometimes loose their money. Financial markets therefore seek to predict future changes of interest rate. Persons responsible for monetary policy seek to understand the market, and market participants seek to predict behaviour of these persons. Some economist elaborated monetary policy rules. According to the Friedman's rule central bank should follow constant growth of money stock. Taylor's rule sets the level of official interest rate based on expected inflation, target inflation (2 %), equilibrium real interest rate (2 %) and production gap. Let's mention other monetary policy rules: autopilot of monetary policy and NAIRU.

10.7.1 Autopilot of monetary policy

We have already mentioned that the experience of last decades show that **expectations** play the essential role in behaviour of economic agents. When estimating future inflation, people do not look only into the past but they also seek to predict behaviour of central bank and to adapt their expectations. Financial markets participants regard central bank representatives to predict the future central bank actions.

Market reacts to the information about economic development, i.e. to the same information as central bank. If market reacts to proclamations of central bank representatives, they do not follow information about economy, i.e. they do not follow some monetary policy rule. Central bank itself does not know how to set rules of its decision-making. **Under the inflation-targeting regime, central bank relies on subjective judgments and not on exact rules.** If there is any monetary policy rule, it should be simple and clear, for otherwise the rule could provoke undesirable surprises. It is not possible to accept such a rule that would cause unpredictable changes of monetary policy. The fundamental requirement is that the **decisions about interest rates should not differ for identical sets of information. If any of such rules proved efficient, central bank could adapt it as autopilot.**

10.7.2 NAIRU

Some economists hold the view that monetary policy should concentrate on the **non-accelerating inflation rate of unemployment** (NAIRU). This concept is close to the so-called natural rate of unemployment. To explain NAIRU, we can use the Phillips curve that represents the relationship between the inflation and unemployment. According to this concept, the rate of unemployment bellow NAIRU coincides with the rise of inflation and vice versa.

Tightening labour market was one of the reasons why the Fed intervened prematurely against inflation in 1994. The federal funds rate jumped from 3 % at the beginning of 1994 to 6 % at the beginning of 1995. According to the Fed it was reaction on information indicating the future increase of inflation. Inflation did not increase. Later, the Fed did not increase interest rate even though the unemployment dropped bellow 4.75 %, i.e. bellow estimates provided by NAIRU.

In macroeconomic models of monetary transmission containing the Phillips curve unemployment plays important role by linking the aggregate demand for goods and services (the demand shock) and inflation. The increased demand increases the real GDP that boosts the demand for labour and thus it reduces unemployment. The increased demand increases consequently inflation. The unemployment thus helps predicting inflation that represents the main monetary policy target.

Some economists believe that NAIRU can provide useful information whereas others argue that such information is misleading. NAIRU opponents base their arguments both on practical and theoretical experience. NAIRU estimates change substantially throughout the time. In the 1960s, it was of 5 % in the United States, in the mid-1970s it increased to 7 %, and in the mid-1990s it fell back to 5.5 – 6 %. NAIRU depends on a variety of factors including demographical trends, government employment policies and regional economic changes.

That means that NAIRU cannot be determined precisely. Based on the thorough empirical analysis of Phillips curve, Staiger, Stock and Watson[28] have drawn a 95 % estimate of NAIRU from 4.8 to 6.6 %. Regarding this uncertainty, NAIRU can provide misleading monetary policy signals. In addition, the short-term trade-off between unemployment and inflation is unstable. The NAIRU also

---

28 Staiger, Douglas, James H. Stock and Mark W. Watson: The NAIRU, unemployment and monetary policy. *Journal of Economic Perspectives*, 1997, 11(1), 33-49.

depends upon the inflation-expectations-generating processes. Any trade-off disappears as soon as the central bank attempts to employ it systematically.

NAIRU can indicate future inflation only when the economy is hit by demand shocks. Nevertheless, the economy can be also hit by supply shocks, i.e. by unexpected changes of the aggregate supply of goods and services – e.g. by the step increase of labour productivity. Initially, this shock increases the volume of goods and services in relation to the current demand. Hence, the prices start falling. The growing GDP boosts the demand for labour, and it reduces thereby the unemployment. Falling unemployment thus coincides with deflationary pressures. If the central bank uses NAIRU, than it can expect wrongly future inflationary pressures and tighten monetary policy.

The arguments that we have mentioned above were opposing the so-called trigger strategy. Under this strategy, the central bank compares the current rate of unemployment with NAIRU, and it consequently adjusts the interest rate. Nevertheless, no central bank bases its monetary policy upon the one sole variable. The question arises as whether the models containing NAIRU are more adequate than other models. Although all models generate errors, it is still hard to say which one provides the best estimates. As inflation is monetary phenomenon the **models based on money stock have some advantage when predicting inflation.**

11 Foreign exchange interventions and dollarization

11.1 Foreign exchange interventions

Foreign exchange intervention (FX intervention) is the action of central bank or another central institution taken in order to affect the spot exchange rate of domestic currency to other currencies at the market. Central bank or another central institution purchases or sells foreign currencies for domestic currency. If it finds the domestic currency too strong, it purchases foreign currencies for the domestic currency and vice versa. **FX intervention is not regarded as a part of monetary policy** as its primary goal is to influence exchange rate and not inflation. But we have already seen (Figure 10.1) that change of exchange rate has indirect effect on inflation.

FX interventions are more frequent in smaller countries. In the USA, the Eurozone, Japan and the United Kingdom are unusual. The reason is that foreign exchange market in developed countries is massive compared to any possible size of FX intervention, and thus central authorities in reality do not have power to influence the spot exchange rate generated on FX market. But there are some exemptions form this rule. For example, the People's Bank of China purchases immense amounts of foreign currency (U.S. dollars) for Chinese yuan in order to weaken Chinese youan and consequently to support Chinese export.

11.1.1 The essentials of foreign exchange interventions

The essentials of FX intervention are very simple as shown in the Examples 11.1 and 11.2. The intervention **to depreciate the domestic currency** is the operation when central bank purchases foreign currency in exchange for the domestic currency. In the Example 11.1 the Czech National Bank purchases $1 billion from some Czech commercial bank for CZK 30 billion. The purchase of foreign currency represents the settlement of foreign-currency part of the contract (adding the value of $1 billion to the nostro account of the central bank) and settlement of domestic-currency part of the contract (adding the value of CZK 30 billion to the clearing account of commercial bank). The liquidity of CZK 30 billion is added to commercial bank clearing account with the Czech National Bank. In order to prevent interbank interest rates falling, Czech National Bank have to witdraw immediately this liquidity (CZK 30 billion) from the clearing accounts on term accounts, e.g. by means of repo operations with one of the Czech commercial banks. Hence we use the term "**sterilized foreign exchange intervention**". Non-sterilized foreign exchange intervention would impact the short-term interest rate of the CZK.

Example 11.1 FX intervention to depreciate the domestic currency

1) Czech National Bank purchases $1 billion from commercial bank for CZK 30 billion

Czech National Bank

Nostro account	
1) $1 bln	

Clearing accounts of commercial banks	
	1) CZK 30 bln

Commercial bank

Clearing account with Czech National Bank	
1) CZK 30 bln	

Nostro account	
Initial balance	1) $1 bln

The intervention **to appreciate the domestic currency** is the operation when central bank sales foreign currency in exchange for the domestic currency. In the Example 11.2 the Czech National Bank sales $1 billion to some Czech commercial bank for CZK 30 billion. The sale of foreign currency represents the settlement of foreign-currency part of the contract (deduction of the value of $1 billion from the nostro account of the central bank) and settlement of domestic-currency part of the contract (deduction of the value of CZK 30 billion from the clearing account of commercial bank). The liquidity of CZK 30 billion is deducted from the commercial bank clearing account with the Czech National Bank. In order to prevent interbank interest rates rising, Czech National Bank have to add immediately this liquidity (CZK 30 billion) to the clearing accounts, e.g. by means of reverse repo operations with some of the Czech commercial bank. Hence we again use the term "sterilized foreign exchange intervention". Non-sterilized foreign exchange intervention would impact the short-term interest rate of the CZK.

Example 11.2 FX intervention to appreciate the domestic currency

1) Czech National Bank sales $1 billion to commercial bank for CZK 30 billion

Czech National Bank

Nostro account	
Initial balance	1) $1 bln

Clearing accounts of commercial banks	
1) CZK 30 bln	Initial balance

Commercial bank

Clearing account with Czech National Bank	
Initial balance	1) CZK 30 bln

Nostro account	
1) $1 bln	

It is obvious that FX intervention does not affect the money stock since bank reserves do not make part of monetary aggregates.

We have to point out that **foreign exchange swap (FX swap)** does not represent instrument of FX intervention but the instrument to influence bank reserves. **Foreign exchange swap composed of the exchange of payments at the beginning and at the end of the contract does not influence the exchange rate since commercial banks include both balance sheet and off-balance sheet items into their foreign exchange positions.** When the central bank purchases dollars for domestic currency, commercial bank has "shorter" dollar balance sheet position (lower amount of dollars at the nostro account), but it has at the same time "longer" dollar off-balance sheet position. Overall dollar position of commercial bank remains unaffected by the currency swap. That means that FX swap do not represent instrument of FX intervention.

11.1.2 The reasons for FX intervention

The reasons for FX interventions are:

- o Maintaining the spot exchange rate within the fixed band under the fixed exchange rate regime; and
- o Preventing the excessive instability under the floating exchange rate regime, e.g. in the case of the so-called overshooting.

It is worth mentioning that the level of interest rate of both currencies influences exchange rate as well.

Central bank should not react to the normal short-term volatility of exchange rate. It should rather concentrate on the elimination of excessive deviations from the long-term trend. In other words, central bank should intervene against fluctuations not against the trend. Central bank is not able to fix permanently the exchange rate by means of interventions if the market finds that such a level does not correspond to fundamental economic variables. The exchange rate can deviate from its equilibrium level even if the FX market is deep and liquid. These fluctuations of the exchange rate are often called **"overshooting"**. Once it occurs, central bank can intervene with a view to correct the exchange rate to its equilibrium level. The disequilibrium exchange rate lasting for longer period of time can influence badly domestic inflation and the overall economic activity.

Once the developed countries have shift to floating exchange rates regimes, financial markets have become considered to keep assets prices consistent with changes of other fundamental variables. The main arguments followed the so-called efficient market hypothesis (EMH). According to this theory, all information relevant to determine market equilibrium is contained already in market prices through trading of rationally thinking participants. Hence, assets markets are always in equilibrium and actions of all market participants "catalyze" the equilibrium. If that is the case, all interventions would be superfluous.

However, the experience shows that markets are not efficient. There is a large number of literature sources proving that trading does not correspond to the efficient markets hypothesis. Markets often generate speculation bubbles and heard behaviour. Although such phenomena do not correspond to the EMH, speculators can profit on inefficient financial markets. In the case of such "overshooting", intervention can be successful since it can bring the exchange rate back to its equilibrium level. Also the extreme volatility of the exchange rate can force central bank to intervene on foreign exchange market.

11.1.3 Effectiveness of Interventions

FX interventions can really affect the exchange rate. However, it is very difficult to predict the magnitude of this impact even if this depends certainly upon the amount of intervention. Experience shows that **FX interventions can help smoothing short-term fluctuations providing that they conform to the long-term trend.** That means that interventions can influence the exchange rate only in the short run providing that they conform to fundamental variables. Interventions cannot determine the exchange rate systematically. Nowadays, the most of economists consider interventions inefficient and thus superfluous. The effectiveness is also hard to estimate since one never knows how the exchange rate would behave if the central bank did not intervene.

Some economists argue that the resources available for intervention are too low with respect to the market size. The argument stems from the fact that intervention work primarily through the restructuring of investors' portfolios. In other words, if the intervention is to affect relative price of one currency, it would have to cause substantial changes of the relative supply of this currency. Nevertheless, researches have shown that the amount of intervention often does not represent the primary factor, and that the news about intervention can affect exchange rate too. The result of intervention depends upon whether investors keep their expectations regardless the intervention or not. Other researches prove that interventions almost never affect the structure of investment portfolios.

In the 1950s Milton Friedman proposed the classical test of efficient and stabilizing intervention consisting in the analysis of gains from intervention. Friedman has shown that central bank should act exactly as a rational speculator. It should buy currency when it is relatively cheap and vice versa. Studies show that interventions are usually profitable for central banks, and that Friedman's test is applicable.

11.1.4 Evidence from some countries

In the **United States**, the magnitude of monetary aggregates, volume of foreign exchange transactions and the overall activity on foreign exchange market make FX interventions very limited, since the Fed or some other central authority is not able significantly to influence these huge variables. Neither the U.S. Department of the Treasury nor the Fed care about exchange rates too much currently.

The possible FX interventions are managed by the Federal open market committee (FOMC) in cooperation with the Department of the Treasury that is responsible for these operations. The Fed then runs the intervention through its foreign exchange desk at the Federal Reserve Bank of New York and through the Exchange Stabilization Fund (ESF) governed by the Department of the Treasury. However, the initiative lies in the hands of ESF that is holding portfolio of FX reserves, which it can sell in order to strengthen the dollar. It is also holding a limited amount of dollar assets that it can use to weaken the dollar. In addition, Fed is holding portfolio of FX assets that it can use to strengthen dollar by selling these FX assets and vice versa. Fed and ESF would intervene in cooperation. The exchange rate policy in the United States thus lies primarily in the hands of the Department of Treasury as a part of its international financial policy. Nevertheless, Fed plays important role through FOMC and Federal Reserve Bank of New York.

Fed is not targeting any level of exchange rate. It concerns only about "incorrect" changes at the currency markets such as speculations that can endanger the efficiency of these markets. Within several preceding decades, Fed intervened several times to support weakening dollar. In such a case, the federal reserve bank of New York sold foreign exchange assets for dollars (Fed debited member banks' accounts at Fed).

But interventions initiated by Fed or by the Department of the Treasury cannot change bank reserves with Fed due to the fact that interventions cannot affect federal funds rate. To avoid the lack or surplus of reserves, Fed uses sterilization operations immediately after the intervention. These operations do not make part of the Fed monetary policy. To neutralize the impact of changing balances of commercial banks accounts at Fed, the Federal Reserve Bank of New York provides or drains reserves automatically in or out of the system.

In September 1985 the G-7 governments of France, West Germany, Japan, the United States and the United Kingdom (G5) have signed the **Plaza Accord** on active interventions to weaken dollar. The United States was often intervening against dollar by the late of the 1980s. In the 1990s there have been interventions on both sides of the market. The last intervention has occured in 2000. Survey of U.S. monetary authorities FX operations can be found in quarterly report *Treasury and Federal Reserve Foreign Exchange Operations.*

In the **Eurozone,** the European Central Bank does not care about exchange rate too much. For example, in 2000 European central bank was concerned about a weak euro. It intervened to appreciate euro on 22 September 2000. This action was supported by the Federal Reserve, the Bank of Canada, the Bank of Japan, and the Bank of England. There were other interventions initiated solely by Euroean Central Bank in November 2000. It follows the principle that central banks should concentrate primarily on inflation and not on exchange rates. The exchange rate should be left on the market. The most of exports of EU member states focuses to other member states so that the exchange rate of euro does not influence the business activity very much.

In **Japan** central bank is acting as the agent of government based on the request made by the Japan Ministry of Finance. Japan has been very interested in keeping the exchange rate of yen lower, i.e. to help exporters, for a long time. Thus, Japan intervened frequently against yen in the 1990s and at the beginning of the 2000s. In March 2004 the Japan Ministry of Finance announced it would no longer routinely intervene on FX market. From that time there was no intervention on FX market.

In the **United Kingdom,** the foreign exchange reserves are historically held by Exchange Equalisation Account. They are owned by Her Majesty's Treasury and the Bank of England is acting as their agent which carries out day-to-day management. Based on the changes of the Bank of England Act of 1998, the Bank of England holds now its small pool of own foreign exchange reserves separately from reserves managed in the name of government. These reserves can be used for monetary policy purposes subject to limits imposed by the Court of Directors. The Bank of England may intervene in the FX market only if the Treasury so instructs the Bank of England. Neither Treasury nor the Bank of England has intervened in this century.

11.2 Dollarization

We talk about **dollarization** when some country abandons its own currency, and it adopts the U.S. dollar as the official currency and legal tender. This type of dollarization is called sometimes official or full dollarization. The unofficial or partial dollarization means that dollar does not become legal tender but the most of money transactions are denominated in dollars. This is the case of some countries of Latin America (whose largest business partner is the United States). Dollarization can sometimes refer to the situation when the domestic currency is officially or unofficially replaced not only by U.S. dollar but by some other currency, e.g. by the euro, Australian dollar, New Zealand dollar and the like.

Countries are generally not willing to give up their currencies. Currency represents a kind of national symbol, and the adoption of dollar could face political aversion. Full dollarization means that central bank has to draw all the domestic currency out of circulation in exchange for dollars. **Then the key functions of central bank disappear, since the central bank ceases as an issuer of currency in cirulation and as a monetary policy maker.** What remain are the less important functions of central bank like banking supervision (if it had been part of central bank already). Central bank can require commercial banks to hold bank reserves. From a view of dollarized country disadvantages of dollarization generally outweight the advantages of dollarization. From a view of the United States dollarization is lucrative.

11.2.1 Advantages and Disadvantages of Dollarization

Let‘s have a look on advantages and disadvantages of dollarization from a view of dollarized country. The dollarization can be the way to avoid currency crisis, to ensure lower costs of foreign loans and to deepen the integration on the world market. On the other hand the dollarization means to give-up a seigniorage in favour of the United States and to loose control over the exchange rates policy of domestic currency (in the case of partial dollarization).

The main advantage of the full dollarization is regarded the **elimination of currency crises**. If there is no domestic currency, there can be no sudden outflow of capital and consequently sharp devaluation of domestic currency. Currency crisis are very expensive for the reason of widening the credit spread and affecting badly the overall economy. Mexican GDP has contracted by 6.9 % in 1995, and Asian countries have experienced the fall of GDP ranging from 5 to 15 %. The most of countries had to devaluate their domestic currencies after the crises and to adopt floating exchange rates regime. Elimination of currency crises makes capital flows more stable.

Elimination of currency crises directly **lowers the costs of foreign loans** since the credit spread gets smaller. The credit spread is lower since the dollarization eliminates FX risk, i.e. the risk of devaluation of some currency. Despite interest rates of dollar-denominated bonds of the country are higher than dollar-denominated bonds issued by the U.S. government for the reason of the higher credit risk. In other words, the sovereign risk of the dollarized country is higher than the sovereign risk of the U.S. government. Higher confidence of foreign investors lowers the costs of loans which lower fiscal expenses and boosts investments and economic growth.

Dollarization can represent other benefit as well. Lower transaction costs and stable dollar prices boost the deeper financial and economic **integration** into the world economy.

We have seen already that the right to issue its own currency enables government to benefit from the so-called **seigniorage**. The seigniorage is the reduction of the expense of central bank corresponding to the zero-interest cost of currency. The central bank generally transfers seigniorage to the central government budget. Dollarization means that domestic central bank (i.e. domestic government) gives up seigniorage in favour of the Fed (i.e. in favour of the U.S. government). For 2007, the seigniorage of Fed amounted to $39.8 billion of which $26.5 billion came from foreign countries through their dollarization. In some years this amount was even higher for the seigniorage of Fed is directly related to the federal funds rate. **The loss of seigniorage is the main obstacle for dollarization.**

There is a case for the U.S. authorities to share part or all of the seigniorage with countries that adopt the U.S. dollar. There is a precedent in the arrangements between South Africa and three other states using the rand (Lesotho, Namibia, and Swaziland). While the United States has no sharing arrangement with Panama or any other officialy dollarized economy, there have been some initiatives in the U.S. Senate to consider legislation providing for seigniorage reimbursement. In 1999 and 2000, there was a heated debate between the Fed, the U.S. Department of the Treasury and politicians. The new legislation was expected. Senator Connie Mack proposed to follow IMF proposal to adopt an act on international monetary stability. According to the proposal, 85 % of seigniorage should be transferred back to the dollarized countries. The major opponent was Secretary of the U.S. Department of the Treasury Larry Summers according to whom there was no reason to transfer seigniorage to dollarized countries. The proposal was rejected.

Dollarization means also that the country **looses its exchange rate policy,** i.e. it looses the possibility to devalue domestic currency. Devaluation of domestic currency can help domestic economy and can reduce the risk of government default. If on the other hand the banks are lending dollars, the banks are not exposed to FX risk but they are exposed higher credit risk as domestic clients become very easy unable to repay dollar-denominated loans, and they often default. This was the case of currency crises in Mexico (1994) and Asia (1997).

The decisive feature of dollarization is its **long-term** character. Dollarization is much harder to leave than currency board. Abandonment of dollarization and U.S. dollar always affects badly the overall economy. **The major benefit of dollarization is that it is supposed to be the irrevocable measure towards lower inflation, fiscal discipline and transparency.** It can bring the stabilized financial and macroeconomic environment. However, in the case of full dollarization, investors can fear of the fiscal deficits or the insufficient regulation. Panama, for example, has faced already several crisis and rescue programs of the IMF.

11.2.2 Dollarized countries

The Table 11.1 shows the list of thirty-two officially dollarized countries as in June 2002. Ecuador, Salvador, Puerto Rico and Panama are the only larger countries of this list. These countries are using U.S. dollar as legal tender. The remaining officially dollarized countries are smaller ones. Many other countries (for example in Latin America) are dollarized unofficially. Dollarized countries of Latin America differ considerably from the United States, and the dollarization does not represent substantial benefits. Before the launch of euro currency, German mark banknotes represented from 10 to 20 % of all currency in circulation in Poland. Some economists have suggested that Canada should dollarize as well.

Table 11.1 Officially dollarized countries as in June 2002

Country	Number of inhabitants	GDP (USD billions)	Political status	Currency	Dollarized since
American Samoa	67,000	0.5	U.S. territory	USD	1899
Andorra	68,000	1.2	Independent	EUR	1278
British Virgin Islands	21,000	0.3	British dependency	USD	1973
Cocos (Keeling) Islands	600	0.0	Australian ext. territory	AUD	1955
Cook Islands	21,000	0.1	New Zealand territory	NZD	1995
Cyprus, Northern	140,000	0.8	De facto independent	TRL	1974
East Timor	857,000	0.2	Independent	USD	2000
Ecuador	13,200,000	37.2	Independent	USD	2000
El Salvador	6,200,000	24.0	Independent	USD	2001
Greenland	56,000	1.1	Danish self-gov. region	DKK	before 1800
Guam	160,000	3.2	U.S. territory	USD	1898
Kiribati	94,000	0.1	Independent	AUD	1943
Kosovo	1,600,000	n.a.	U.N. administration	EUR	1999
Liechtenstein	33,000	0.7	Independent	CHF	1921
Marshall Islands	71,000	0.1	Independent	USD	1944
Micronesia	135,000	0.3	Independent	USD	1944
Montenegro	700,000	1.6	Semi-independent	EUR	2002
Monaco	32,000	0.9	Independent	EUR	1865
Nauru	12,000	0.1	Independent	AUD	1914
Niue	2,000	0.0	New Zealand territory	NZD	1901
Norfolk Island	2,000	0.0	Australian ext. territory	AUD	before 1900
North Mariana Islands	75,000	0.9	U.S. commonwealth	USD	1944
Palau	19,000	0.1	Independent	USD	1944
Panama	2,800,000	16.6	Independent	USD	1904
Pitcairn Island	42	0.0	British dependency	NZD	1980s
Puerto Rico	3,900,000	39.0	U.S. commonwealth	USD	1899
San Marino	27,000	0.9	Independent	EUR	1897
Tokelau	1,500	0.0	New Zealand territory	NZD	1926
Turks and Caicos Islands	18,000	0.1	British colony	USD	1973
Tuvalu	11,000	0.0	Independent	AUD	1892
U.S. Virgin Islands	120,000	1.8	U.S. territory	USD	1934
Vatican City	1,000	0.0	Independent	EUR	1929

Source: http://www.dollarization.org

After the economic stagnation in 1998, the economy of **Ecuador** collapsed into the deep crisis in 1999 (real GDP shrunk 8 % in this year). The reason was that banks went bankrupt which caused credit crunch. The unemployment increased to almost 17 % at the end of 1999. The year-to-year inflation increased from 45 % by the end of 1998 to 60 % by the end of 1999. Public finances were in a bad condition which was caused, among other reasons, by the long-lasting low oil prices. In 1998, the government introduced the indexation of oil-product and gas-product prices to the exchange rate of U.S. dollar.

In August 1999 Ecuador announced that it could not service its debt and that it would not meet a payments on its Brady bonds. Ecuador was the first country to default on Brady bonds. In October 1999 Ecuador failed in coupon payments on its eurobonds. Ecuador adopted the U.S. dollar as its official currency in January 2000. Domestic banknotes were slowly replaced by dollar banknotes. Nevertheless, the inflation during the first half of 2000 was on the level of inflation of 1999. According to Stanley Fisher, the dollarization in Ecuador should serve as a good example to be followed by the whole Latin America.

Panama is the country with strong and close historical, political and economic relations to the United States. It has adopted officially the U.S. dollar as the only legal tender already in 1904. In Panama, the dollarization has helped to maintain as stable currency and low inflation as in the United States.

Among the unofficially dollarized countries, we can mention **Argentina**. In January 1999, Argentine president announced the intention to dollarize the country. His intent was to protect the economy from speculative attacks on domestic currency. At that time 60% of private nonfinancial sector deposits were in dollars. If Argentina decided to adopt the full dollarization, it would have lost 750 million pesos a year in seigniorage. The key question was whether the dollarization would sufficiently lower the credit spread of dollar-denominated bonds by reducing the FX risk to investors.

12 Monetary policy in some countries

12.1 Monetary policy in the USA

The contemporary Fed differs substantially from the conceptions of authors of the Federal Reserve Act of 1913. Priorities of Fed were strongly affected by consequences of the world wars, the Great Depression of the 1930s and inflation of the 1970s and 1980s. The decentralized system was gradually centralized. The current objective of the Fed is to maintain long run growth of the monetary and credit aggregates commensurate with the economy's long run potential to increase production, so as to promote effectively the goals of maximum employment, stable prices and moderate long-term interest rates (section 2A of Federal Reserve Act).

12.1.1 Monetary policy till the 1960s

Figure 12.1 shows the development of monetary aggregates in the USA from 1867 till 1958 according to data of Friedman and Schwartz (for period from 1867 till 1947) and Rasche (for period from 1948 till 1958). The money stock grew at a higher rate than the growth of nominal GDP. The money stock has tended to rise more rapidly during business cycle expansions than during business cycle contractions. An actual decline of the money stock has occurred only during three economic cycle contractions: 1920 to 1921, 1929 to 1933, and 1937 to 1938. The severity of any economic decline was a consequence of the reduction in the money stock, particularly in the case of Great Depression which started in 1929. The price development from 1800 till 1916 was mainly deflationary Figure 8.1). World War I (1914 to 1920) caused the first period of higher inflation. Nevertheless, since 1920 to 1939, deflation was dominating again. Then there was inflation from 1940 to 1948. Each of the price inflations has been preceded and accompanied by a corresponding increase in the rate of growth of the money stock. An acceleration of money growth in excess of real output growth has invariably produced inflation in these periods.

The most well-known part is the monetary policy during 1929–33. The money stock price level fell by one-fourth, real interest rates reached double digits, and thousands of banks failed. Some economists blame the Fed's policy. There are many expalanations of the Fed behaviour during the Great Depression. The one is that of Friedman and Schwartz (1963). According to them a significant shift in policy occurred after the death in 1928 of Benjamin Strong, Governor of the Federal Reserve Bank of New York. They argue that he understood how to employ the tools of monetary policy to minimize cyclical fluctuations in output and prices. But nobody can tell what kind of policy Strong would prefer.

Figure 12.1 Development of monetary aggregates in the USA from 1867 till 1958 according to Anderson[29], Friedman and Schwartz[30] and Rasche[31]

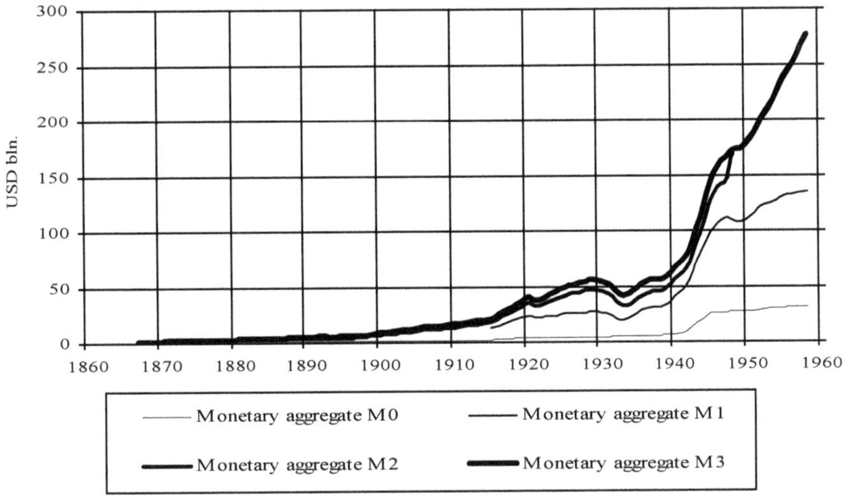

In 1931, uncertainty about the ability or willingness of the United States to remain on the gold standard accelerated gold outflows associated with the decline of bank reserves. It forced the Fed to make a decision. The Fed could choose either to defend their gold reserve by rising interest rate or suspend the convertibility of the dollar into gold. The Fed understood that a tighter monetary policy might worsen the depression, but to preserve the gold standard it chose not to increase bank reserves which resulted in the **rise of interest rate.** The Fed viewed the gold standard as fundamental to long-run economic prosperity and was willing to defend the system even if it took actions that worsened the ongoing depression. The Fed made virtually no open-market purchases of government securities during the crisis to lower interest rate.[32]

29 Anderson Richard G.: *Some Tables of Historical U.S. Currency and Monetary Aggregates Data.* Working Paper. Federal Reserve Bank of St. Louis, St. Louis, 2003.

30 Friedman, Milton and Anna J. Schwartz: *A Monetary History of the United States, 1867–1960.* Princeton University Press, Princeton 1963.

31 Rasche, Robert H.: Demand Functions for Measures of U.S. Money and Debt. In: Proceedings of the Board of the Governors of the Federal Reserve System. 1990, 113-172.

32 Wheelock, David C.: *Monetary Policy in the Great Depression and Beyond: The Sources of the Fed's Inflation Bias.* Working Paper 1997-011A. Federal Reserve Bank of St. Louis, St. Louis 1997.

12.1.2 Monetary policy from the 1960s

Figures 12.2 to 12.6 show the development of federal funds rate, monetary aggregates, consumer price index (CPI), inflation derived from CPI and ex post real interest rate in the U.S from 1960 till 2008.

The USA in the period from 1965 till 1980 sustained the rise of inflation from 2 % to over 12 % (**the Great Inflation of the 1970s**). There was a similar historical pattern for inflation in Japan, the United Kingdom, Canada and other countries. But in Japan the desinflation occurred earlier (in the mid-1970s) as opposed to the early 1980s in the USA other countries.

In August 1971 President Nixon announced his "New Economic Policy." The plan included two features:

- o To combat inflation. Nixon imposed wage and price controls; and
- o To suspend convertibility of the dollar into gold in response to the USA's long-standing and worsening international payments deficit.

Both policies were intended to be temporary. The wage and price controls were temporary, but the dollar convertibility into gold appeared to be permanent. The dollar floated against other currencies since 1973. Both measures were directed to control inflation under the Bretton Woods System. The post-war gold standard did not impose the same level of discipline on commercial bank's loans that the pre-war gold standard had. The monetary policy was too expansionary in the 1970s, and a tighter monetary policy had been required to produce lower growth of monetary aggregates, lower growth of aggregate demand, and, hence, to curb inflation.[33]

In October 1979, the Fed decided to take decisive actions against inflation. The Fed chose to manage money base and M1 as an intermediate target (see 8.2.2). Inflation sharply fell at the expense of the economic recession in 1981–82 when GDP dropped by 2.9 %. Nevertheless, M1 was still growing. Since 1983 price level in the United States (as well as in some other countries facing high inflation) stabilized.

In the mid-1980s the relationship between M1 and real GDP and inflation proved too be week, and the Fed started, therefore, to target M2 and M3 aggregates. These aggregates were used until the 1990s when Fed observed troubles

33 Nelson, Edward: *The Great Inflation of the Seventies: What Really Happened?* Working Paper 2004-001. Federal Reserve Bank of St. Louis, St. Louis 2004.

resulting from monetary aggregates. The growth of M2 and M3 slowed down considerably to almost zero growth at the beginning of the 1990s whereas Federal funds rate lowered below 4 %. Commercial banks reduced their loan expansion in order to improve their profits. This could also be caused by the new capital adequacy measures (International convergence of capital measurement and capital standards) initiated by the Basel Committee on Banking Supervision. The Fed has been gradually eliminating the reliance on monetary aggregates as indicators of monetary policy and has been paying more attention to the data of employment, expenditures, wages, foreign trade and other economic variables. This policy represents a certain shift to inflation targeting.

The period from 1991 to 2001 was the period of economic expansion, which was the longest one in U.S. history. The economy was growing at a rate that was thought to be unsustainable. To curb growth, the Fed raised the interest rate from 4.75 % to 6.50 % between mid-1999 and May 2000. Apparently this tightening of monetary policy was too severe, for economic growth collapsed soon thereafter. In the presence of a low economic growth, falling industrial production, and an increasing unemployment rate, the Fed began aggressively easing monetary policy. Between 3 January and 11 December 2001, the interest rate was reduced from 6.50 % to 1.75 %. Economic growth was sluggish during the second half of 2000, and it remained sluggish through 2001.

During 2002 and 2003 the Fed lowered interest rate further. Positive growth resumed at the fourth quarter of 2001, and it has continued throughout 2002 and 2003. From 2004 the Fed was tightening monetary policy again till the middle of 2006 when the Federal funds rate had reached 5.25 %. Starting 18 September 2007 the Fed had been aggressively cutting Federal funds rate to the final level 0–0.25 % on 16 December 2008.

In April 2009, the Fed declared policy of quantitative easing. It announced that to provide support to mortgage lending and housing markets and to improve overall conditions in private credit markets, it will purchase a total of up to $1,250 billion of agency mortgage-backed securities and up to $200 billion of agency debt by the end of the year. In addition, the Federal Reserve will buy up to $300 billion of Treasury securities by autumn.

Figure 12.2 The development of federal funds rate in the USA

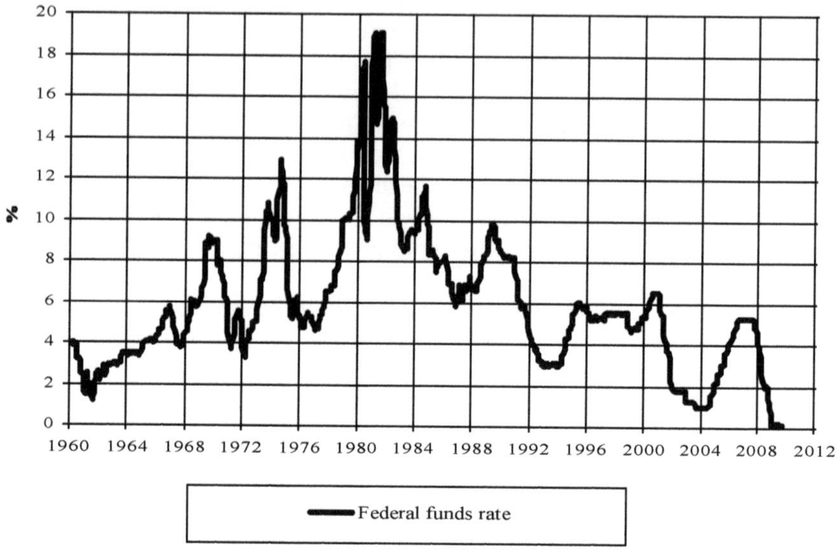

Figure 12.3 Development of monetary aggregates in the USA

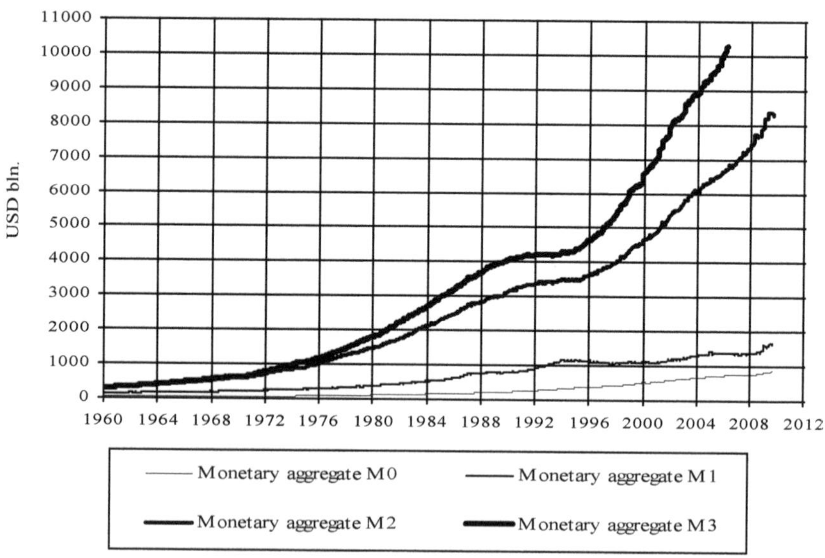

Figure 12.4 Development of consumer price index (CPI) in the USA

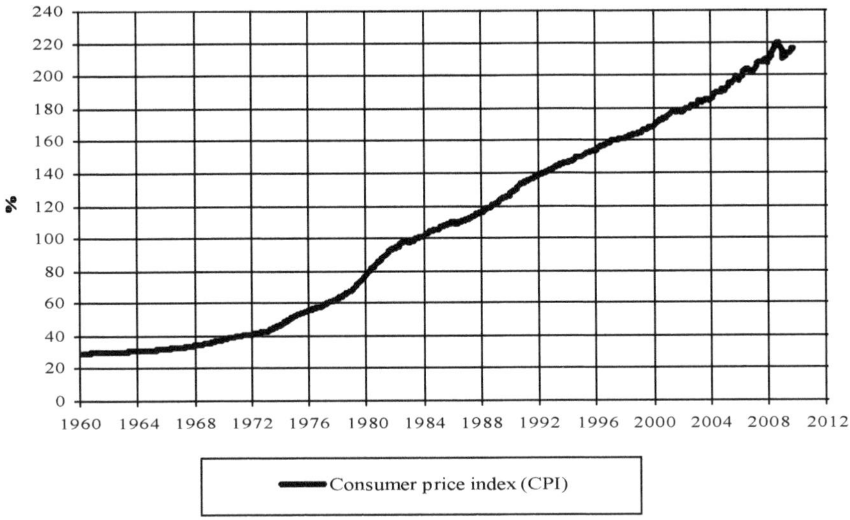

Figure 12.5 Development of inflation derived from CPI in the USA

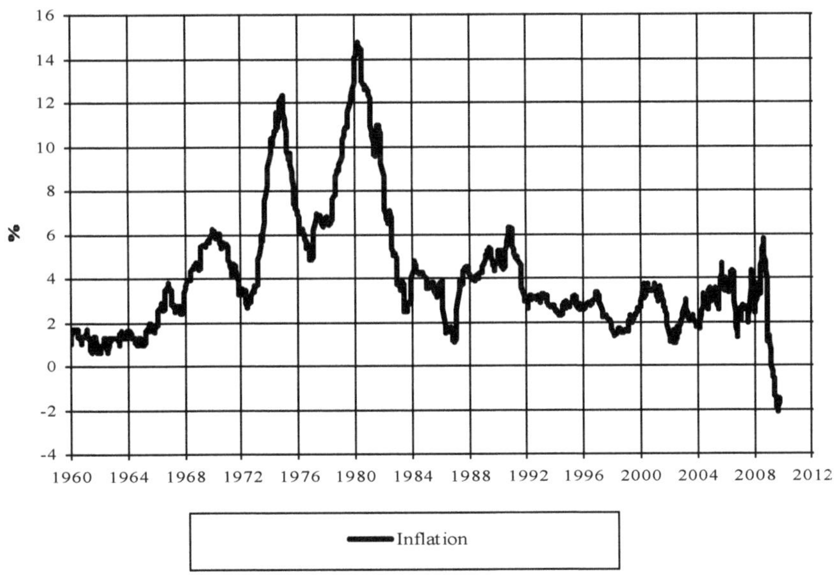

Figure 12.6 Development of ex post real interest rate in the USA

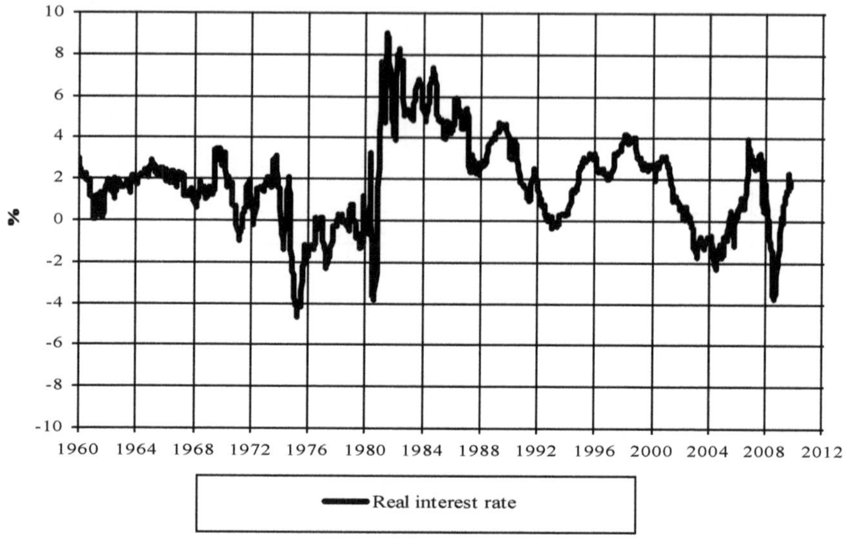

12.2 Monetary policy in the Eurozone

Figures 12.7 to 12.11 show the development of main refinancing operations interest rate, monetary aggregates, harmonized index of consumer prices (HICP), inflation derived from HICP and ex post real interest rate in the Eurozone till 2008.

The **Eurozone** with euro as legal tender has been established on **1 January 1999** when sixteen member states of the European Union have adopted the euro as their currency. The ECU currency was replaced by euro by the ratio 1:1. Payments based on transfers of funds on accounts had been converted to euro. There were no euro banknotes and coins. European Central Bank (ECB) started its monetary policy. A part of foreign reserves held by national central banks was transferred to ECB. Starting **1 January 2002** euro banknotes and coins have been issued. The transition to euro banknotes and coins had finished on **1 March 2002.**

According to the article 105 of the Maastricht Treaty on European Union (1992) the primary objective of the European System of Central Banks (ESCB[34]) shall be price stability. In addition, the ESCB is supposed to support the overall economic policy of the European Union. In doing so, ESCB shall act with accordance with the principle of an open market economy with free competition, favouring an efficient allocation of resources. The Treaty does not set what is meant by the price stability. Hence, in 1998, the Governing Council of ECB defined quantitatively the price stability as a yearly increase of the harmonized index of consumer prices (HICP) in the Eurozone of **below 2 %.** Later in 2003, the Governing Council further clarified that, within the definition, it aims to maintain inflation rates below but close to 2% over the medium term in order to prevent deflationary expectations.

Monetary policy of ECB is based on two pillars. The **first pillar** is the role of money. According to ECB, there was stable long-term relationship between the price level and monetary aggregates at the time of euro implementation. Monetary aggregates allegedly contained information about the income and represented the basis of inflation. This monetarist pillar was supported mainly by the Otmar Issing (member of the Executive Board of the ECB and former member of the Board of the Deutsche Bundesbank). ECB took over the policy of the German Bundesbank that was successful for a long time. The policy assured low inflation together with strong economic growth.

The Governing Council of the ECB decided on 1 December 1998 to set the reference rate for the annual growth of a broad monetary aggregate M3 in the eurozone at **4.5 %.** This value was subsequently confirmed in 1999 and 2000. But this reference value did not represent the monetary target, and ECB thus did not attempt to maintain it at any cost. The value resulted from the following calculation:

$$\textit{M3 growth} = \textit{real GDP growth} + \textit{inflation} - \textit{change of the velocity of money},$$
$$\textit{M3 growth} = 2.0\ \% + 2.0\ \% - (-0.5\ \%),$$
$$\textit{M3 growth} = 4.5\ \%.$$

34 **The European System of Central Banks (ESCB)** consists of the European Central Bank and the national central banks of all 27 European Union member states. **The Eurosystem** comprises the ECB and the NCBs of those countries that have adopted the euro

Figure 12.7 The development of main refinancing operations interest rate in the Eurozone

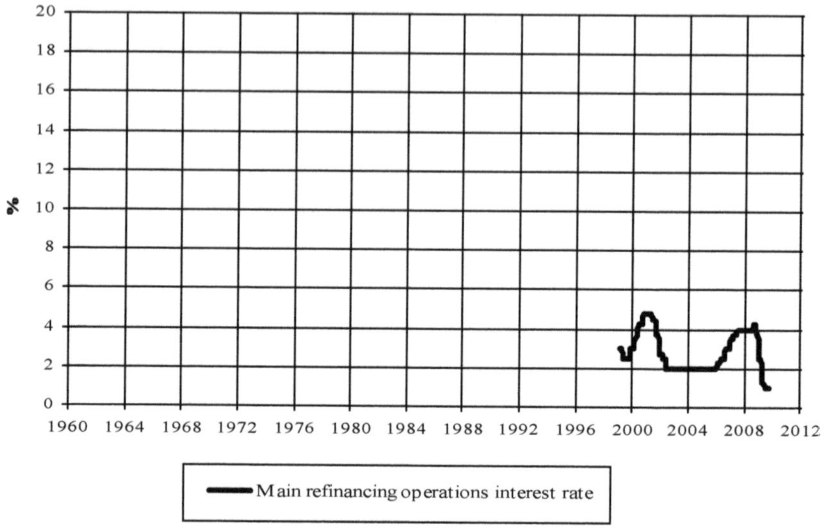

Figure 12.8 Development of monetary aggregates in the Eurozone

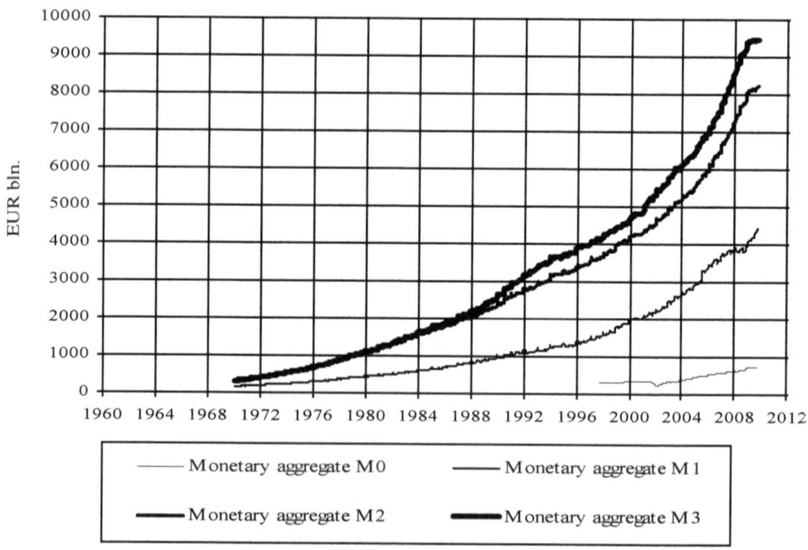

Figure 12.9 Development of harmonized index of consumer prices (HICP) in the Eurozone

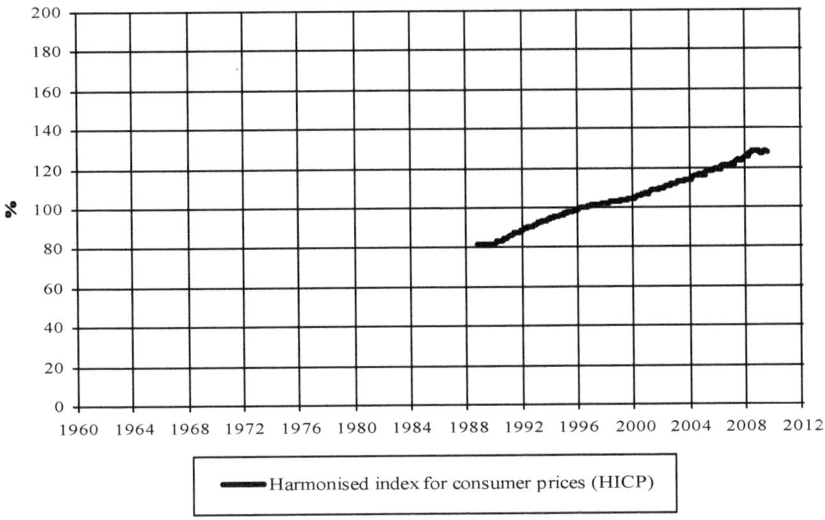

Figure 12.10 Development of inflation derived from HICP in the Eurozone

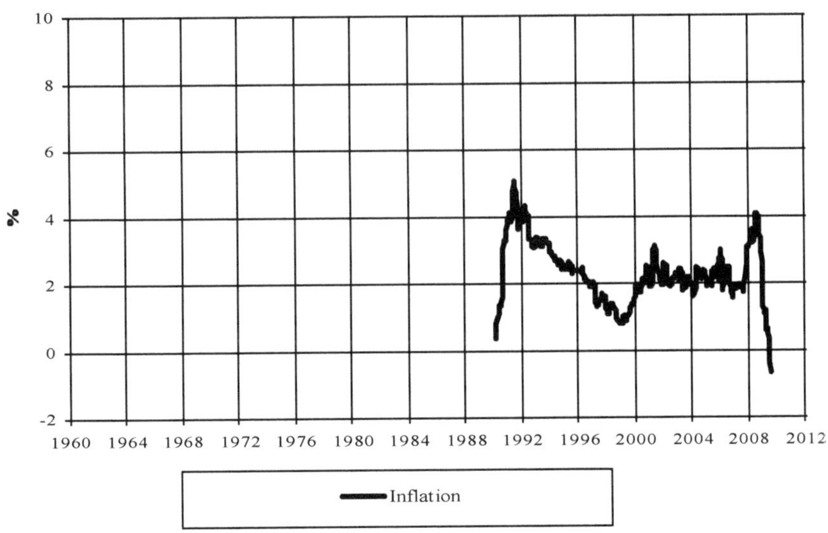

Figure 12.11 Development of ex post real interest rate in the Eurozone

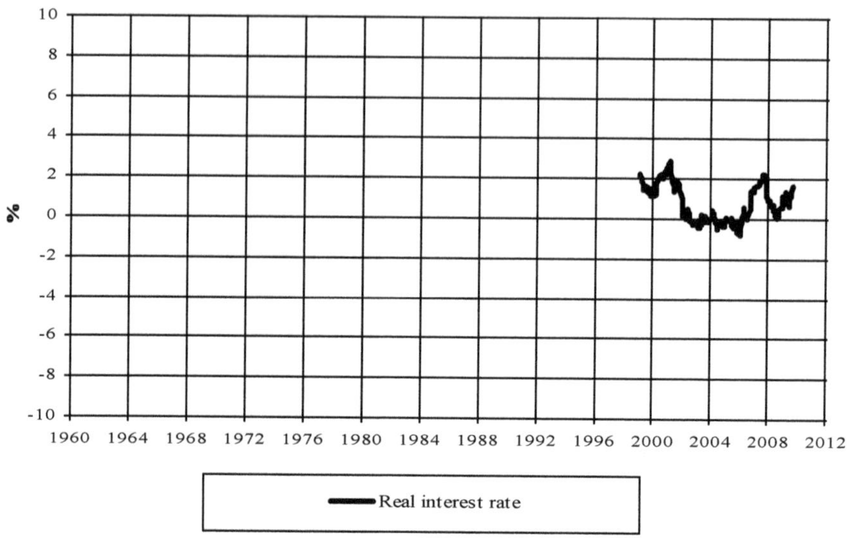

The ECB supposed that the real GDP should grow at 2 %, inflation measures through HICP should be 2 %, and the drop of the velocity of M3 was suggested to be 0.5 %. The M3 growth was close to the reference rate only in the first a few months of euro implementation. In the period from 1999 to 2008 the annual M3 growth substantially increased, and average annual M3 growth for this period had reached 7.7 %.

The **second pillar** of monetary policy represents a wide-ranging set of other price-determining variables, e.g. GDP, labour market, indicators of expenditures and prices, fiscal policies, balance of payments and asset prices. The former Bundesbank had used also other variables next to monetary aggregates. This double-pillar strategy of the ECB is subject to some criticism. Some critics consider reference rate for M3 as a vestige of the monetarist policy of Bundesbank.

In May 2009 the ECB announced that the Eurosystem shall purchase eligible covered bonds with a targeted nominal amount of 60 billion eur. In substance the ECB announced quantitative easing without referring to it as such. There was criticism from Germany.

12.3 Monetary policy in Japan

Figures 12.12 to 12.16 show the development of uncollaterised overnight call rate, monetary aggregates, consumer price index (CPI), inflation derived from CPI and ex post real interest rate in Japan till 2008.

In 2008, Japan was 15 years in economic crisis with no economic growth. The roots of the crisis were soon after the high-growth period of the 1980s when the Japanese stock market and real estate experienced a bubble. From a peak in December 1989 to a bottom in April 2003 stock market crashed to a level of less than 20 %. It means that more than 80 % of equity value had evaporated during this period. Real prices of Japanese real estate reached their peak in the first quarter of 1991, and from that time real estate prices have been sinking till now. At the end of 2008, their level was only 54 % of the peak in 1991.

This led to negative effects on both consumption and investments. In reaction, the Bank of Japan gradually eased monetary policy. The benchamrk official intereset rate (uncollaterised overnight call rate) had lowered from 8.0 % in 1991 to 0.5 % in 1995 and to 0.0 in 1999. From that time the Bank of Japan applies zero-interest rate policy with some minor exceptions. In 1995 Japan plunged into deflation.

The reduced activities of banks in lending led to credit crunch at the beginning of the 1990s. Enterprises were repaying their debts as much as possible. It was fundamental for their survival. According to some authors credit crunch was influenced also by the attempts of banks to comply with the Basel capital adequacy requirements. Banks were also suffering the consequences of the crash of the stock and real estate bubble. They experienced large losses on their portfolios of loans and shares. No economic growth reduced the borrowers' ability to service the loans. The value of the collateral (often land) lowered significantly. In 1997 this led to a banking crisis. Some banks bankrupted, and the government had to provide capital to banks.

In view of an economic upswing the Bank of Japan raised the benchmark interest rate to 0.25 % in the summer 2000. Shortly afterwards the economy weakened again as a result of the global economic slowdown. In early 2001, the interest rate was lowered to 0.15 %, and in March 2001 the Bank of Japan introduced a "new" monetary policy operational target. It is sometimes referred to as a "quantitative target", and it is a target for counterparty deposits on clearing accounts at the Bank of Japan. The policy is called "quantitative easing". From the mid 2001 the benchmark interest rate was 0.0 %. At the end of 2007 the benchmark interest rate has increased temporarily to 0.5 %.

Figure 2.17 Development of uncollaterised overnight call rate in Japan

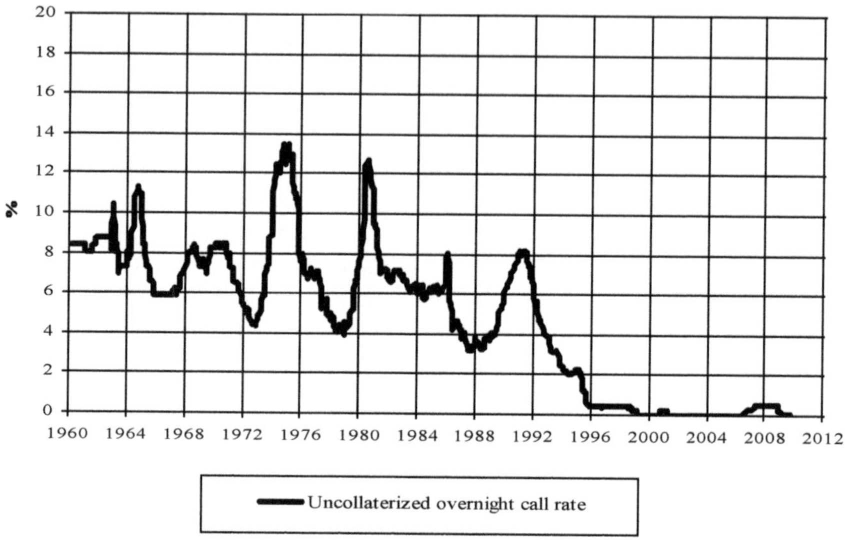

Figure 2.18 Development of monetary aggregates in Japan

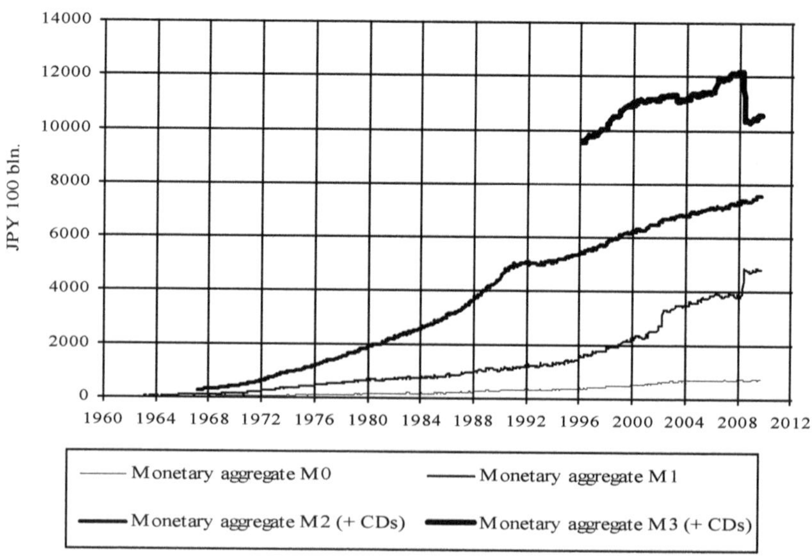

Figure 2.19 Development of CPI in Japan

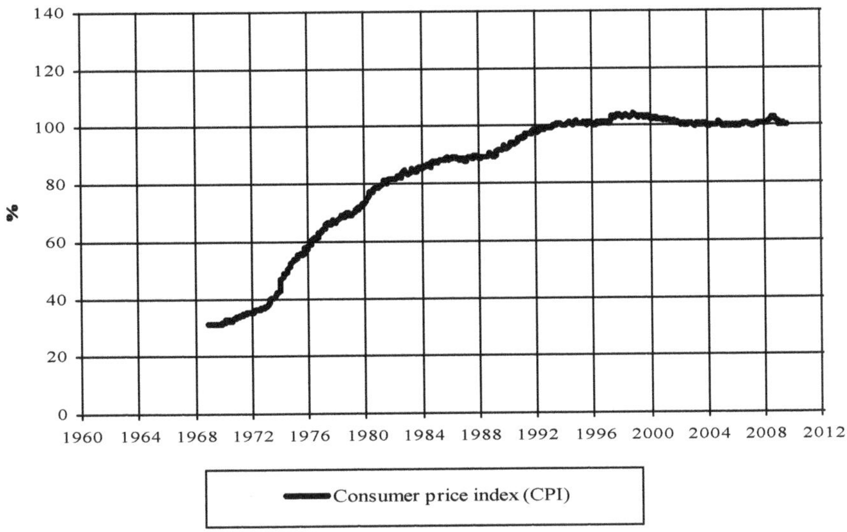

Figure 2.20 Development of inflation derived from CPI in Japan

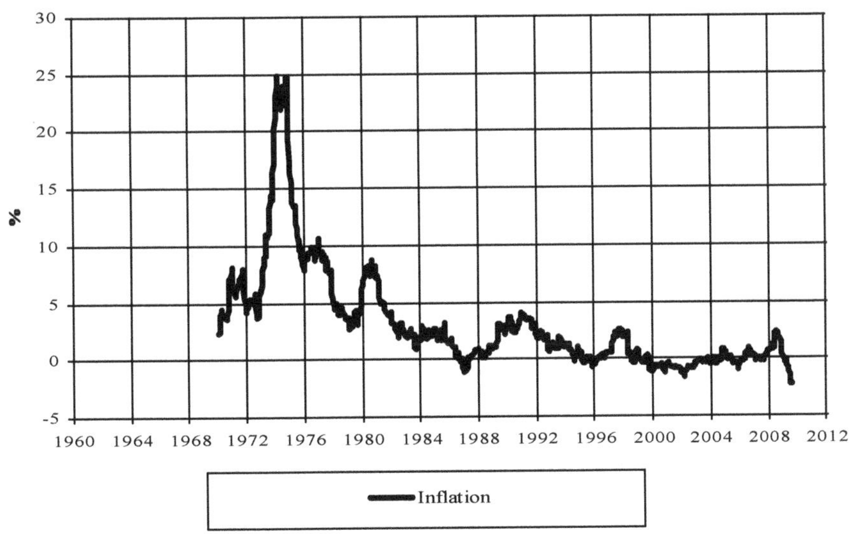

Figure 2.21 Development of ex post real interest rate in Japan

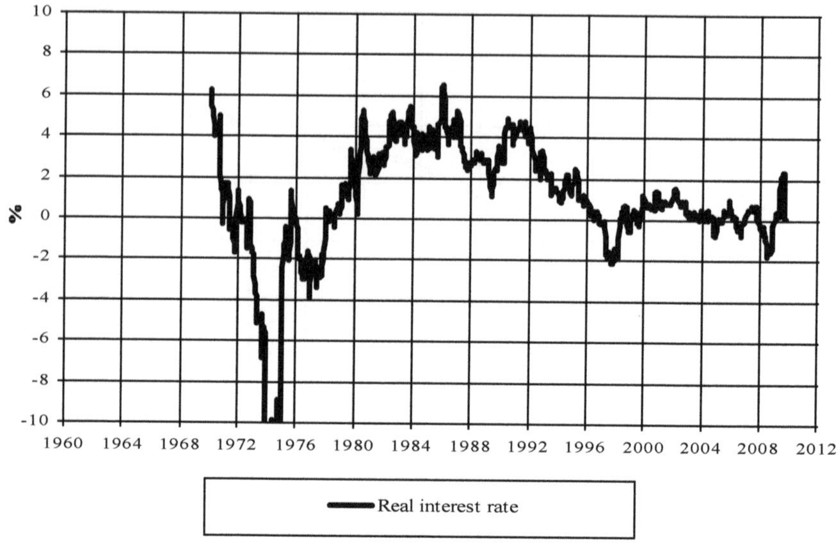

Fiscal policy was eased significantly, resulting in the official public debt of approximately 180 % of GDP by the end of 2008. Japan is in Keynesian liquidity trap. Estimates vary as to the scale of the bad loans. Officially, they are assessed at 6–7 % of GDP, while market participants consider the volume to be much larger. The immediate prospects for the Japanese economy are miserable. There is a recession, prices are falling, the public debt is growing up, and the banking sector is weak.

12.4 Monetary policy in the United Kingdom

It is appealing to compare monetary policy of the USA with monetary policy of the United Kingdom[35]. Both countries did not experience hyperinflation. But inflation in the United Kingdom was generally substantially higher than in the USA (Figure 8.1). From 1800 to 1914, the price level in the United Kingdom was mostly lowering. There was inflation during the World War I. From 1921 to 1933, the United Kingdom experienced deflation again.

35 Balls, Edward and Gus O'Donnell (eds): Reforming Britain's Economic and Financial Policy – Towards Greater Economic Stability. Palgrave, Basingstoke 2002.
Bean, Charles and Nigel Jenkinson: The formulation of Monetary Policy at the Bank of England. *Bank of England Quarterly Bulletin*, 2001, Winter, 434-41.

Figures 12.17 to 12.21 show the development of repo rate, monetary aggregates, retail price index excluding mortgage payments (RPIX), inflation derived from CPI and ex post real interest rate in the United Kingdom till 2008.

By the end of the 1960s, the inflationary development was quite modest. But in the 1970s and in the early 1980s inflation in the United Kingdom shot up into double-digits, and it highly exceeded inflation in the USA. In the middle of 1975 inflation reached extremely high value 27 %. It took many years when inflation landed on the value 5 % (in 1983). It seems that inflation was out of control of the Bank of England for more than decade. In summer 1991 inflation was again on high values (9.5 %). But then inflation calmed down, and from 1993 till 2008 inflation was generally in a range from 2 % to 4 %.

The key difference between the USA and the United Kingdom is non-monetary view on inflation and scepticism about the control of aggregate demand through monetary policy in the 1950s. At that time policy advisers and academics adhered to the "Neanderthal Keynesian" view[36]. This view was based on assumption that consumption and investment were quite insensitive to monetary policy actions. Monetary policy was considered as a tool to influence the exchange rate. The United Kingdom adhered on a fixed exchange rate also in the 1960s. Some tightening of monetary policy had a source in exchange rate considerations. But high monetary aggregates growth and inflation during the 1960s made further adherence to a fixed exchange rate impossible.

In the 1960s the "main instrument" of monetary policy was considered the credit control. It was the requirement that the commercial banks should keep their increase in loans to the private sector to a specified limit. This control was applied to the "clearing banks" up to 1961, and it was extended thereafter to other commercial banks. Credit control was abolished in 1971.

But the United Kingdom gradually made higher reliance on classical monetary policy. Targets for broad money growth (M3) were formally announced in July 1976, even if monetary targets had been used since 1973. These developments occurred despite continuing strong reliance on the non-monetary variables. The details of internal discussions were not disclosed at that time (thus the term "Kremlinology"). The dissent between advocates of classical monetary policy and traditional hardliners continued. According to Goodhart[37] soon after the introduction of monetary targets, the short term rates were used to almost fix the dollar/sterling exchange rate.

---

36 Batini, Nicoletta, and Edward Nelson: *The U.K.'s Rocky Road to Stability.* Working Paper 2005-020A. Federal Reserve Bank of St. Louis, St. Louis 2005.

37 Goodhart, Charles.: *Monetary Theory and Practice: The U.K. Experience.* Macmillam, London 1984.

Figure 2.22 Development of repo rate in the United Kingdom

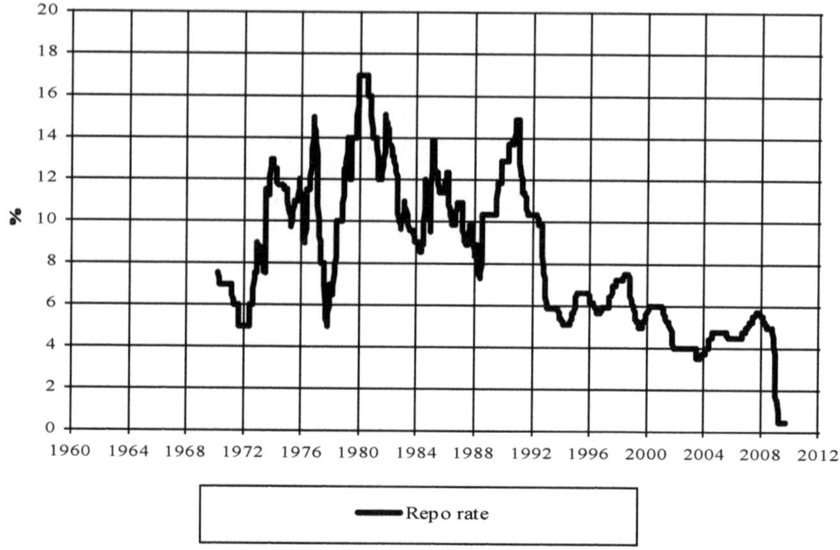

Figure 2.23 Development of monetary aggregates in the United Kingdom

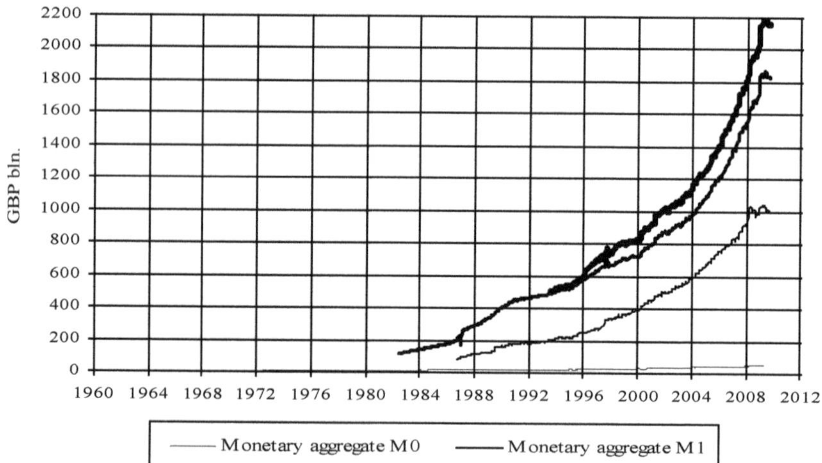

Figure 2.24 Development of retail price index excluding mortgage loans (RPIX) in the United Kingdom

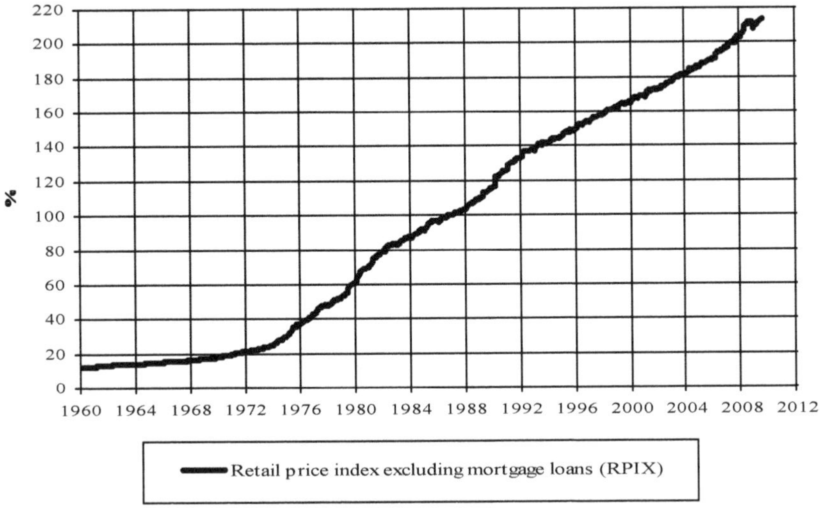

Figure 2.25 Development of inflation derived from the RPIX in the United Kingdom

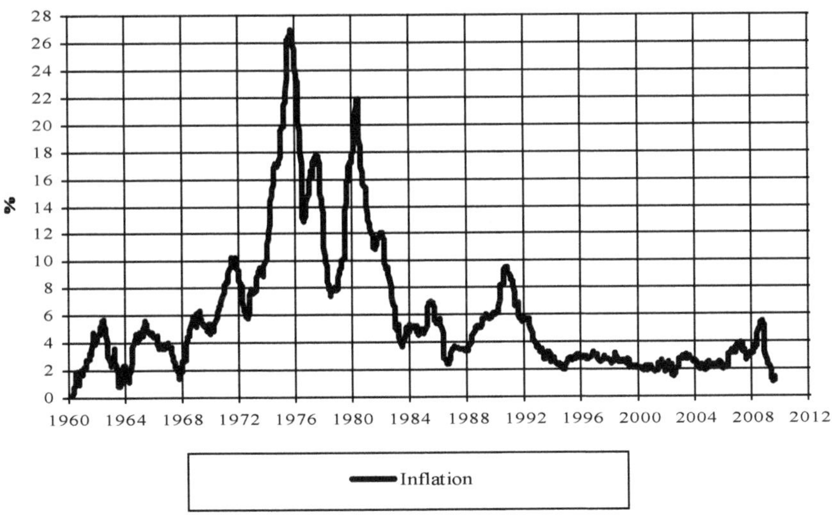

Figure 2.26 Development of ex post real interest rate in the United Kingdom

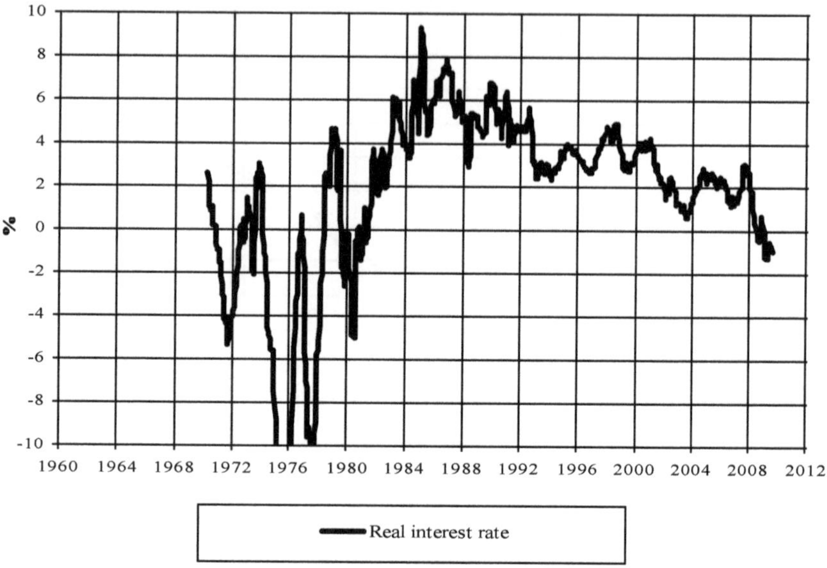

In late 1973 the Supplementary Special Deposits Scheme (the „corset") was introduced with the aim to lower M3 growth without changing interest rates. Banks and finance houses were required to place special non-interest-bearing deposits with Bank of England if their growth in interest bearing liabilities exceeds specified limits. It is doubtful whether the corset had a restrictive effect but it led the banks to evade the new control (creation of deposit substitutes). The corset was abolished in mid-1980.

In October 1990 the United Kingdom entered the Exchange Rate Mechanism, and in September 1992 it was forced to exit due to attack of currency speculators. Pound sterling depreciated deeply. In October 1992 inflation targeting was introduced, and in 1997 Bank of England became public organization wholly-owned by the Government with independence in setting monetary policy. In December 2003 HM Treasury changed the inflation target from 2.5 % measured by RPIX to a 2 % measured by the new CPI (UK HICP). In March 2009, the Monetary Policy Committee announced that, it would start to use quantitative easing (purchase of gilts) in order to meet the inflation target.

12.5 Some general trends

Let's compare the development of broad monetary aggregates (M2, M3) in the USA, the Eurozone, Japan and the United Kingdom in the last five decades. In the 1960s, 1970s and 1980s the broad monetary aggregates had been increasing **exponentially.** The pattern had been changed by the American and Japanese credit crunch at the beginning of the 1990s. The growth of broad monetary aggregates had been heavily suspended in the USA and in Japan for five years.. Commercial banks reduced lending activities and enterprises were repaying their debts. According to some authors credit crunch was influenced also by the attempts of banks to comply with the Basel capital adequacy requirements. There was no suspension of broad monetary aggregates in the Eurozone and in the United Kingdom, and broad monetary aggregates slowed down insignificantly

Afterwards (from 1995 to 2008), the broad monetary aggregates in the USA and in Japan grew following **a linear pattern**. Annual growth of M2 was 9.4 %, and annual growth of M3 was extremely high, and it reached 12.0 % in the USA. Annual growth of broad monetary aggregates was very low in Japan as annual growth of 2.8 % for M2 + CDs was achieved.

The broad monetary aggregates in the Eurozone and in the United Kingdom experienced **an exponential pattern** in the period from 1995 to 2008, i.e. the same pattern as before but in a smaller pace. Annual growth of M2 was 6.9 %, and annual growth of M3 reached 7.1 % in the Eurozone. Annual growth of broad monetary aggregates was very high in the United Kingdom as annual growth of 9.4 % for M2 and 10.3 % for M3 were achieved.

Let's compare the growth of broad monetary aggregates with the growth of nominal GDP (Table 12.1) in the USA, the Eurozone, Japan and the United Kingdom for a decade **from 1999 to 2008.** The growth of the monetary aggregate M2 exceeded the growth of the nominal GDP from 1.3 % to 5.0 %. The growth of the monetary aggregate M3 exceeded the growth of the nominal GDP from 2.6 % to 5.3 %. Looking into the period **from 1960 to 1998** in the USA, the growth of the broad monetary aggregates approximately matched the growth of nominal GDP.

Table 12.1 Average growth of broad monetary aggregates and average growth of nominal GDP in some countries (in percent per annum)

Country	Period	Growth of M2 (1)	Growth of M3 (2)	Growth of nominal GDP (3)	(1) − (3)	(2) − (3)
United States	1960–1998	7.1	8.0	7.6	**−0.5**	**+0.5**
	1999–2008	6.4	7.7*	5.1	**+1.3**	**+2.6***
Eurozone	1999–2008	7.3	7.8	4.2	**+3.1**	**+3.6**
Japan	1999–2008	2.0	–	0.1	**+1.9**	**–**
United Kingdom	1999–2008	10.1	10.4	5.1	**+5.0**	**+5.3**

* Till the end of 2005 only.

Part IV: Payment systems

13 Payment systems

This chapter describes essentials of payment systems. Gross and net settlement systems and payment systems in the United States, the Eurozone, Japan and the United Kingdom are explained.

13.1 Essentials of payment systems

Payment means the transfer of money or liquidity. The payment is carried out by means of a **currency** or by transfer of a bank deposit (the so-called **bank payment**). Currency is used usually to realize small retail payments. The large retail payments and all wholesale payments take the form of deposit transfer. In this chapter we will concentrate solely on bank payments.

Payment system or **funds transfer system** (FTS) is the system of transfers of deposits or liquidity between current accounts. It can operate either on the basis of settlement of individual (gross) payments while checking balances on the current accounts (gross payment system), on the basis of settlement the net payment calculated as a difference between mutual claims and obligations (net payment systems), or on the basis of combination of both systems.

13.1.1 Interbank payment systems

The **interbank payment system** or the **interbank funds transfer system** (IFTS) is the system of transfers of liquidity whose participants are mostly or exclusively banks. This system operates usually on the basis of **correspondent banking** through mutual nostro and vostro accounts. Within individual countries, the system of nostro and vostro accounts gets simplified so that there is at least one bank or some special entity (usually owned by banks) in which the banks hold their nostro accounts. Then, there is one-tier or two-tier system architecture. In one-tier system architecture, all banks are directly connected to the central payment system operated usually by central bank. In two-tier system architecture, the central payment system is restricted on some banks while other banks are connected through satellite payment systems.

The simplest transfer comprises usually three partners. That is the case of payer and payee (beneficiary) being clients of the same bank. More complicated transfers are, however, more common. Let's look to the transfer with two banks: the payer's bank and the payee's bank. This case is covered by the term of correspondent banking which is a situation when one bank has the current account in another bank, and through this account banks operate payments of their clients (or their own payments). One bank considers this account as its nostro account and the second bank as its vostro account. Example 3.16 (the first chapter) shows the cross-border payment in U.S. dollars through vostro account of payer's bank, and Example 13.1 shows the cross-border payment in U.S. dollars through nostro account of payer's bank. In both cases U.S. resident pays $1,000 to the Eurozone resident. No clearinghouse is needed. In reality more banks can be involved in the transfer. This type of **correspondent banking is mainly used for domestic payments in foreign currencies and for cross-boarder payments**.

For **domestic payments in domestic currencies** the former system is usually simplified so that there is one bank or some special entity (usually owned by banks) in which the banks hold their nostro accounts. It is **central payment system** (nostro accounts are held with the central bank) or **satellite payment system** (nostro accounts are held with special entity usually owned by banks). The central payment system with clearing house with the Fed is demonstrated on Figure 3.15.

The central interbank payment system operates on the basis of liquidity transfer from the account of payer bank to the account of recipient bank within the clearing house. The banks carry out payments following their own orders, their clients' orders in the form of written document (transfer order, cheque etc.) or in the form of other types of orders (electronic order, phone order etc.). If both payer and recipient hold their accounts at the same bank, the transfer is carried out inside the bank's clearing centre without using the interbank payment system.

Figure 13.1 shows the U.S. dollar payment between the two Eurozone residents. The transfer of funds is based on:

- Two correspondent relationships (the Eurozone bank A with its correspondent bank in the USA and the Eurozone bank B with its correspondent bank in the USA); and

- One central payment system. The transfer between correspondent banks in the United States is carried out through the standard payment system of the United States, i.e. through the Fedwire, automated clearing house (ACHs) and other clearing houses.

Example 13.1 Foreign currency cross-boarder payment between clients of two commercial banks

1) Client X (U.S. resident) pays $1,000 for real estate to client Y (Eurozone resident)

Bank A in the USA

Nostro account with bank B

Initial balance	1) $1,000

Client X's current accounts

1) $1,000	Initial balance

Client X in the USA

Current account with bank A

Initial balance	1) $1,000

Real estate

1) $1,000	

Bank B in the Eurozone

Vostro account of bank A

1) $1,000	Initial balance

Client Y's current accounts

	1) $1,000

Client Y in the Eurozone

Current account with bank B

1) $1,000	

Real estate

Initial balance	1) $1,000

Figure 13.1 The payment in U.S. dollars between the two Eurozone entities

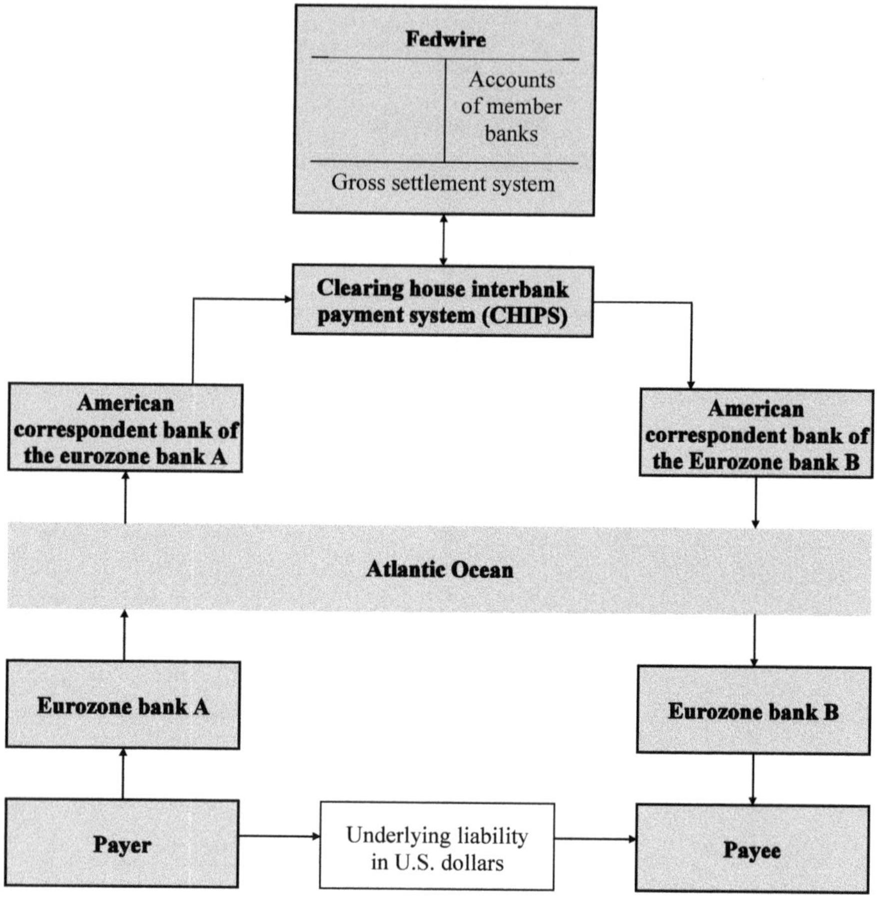

Theoretically the Eurozone banks A and B can have mutual nostro and vostro foreign currency accounts, and they can make their foreign currency payments through these accounts. In practice, however, commercial banks do not have direct relationships with each other, and they make their payments through two or more correspondent banks in countries where the currency of transfer represents the domestic currency (the so-called U-turn).

Anyway, there must be an uninterrupted chain of banks having correspondent relationships to carry out the transfer. Moreover, each of these correspondent relationships can be subject to a different legislation and different terms and conditions. It is necessary to distinguish the chain of mutual correspondent relationships from the underlying obligation between payer and payee. The underlying obligation is subject to some legislation and the transfer of funds to some other legislation(s). It is necessary to point out that the transfer of funds does not need to coincide necessarily with any underlying obligation. Depositor, for instance, can wish only to transfer money from one bank to another one.

The **large-value payment** is the payment between bank (or some other important player on the financial market) and other bank (or some other important player). This payment requires the early and preferred settlement. **Large-value funds transfer system** (wholesale funds transfer system) is the system enabling large-value payments, i.e. transfers of large sums of money or liquidity of high priority. Although there is no bottom limit for transferred amounts, the average amount of payments carried through this system is relatively large.

The **retail funds transfer system** (bulk funds transfer system) is the system enabling transfers of a large number of smaller payments in the form of credit transfers, direct debits, cheques and payment cards. **The retail payment** is typically payment on behalf of bank customer, such as individual, company and public authority. The value of the individual orders tends to be low, and they are usually not time-critical.

Some payment systems are operated by central banks. In such a case, there is usually the facility known as **collaterised intraday credit** (daylight credit, daylight overdraft). It is the credit granted by central bank to commercial banks for period shorter than one day for the purpose of delivering liquidity on clearing accounts with central bank. The facility is important when reserve requirements are zero or small. In such a way payment system runs smoothly. The credit is fully collaterised.

13.1.2 Forms of bank payments

There is a variety of current accounts (checking accounts) used to carry out bank payments. Term deposits and saving deposits are designed primarily for saving, and they are usually not used for payments. Bank payments take usually the form of credit transfer, direct debit, cheque, and payment card.

a) Credit transfer

Credit transfer, giro transfer or **direct credit** is the payment order made by payer through his bank in order to transfer money to the account of payee at the same or another bank. Payment order is headed from the payer to payee and sometimes even through several payment systems. The payer's bank debits the amount from the account of its client. The payee's bank credits the amount to the account of its client. In other words, the payer's bank looses obligation to its client, and the payee's bank accepts the obligation to its client. The system is called **credit transfer system** or **giro transfer system**. The problem with dishonoured cheques does not exist, for the payer cannot transfer more money than he has.

b) Direct debit

Direct debit, debit transfer or **debit collection** is a client's instruction to his bank authorising a payee to collect varying amounts from his current account. Any payment is then initiated by payee, and the debit order is transferred from the payee's bank to payer's bank, and the payment hence follows. The corresponding system is called **debit transfer system** (or debit collection system).

Payee makes the payment order in the same way as payer would make the credit transfer order (written or electronic form). Payee's bank then sends this order to the payer's bank through the interbank electronic clearing system, and the payer's bank then debits payer's account. Debiting is possible only if payer authorized his bank in advance to do so. The bank is obliged to prevent any debiting of its client's account without the explicit agreement.

c) Cheque

Cheque is a written order of a maker (drawer) to drawee (usually a bank) to pay an amount to payee. In the case of banking cheque it is in general an order to transfer money from payer's current account to payee's current account held with the same or another bank. The problem is that sometimes, banks have to deal with dishonoured cheques. The cheque guarantee system is the system guaranteeing cheques up to the amount set by the client. Some countries (like the United States) still heavily rely on cheques.

Cheque clearing represents the process of sending the cheque from the institution where it was presented back to institution that had issued it and the subsequent transfer of money. There is a wide variety of national cheque clearing systems.

Cheque truncation means that the institution where the cheque was presented keeps the paper cheque and sends electronically all necessary information to the bank which has issued the cheque. Truncated cheque does not return to the issuing institution.

Cheque payments are widely used in the United States, for example. If the payer's account is outside the local clearing house, the payment goes usually through the Fed. The money that exists both at the payer's account and at the payee's account during the transaction is called "Fed's float". Once the payee presents the cheque to her bank, he gets her money immediately. Payer thus gets the interest-free credit for the time of cheque transaction, i.e. until the time when the money is debited from his account. Credit cards offer much longer interest-free credit period.

Cheques have been in decline in the last decade. Paper-based cheques are costly to process in comparison to electronic payments. Banks discourage the use of cheques. In the United Kingdom, it seems that cheques will be phase out in 2018.

d) Payment card

The term **payment card** is used for debit card, credit card and charge card.

The **debit card** deducts directly an amount from a bearer's current account or from the remaining balance on the card. These cards have become widespread in some countries, and they have surpassed the cheques by volume. Debit cards are also used for telephone and internet purchases, and they allow for instant withdrawal of currency. There are three ways of debit card processing of the transaction: online debit (PIN debit), offline debit (signature debit) and electronic purse card system. One debit card can combine all kinds of processing.

The **credit card** card allows spending an amount on credit of the issuing institution (mostly bank). While debit card uses the money that a card bearer has the credit card uses the money that card bearer receives through credit. The issuing institution grants a line of credit to the card bearer. The card bearer has to pay a defined minimum proportion of the bill by a due date or may pay a higher amount up to the entire amount owed. The issuing institution charges interest on the amount owed if the amount is not paid in full each month. Interest rate is much higher than most other forms of debt, often 20 to 30 %. A grace period is the time the holder has to pay the amount before interest is charged. Grace period is usually a range from 20 to 50 days. Some credit card holders become heavily encumbered with their credit debt service and are driven to bankruptcy.

The **charge card** insures purchase of good and services on credit under the condition that debt incurred will be paid in full by due date each month. Late payment is subject to severe fee.

13.2 Settlement systems

Fundamentally, there are two basic types of settlement systems, namely the gross settlement systems and net settlement systems. Any settlement system operates either on a real-time or on a batch basis.

13.2.1 Gross settlement systems

The **gross settlement system** is a settlement system in which settlement takes place on an order-by-order basis (without netting). The gross feature of the system refers to the fact that each transaction is settled separately. The structure of the gross payment system is simple (Figure 13.2). Every single payment is processed separately and immediately when the payer's bank has sufficient liquidity. The settlement does not depend upon any netting mechanism. Moreover, any settlement is final, and there is no mechanism of unwinding (see further). The gross settlement system features a disadvantage resulting from higher liquidity requirements.

In the world, the vast majority of interbank gross settlement systems are the real-time gross settlement systems (RTGS). The RTGS is the system where payment orders are processed and settled continuously in a real-time. The modern information technology has almost eliminated any delays. The queuing of payment orders is usually based on principle the principle "first in, first out" Any payment system operated by the central bank is the RTGS. In such a system, liquidity is transferred by payer's bank on behalf of its customer (or on behalf of its own) to payee's bank. The real-time feature of the system means that the funds are transferred immediately if there is sufficient amount of the liquidity on the account of payer's bank. Te RTGS essentially eliminates settlement risk. In the case of central bank payment system, the commercial banks actually transfer bank reserves (liquidity) from and to their accounts on the books of the central bank. To improve the liquidity of the RTGS, the central bank typically provides participants with some access to collaterised intraday credit.

Figure 13.2 Gross settlement system
(Number of payments = 9, value of payments = 430)

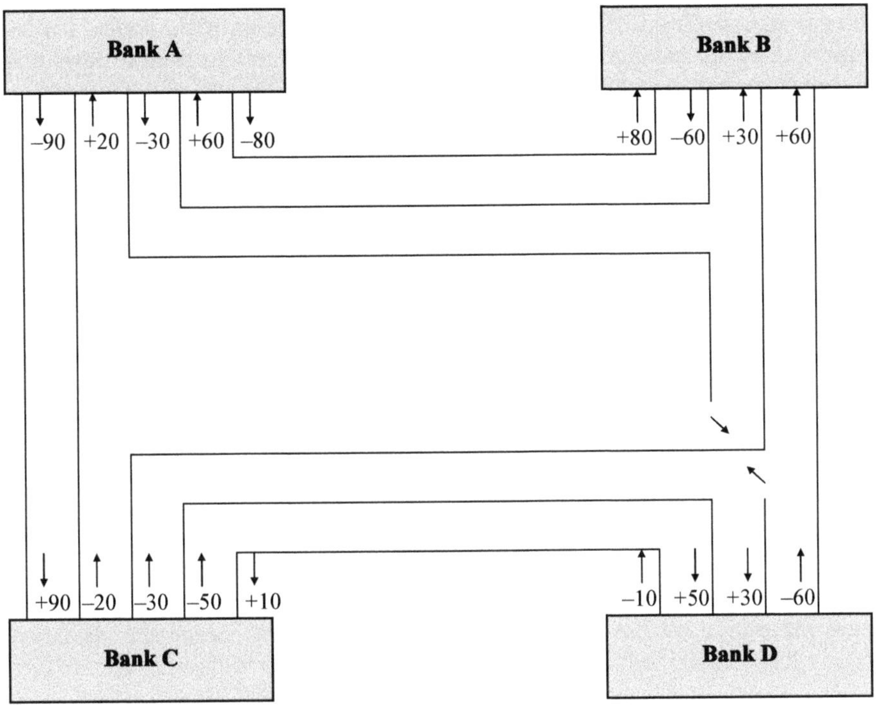

13.2.2 Net settlement systems

The **netting** means an offset of an amount of positive value (asset) with an amount of negative value (liability) and partial or entire cancellation each other. The assets and liabilities covered by the netting arrangement may arise from financial contracts. The netting can reduce a large number of individual obligations to a smaller number of obligations. Netting may take several forms which have varying degrees of legal enforceability in the event of the default of one of the parties. There are bilateral and multilateral netting. Multilateral netting is an arrangement among three or more parties to net their obligations. The multilateral netting of payment obligations normally takes place in the context of a multilateral net settlement system. Such netting is conducted through a central counterparty.

The **net settlement system** is a settlement system in which settlement takes place on a net basis. The system requires less liquidity for the participants involved. Payments to and from any participant accumulate, and only the net difference is transferred. What that means is that, on receipt of the funds, the recipient does not have access to those funds until the accumulated inflows and outflows are netted and settled. Transfers are settled at the end of the processing cycle, with all transfers being provisional until all participants have discharged their settlement obligations.

If a participant fails to settle, some or all of the provisional transfers involving, the participant is deleted from the system, and the settlement net obligations from the remaining transfers are then recalculated. Such an **unwinding** procedure has the effect of unpredictable liquidity pressure and possible losses arising from the failure to settle to the remaining participants, and it may in an extreme case result in defaults by other participants. In order to avoid unwinding procedures, a system could set up a guarantee fund, paid by the participants, in combination with a limit system on net open debit positions, which would make sure that settlement would take place even if the largest debtor in the system defaults.

There are two basic systems of net settlement, namely a bilateral net settlement system and a multilateral net settlement system.

The **bilateral net settlement system** is a settlement system in which settlement takes place on a net basis between every combination of participants. Bilateral net settlement positions are calculated between every two participants (Figure 13.3).

The **multilateral net settlement system** is a settlement system in which settlement takes place on a net basis between three or more parties (Figure 13.4 – 13.6). Calculations of multilateral net positions are provided usually by the clearing centre operating as a central party place in the middle of the system. Every operation between participants X and Y is thus divided into two separate operations: operation between X and clearing centre and operation between the clearing centre and Y.

The **multilateral net settlement position** is the sum of the amounts of all the transfers a participant in a net settlement system has received during a certain period of time less the amounts of the transfers made by the participant to all other participants. If the sum is positive, the participant is in a multilateral net credit position; if the sum is negative, the participant is in a multilateral net debit position. The net credit or debit position is called net settlement position. The multilateral net position is also the bilateral net position between each participant and the central counterparty.

Figure 13.3 Bilateral net settlement system
(Number of payments = 6, value of payments = 250)

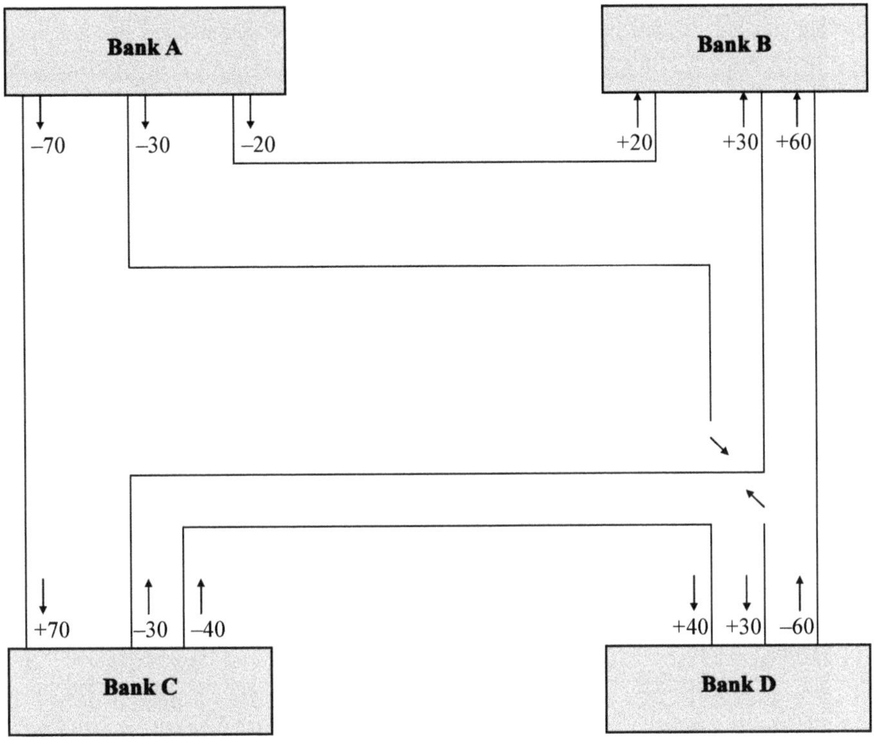

The multilateral net settlement system is much more complicated than gross settlement system from the point of view of their legal structure. There are two ways how to calculate the multilateral net settlement positions:

- o The multilateral net settlement positions are calculated indirectly, i.e. there is prior calculation of bilateral net settlement positions (Figure 13.5); and
- o The multilateral net settlement posisitons are calculated directly, i.e. there is no prior calculation of bilateral net settlement positions (Figure 13.6).

Figure 13.4 Multilateral net settlement system

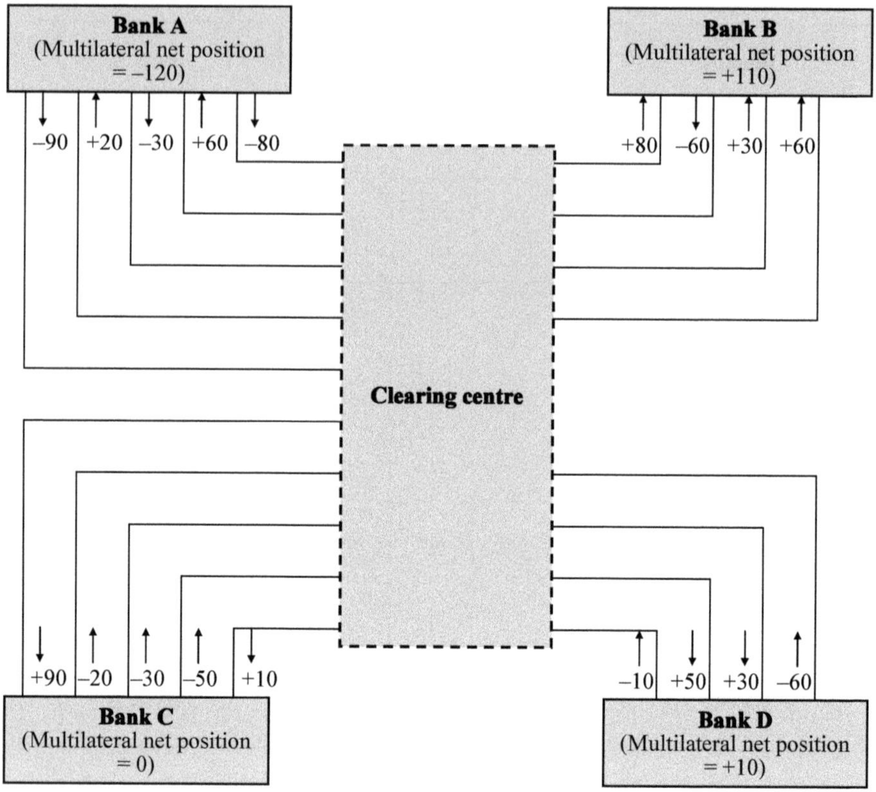

Operations of the multilateral settlement systems can be divided into two separate phases, namely the netting and the settlement. Payment orders are electronically transferred into the clearing centre. Clearing centre calculates multilateral net settlement positions of each participant (debit, credit, or zero). Such positions are usually not legally enforceable. Afterwards, participants having the net debit positions are expected to initiate payments in favour of participants having the net credit positions.

Figure 13.5 Multilateral net settlement system based on indirect calculation of multilateral net positions (Number of payments = 3, value of payments = 120)

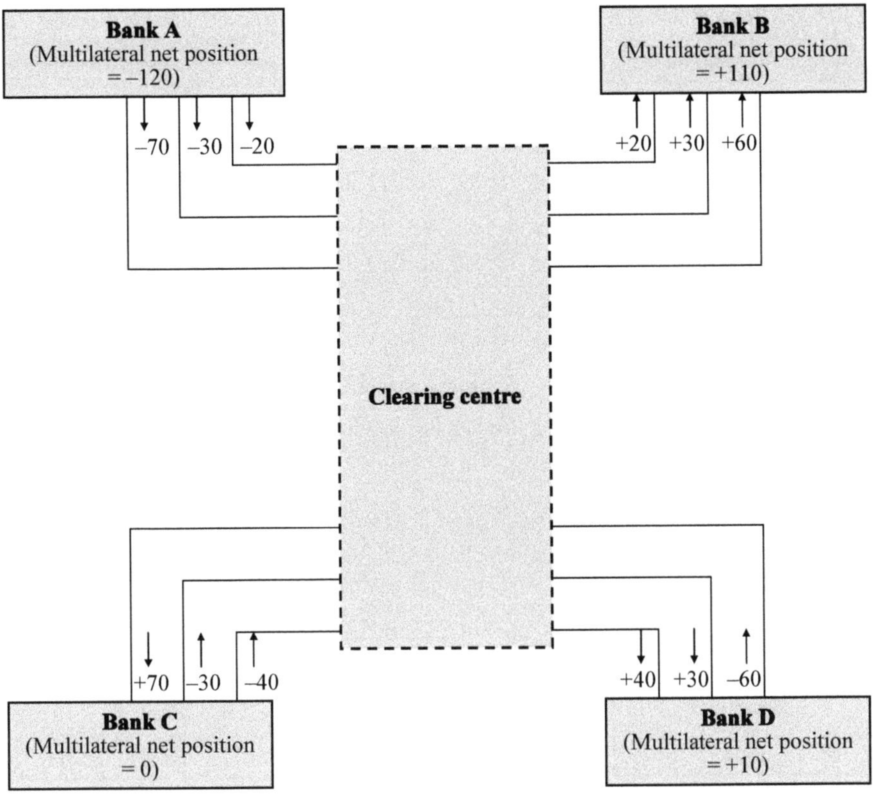

Once the system has settled all net positions, individual payment orders included are considered to be legally enforceable. If any of the participant is unable to settle her net position, unwinding follows. By cancelling some payments, some creditors can loose part of their payments due. But unwinding does not represent the only possible solution. There is also possibility that all other participants can share loses equally through the guarantee fund.

Figure 13.6 Multilateral net settlement system based on direct calculation of multilateral net positions (Number of payments = 3, value of payments = 120)

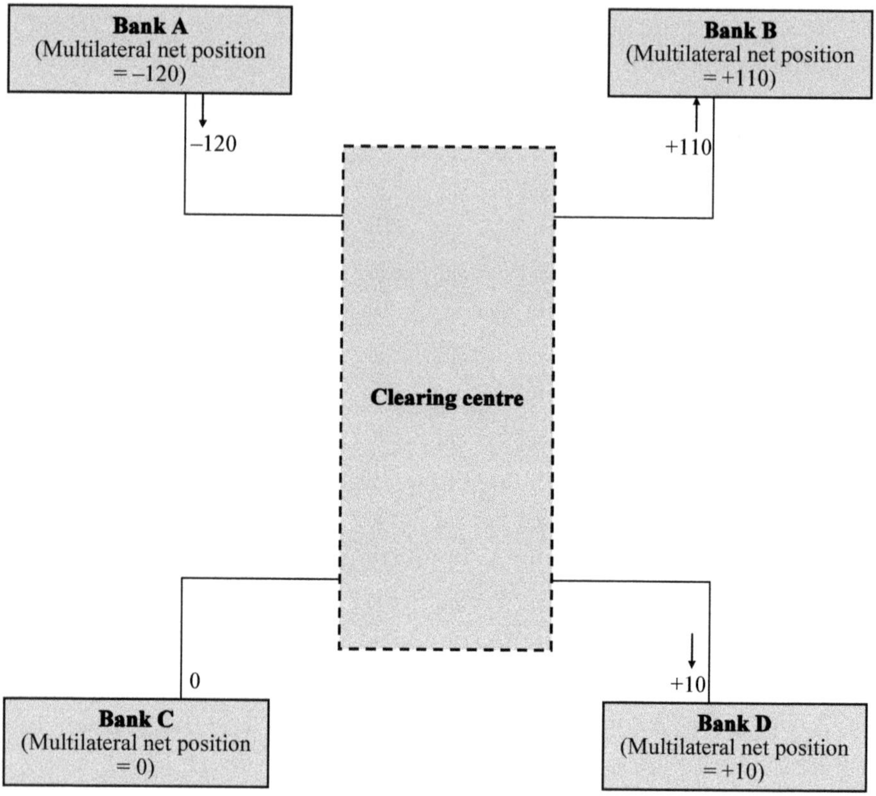

Let's compare the gross settlement system, bilateral net settlement system and multilateral net settlement system:

- In the case of gross settlement system (Figure 13.2), the number of payments is 9, and the value of payments is 430;
- In the case of bilateral net settlement system (Figure 13.3), the number of payments is 6, and the value of payments is 250; and
- In the case of multilateral net settlement system (Figure 13.4 – 13.6), the number of payments is 3, and the value of payments is 120.

The main advantage of the net settlement system consists in the substantial reduction of the number and the value of interbank settlement operations and reduction of the liquidity requirements. However the multilateral settlement systems carry the risk for all participants relying on the net position estimates. These positions are usually not legally enforceable (till the settlement), and they are subject to the subsequent settlement between all participants. In other words, the time lag between netting and settlement causes those participants **with the net credit positions grant implicit credits to participants with the net debit position**.

We can conclude that bilateral and multilateral net settlement systems can save large amounts of liquidity and it can reduce settlement risk. However, the real-time gross settlement systems are now considered more convenient.

13.3 Payment systems in the United States

There are two major large-value payment transfer systems in the United States:

- o Fedwire; and
- o CHIPS.

Generally, these payment systems are used by financial institutions and their customers to make large-dollar, time-critical transfers. The Federal Reserve National Settlement Service and Automated Clearing Houses are also mentioned.

The **Fedwire** funds transfer system is a real-time gross settlement system that enables participants to send and receive final payments through liquidity at the Fed between each other. The system is operated by Federal Reserve banks. The Fedwire processes and settles payment orders individually. The Payment to the receiving participant is final and irrevocable when the amount is credited to the receiving participant's account or when notice is sent to the receiving participant, whichever is earlier. The Fedwire transfers are generally initiated online, via an electronic connection to the Fed communications network. Approximately 9,300 participants are able to send or receive funds over the system.

CHIPS (Clearing House Interbank Payments System) is owned and operated by the Clearing House Interbank Payments Company L.L.C. (CHIPCo). All participants are members of CHIPCo. In 2001, CHIPCo converted CHIPS from an end-of-day, multilateral net settlement system to one that provides real-time final settlement for payment orders. Participation in CHIPS is available to commercial banking institutions or Edge Act corporations. A non-participant wishing to send payments over CHIPS must employ a CHIPS participant to act as its correspondent or agent. There are approximately only 50 participants. The payments transferred over CHIPS are often related to international interbank transactions, including the dollar payments resulting from foreign currency transactions (such as spot and currency swap contracts) and Eurodollar placements and returns. Payment orders are also sent over CHIPS for the purpose of adjusting correspondent balances and making payments associated with commercial transactions, bank loans and securities transactions.

The Fed allows participants in private clearing arrangements to settle transactions on a net basis using account balances held at the Fed through the **Federal Reserve National Settlement Service** (NSS). Participants include cheque clearing houses, ACH networks and some bank card processors. Approximately 70 local and national private sector clearing and settlement arrangements use NSS. NSS offers finality that is similar to that of the Fedwire funds transfer service, and it provides an automated mechanism for submitting settlement files to the Fed.

The **Automated Clearing Houses** (ACHs) are nationwide electronic file transfer mechanisms that process transfers initiated by depository institutions through electronically originated batches. Only banks may have direct links to the ACH, and, through them, more than 3 million businesses and 100 million consumers originate and receive ACH transactions. The first ACH was created in the mid-1970s as part of the government efforts to begin dispersing electronically the growing number of government payments (such as Social Security). There are two ACH operators: the Fed and Electronic Payments Network (EPN) – formerly the New York Automated Clearinghouse. The Fed is the large ACH operator and processes approximately 60 % of the commercial interbank ACH transactions. ACH transactions processed by the Fed are settled through deposit-taking institutions' accounts held at the Fed. Even if EPN is not a bank, it is bank-owned. For transactions sent through the Fed, settlement may take place in the Fed account of each bank or in the Fed account of designated correspondent bank. EPN ultimately relies on the Fed for settlement.

13.4 Payment system in the Eurozone

There are five large-value payment systems operating in euro:

- TARGET2 of the Eurosystem;
- The Euro System of the EBA Clearing Company (EURO 1);
- The French Paris Net Settlement (PNS);

- o The Finnish Pankkien On-line Pikasiirrot ja Sekit-järjestelmä (POPS); and
- o CLS.

The **TARGET2** is the RTGS system for the euro, managed by the Eurosystem. The TARGET2 is an upgraded vwersion of the former TARGET sysstem The TARGET stands for **T**rans-European **A**utomated **R**eal-time **G**ross settlement **E**xpress **T**ransfer system. It is used for the settlement of central bank operations, large-value euro interbank transfers and other euro payments. It is real-time system with settlement in accounts at central banks and with immediate finality. The TARGET was created by connecting national euro real-time gross settlement systems and the ECB payment mechanism. It started in January 1999. The launch of the single currency necessitated a real-time payment system for the euro area.

The **EURO 1** is a large-value payment system for euro payments. It is a net settlement system, and it is managed by the EBA Clearing Company which was set up by the Euro Banking Association (EBA). The EBA is a cooperative undertaking between EU-based commercial banks and EU branches of non-EU credit institutions. It covers over 70 banks from the EU-15 Member states and 5 non-EU countries. It processes credit transfers and direct debits. Payments are processed throughout the day, and net balances are settled at the end of the day in clearing accounts at the European Central Bank.

PNS is a French settlement system. Participants can set bilateral limits. Transfers are settled in real-time if there is sufficient liquidity on the participant's account, and if bilateral limits are met. Otherwise, transactions are queued. At the opening of the system, participants need to make a transfer of liquidity from their clearing accounts at the Banque de France through the French TARGET component TBF to their accounts in PNS. Participants may transfer liquidity between TBF and PNS during the day. Balances in PNS are always positive. End-of-day balances are credited the participants' clearing accounts at the Banque de France. PNS started in April 1999.

POPS is a real-time system operated by the banks on a basis of both gross and net settlement. The banks send payment orders bilaterally. Payment orders are netted bilaterally. In the case a payment exceeds the agreed limit, the bank should make a corresponding transfer in the Finnish TARGET component BoF-RTGS. If bilaterally agreed net debit limits is reached, a transfer is made through the BoF-RTGS. At the end of the day a settlement of net amounts is made.

CLS is the continuos settlement system for foreign exchange transactions. Generally, the two legs of a foreign exchange transaction are settled separately. There is settlement risk which relates to the fact that one party can default before both sides of the trade are settled. CLS eliminates this risk. It settles both sides of a foreign exchange transaction simultaneously (payment-versus-payment, PvP). Settlement in CLS is final and irrevocable. Participating banks receive real-time settlement information. This helps them to better manage liquidity. CLS started in September 2002. The ECB acts as the settlement agent. The ECB has opened an account for CLS Bank. All payments to and from CLS are processed through the ECB payment mechanism.

The major retail payment systems in the euro area are:

- CEC (Centre for Exchange and Clearing) of Belgium;
- CHS (Brussels Clearing House);
- PMJ (Banks Payment System) of Finland;
- SIT (Systeme Interbancaire de Telecompensation) of France;
- RPS (Retail Payment System) of Germany;
- ACO (Athens Clearing Office) of Greece;
- DIAS (Interbanking System) of Greece;
- IRECC (Irish Retail Electronic Payments Clearing Company Limited) of Ireland;
- IPCC (Irish Paper Clearing Company Limited);
- BI-COMP (Clearing system for interbank payments) of Italy;
- LIPS-Net (Luxembourg Interbank Payment System on a net basis) of Luxembourg;
- CSS (Clearing and Settlement System) of the Netherlands;
- SICOI (Interbank Clearing System) of Portugal;
- SNCE (National Electronic Clearing System) of Spain; and
- STEP 2 system of the EBA Clearing Company.

Retail payment systems generally cover only one country. The first European automated clearing house is the STEP 2 system, which started in April 2003.

13.5 Payment system in Japan

There are four major interbank clearing systems in Japan. The first system is operated by the central bank (gross settlement system), and three systems are in the private sector (net settlement systems):

- BOJ-NET Funds Transfer System;
- Foreign Exchange Yen Clearing System (FXYCS);
- Zengin Data Telecommunication System (Zengin System); and
- Bill and check clearing systems.

The **BOJ-NET Funds Transfer System** permits electronic settlement of transactions for participants with accounts at the Bank of Japan. Transfers through BOJ-NET may be settled immediately (RTGS) or at a designated time depending on participant instructions. In both cases settlement is final and irrevocable. Payment transactions are initiated through BOJ-NET terminals. It also settles net amounts from private net settlement systems.

The **Foreign Exchange Yen Clearing System** (FXYCS) is operated by the Tokyo Bankers Association (TBA). The FEYCS is a net settlement system which accepts SWIFT formats for message transmission, and it uses Bank of Japan accounts for settlement. It is used mainly for the settlement of yen legs of foreign exchange transactions, and it is similar to CHIPS. Net settlement is realised through the BOJ-NET.

The **Zengin Data Telecommunications System** is operated by the TBA. It is a completely electronic payment system for domestic third party transfers, and it uses a communications and network from NTT Data Communications Systems Corporation. Transactions are entered and processed online but settlement does not take place until after the Zengin System has closed for the day. Net settlement is realised through the BOJ-NET.

The **Bill and check clearing systems** are used by financial institutions to clear bills of exchange and checks drawn by individuals or firms and presented at regional clearing houses. There are more than 600 clearing houses in Japan. More than 70 % of the total clearing value is concentrated within the Tokyo Clearing House. Any clearing house serves a specific geographical area. Member institutions gather at a specific time exchange bills, and they checks and calculate their net settlement positions. Clearing houses are operated, among others, by local bankers associations. Net settlement is realised through the BOJ-NET.

13.6 Payment system in the United Kingdom

In the United Kingdom, the main interbank payment networks are:

- the CHAPS;
- the BACS; and
- Cheque and Credit Clearing Company.

The BACS and the cheque and Credit Clearing Company deal with high volumes of relatively small-value payments, although they are able to accommodate non-urgent large value transfers.

The **Clearing House Automated Payment System** (CHAPS) is RTGS system primarily designed for high-value payments, although there is no lower (or upper) limit on the value of payments. It is operated by CHAPS Clearing Company Ltd., and infrastructure is run by the Bank of England. The CHAPS now handles nearly all large-value same-day sterling payments between banks. There are 14 direct participants in CHAPS (excluding the Bank of England).

Prior to April 1996 payments were processed as a single net transaction at the end of the day and exposed the settlement risk (if one of the banks were to fail). In January 1999 the RTGS system was developed to accommodate euro accounts (CHAPS Euro) so that members could make domestic and cross-border euro payments. CHAPS Euro connected to the TARGET system, which linked together the RTGS systems of the 15 EU states and the European Central Bank. This provided member banks with the ability to make and receive cross-border as well as domestic payments in euros. A total of 20 banks, including two remote participants, were members of CHAPS Euro. Of these, 12 banks (including the Bank of England) were also members of CHAPS Sterling. CHAPS Euro closed in May 2008 as part of the final phase of the TARGET2.

A significant proportion of CHAPS payments, by value, originate in the foreign exchange market and other wholesale markets owing to their requirement for a prompt settlement service. The CHAPS system is, however, also used to facilitate same-day transfers arising from a wide range of other activities as general commercial transactions.

The **BACS** (known as Bankers' Automated Clearing Services Ltd until 1986) is the largest retail payment system in the United Kingdom. It is a deferred multi-lateral net settlement system, with a three-day clearing cycle. Net settlement is realised through the accounts at the Bank of England. The system is responsible for clearing bulk electronic transfers (credit transfers and direct debit). The membership of BACS consists of the Bank of England, 13 commercial banks and one building society. These credit institutions are responsible for settling all interbank obligations arising from the BACS clearing process. Users are allocated a user number, and they are able to submit payment instructions directly to the system. There are many organizations using the system, including a wide range of commercial and public sector bodies, along with many other indirect users who submit instructions through an intermediary.

The **Cheque and Credit Clearing Company** is responsible for clearing of cheques, bankers' drafts, building society cheques, postal orders, warrants and government payable orders in Great Britain. It has 12 direct members: Bank of England, 10 commercial banks and one building society. Other banks and building societies can have access through agency arrangements with the direct members.

References

Anderson, Richard G.: *Some Tables of Historical U.S. Currency and Monetary Aggregates Data.* Working Paper. Federal Reserve Bank of St. Louis, St. Louis, 2003.

Arestis, Philip and Alfred Eichner: The Post-Keynesian and Institutionalist Theory of Money and Credit. *Journal of Economic Issues*, 1988, 22(4), 1003–21.

Arestis, Philip and Peter Howells: The Supply of Credit Money and the Demand for Deposits: a Reply. *Cambridge Journal of Economics*, 1999, 23(1), 115–19.

Arestis, Philip and Malcom Sawyer (ed): *Money, Finance and Capitalist Development.* Edward Edgar, Cheltenham 2001.

Bagehot, Walter: *The Lombard Street: A Description of the Money Market.* Henry S. King and Co., London 1873.

Balls, Edward and Gus O'Donnell (eds): *Reforming Britain's Economic and Financial Policy – Towards Greater Economic Stability.* Palgrave, Basingstoke 2002.

Banking Reform – Discussion. *The American Economic Review*, 1913, 3(1), 64–88.

Batini, Nicoletta, and Edward Nelson: *The U.K.'s Rocky Road to Stability.* Working Paper. Federal Reserve Bank of St. Louis, St. Louis 2005.

Bean, Charles and Nigel Jenkinson: The formulation of Monetary Policy at the Bank of England. *Bank of England Quarterly Bulletin*, 2001, Winter, 434–41.

Beckhart, Benjamin H.: Monetary Policy and Commercial Bank Portfolios. *The American Economic Review,* 1940, 30(1) Supplement, 17–26.

Bell, Stephanie: The Role of the State and the Hierarchy of Money. *Cambridge Journal of Economics*, 2001, 25(2), 149–163.

Bellofiore, Riccardo: Between Wicksell and Hayek: Mises' Theory of Money and Credit Revisited, *The American Journal of Economics and Sociology*, 1998, 57(4), 531–78.

Bernanke, Ben S. and Michael Woodford (eds): *The Inflation Targeting Debate.* The University of Chicago Press, Chicago 2005.

Between Wicksell and Hayek: Mises' Theory of Money and Credit Revisited, *The American Journal of Economics and Sociology*, 1998, 57(4), 531–78.

Bernholz, Peter: *Monetary Regimes and Inflation: History, Economic and Political Relationships.* Edward Elgar, Cheltenham 2003.

Bessis, Joel: *Risk Management in Banking.* John Wiley & Sons, Chichester 1998.

Bindseil, Ulrich: *Monetary Policy Implementation: Theory Past and Present.* Oxford University Press, Oxford 2004.
Bisschop, W. R.: *The Rise of the London Money Market, 1640 to 1826.* Batoche Books Limited, Ontario 1896 (2001).
Black, Fischer: Active and Passive Monetary Policy in a Neoclassical Model. *Journal of Finance*, 1972, 27(4), 801–814.
Black, Fischer: The Trouble with Econometric Models. *Financial Analysts Journal*, 1982, 38(2), 29–37.
Black, Fischer: *Business Cycles and Equilibrium.* Basil Blackwell, New York 1987.
Blomquist, Thomas W. Commercial Association in Thirteenth-Century Lucca. *Business History Review*, 1971, 45(2), 157–178.
Bruun, Charlotte: *Logical Structures and Algorithmic Behaviour in a Credit Economy.* Ph.D. dissertation. Department of Economics, Politics and Public Administration, Aalborg University 1995.
Champ, Bruce, and Scott Freeman: *Modelling Monetary Economics.* John Wiley & Sons, New York 1994.
Chown, John F.: *A History of Monetary Unions.* Routledge, London 2003.
Clower, Robert W.: Theoretical Foundations of Monetary Policy. In: Monetary Theory and Monetary Policy in the 1970s. Oxford University Press, London 1971, 15–28.
Collins, Michael: *Central Banking in History.* Edward Edgar, Cheltenham 1993.
Cook, Robert M.: Speculation on the Origins of Coinage. *Historia*, 1958, 7, 257–62.
Cottrell, Allin: Post-Keynesian Monetary Economics. *Cambridge Journal of Economics*, 1994, 18(6), 587–605.
Cramp, A. B.: Two Views on Money. *Lloyd's Bank Review*, 1962, July, 1–16.
Crick, W. F.: The Genesis of Bank Deposits. *Economica*, 1927, 20, 191–202.
Chrystal, Alec (ed): *Monetarism.* Edward Edgar, Cheltenham 1990.
Dahlberg, Arthur O.: *When Capital Goes on Strike. How to Speed up Spending.* Harper & Brothers, New York 1938.
Dahlberg, Arthur O.: *Money in Motion.* John de Graaf, New York 1962.
Dalton, George: Barter. *Journal of Economic Issues*, 1982, 16(1), 181–90.
Davenport, Herbert J.: *Value and Distribution. A Critical and Constructive Study.* University of Chicago Press, Chicago 1908.
Davenport, Herbert J.: Velocities, Turnovers and Prices. *The American Economic Review*, 20(1), 1930, 9–19.
Davidson, Paul: *Money and the Real World.* London, Macmillan 1972.
Davidson, Paul: Reforming the World's Money. *Journal of Post-Keynesian Economics,* 1992/93, 15(2), 153–79.
Davidson, Paul and Jan A. Kregel (eds): *Full Employment and Price Stability in a Global Economy.* Edward Edgar, Cheltenham 1999.

Davies, Glyn: *A History of Money from Ancient Times to the Present Day.* University of Wales Press. Cardiff 1994.
Davies, Glyn: *Credit: 6,000 Years Old and Still Evolving Vigorously.* Business Credit, 1996, June, 16–19.
Davies, Glyn and Roy Davies: A Comparative Chronology of Money. Part 1: From the Origins of Agriculture to the Industrial Revolution, *Journal of Management History*, 1998, 4(3), 160–85.
Davies, Glyn and Roy Davies: A Comparative Chronology of Money. Part 2: From the Industrial Revolution to the Present Day, *Journal of Management History*, 1998, 4(3), 186–232.
Day, Alan Charles Lynn: *Outline of Monetary Economics.* Oxford University Press, Oxford 1957.
Douglas, Clifford Hugh: *The Monopoly of Credit.* Chapman and Hall, London 1931.
Dunbar, Charles F.: Deposits and Currency. *Quarterly Journal of Economics,* 1887, 1, 401–18.
Dunbar, Charles F.: *The Theory and History of Banking*, Putman, New York 1891.
Edwards, James D.: Early Bookkeeping and its Development into Accounting. *Business History Review,* 1960, 34(4), 446–58.
Fendel, Ralf: *Monetary Policy, Interest Rate Rules, and the Term Structure of Interest Rates.* Peter Lang, Frankfurt am Main 2007.
Ficek, Karel K.: The Quantity Theory and the Wages Fund. *The American Economic Review*, 1934, 24(4), 631–34.
Financial Structure and the Monetary Policy Transmission Mechanism. Bank for international settlements, Basel 1995.
Fontana, Giuseppe: La théorie du credit d'Emile Mireaux: 'Les miracles du credit', *Revue d'Économie Politique*, 1997, 107(2), 285–94.
Forstater, Mathew: *Tax-Driven Money: Additional Evidence From the History of Thought, Economic History, and Economic Policy.* Working Paper. University of Missouri, Kansas City 2004.
Friedman, Benjamin M. and Frank H. Hahn (eds): *Handbook of Monetary Economics I – II.*. Elsevier, Amsterdam 2000.
Friedman, Milton and Anna J. Schwartz: *A Monetary History of the United States, 1867– 1960.* Princeton University Press, Princeton 1963
Friedman, Milton et al (eds): *Milton Friedman's Monetary Framework: A Debate with his Critics.* University of Chicago Press Journals, Chicago 1975.
Friedman, Milton: *Price Theory.* Aldine, Chicago 1976.
Friedman, Milton: Lessons from the 1979–82 Monetary Policy Experiment. The *American Economic Review*, 1984, 74(2), 397–400.
Fullarton, John: *On the Regulation of Currencies.* Kelley. New York 1844.

Galbraith, John K.: *The Unfinished Business of the Century*. London School of Economics, London 1999.

Ghosh, Atish R., Anne-Maria Gulde and Holger C. Wolf: *Exchange Rate Regimes: Choices and Consequences*. MIT Press, Cambridge 2003. .

Giovannini, Alberto: *The Debate on Money in Europe*. MIT Press, Cambridge, 1996.

Goodhart, Charles.: *Monetary Theory and Practice: The U.K. Experience*. Macmillam, London 1984. .

Goodhart, Charles: The Conduct of Monetary Policy, *The Economic Journal*, 1989, 99(396), 293–346.

Goodhart, Charles: Has Moore Become too Horizontal? *Journal of Post Keynesian Economics*, 1989, 12(1), 29–34

Goodhart, Charles: The Two Concepts of Money: Implications for the Analysis of Optimal Currency Areas. *European Journal of Political Economy*, 1998, 14(3), 407–32.

Goodhart, Charles: Myths about the Lender of Last Resort. *International Finance*, 1999, 2(3), 339–60.

Goodhart, Charles: Can Central Banking Survive the IT Revolution? *International Finance*, 2000, 3(2), 189–209.

Graziani, Augusto: The Monetary Theory of Production. Cambridge University Press, Cambridge 2003.

Greco, Thomas H.: *Money: Understanding and Creating Alternatives to Legal Tender*. Chelsea Green, White River Junction 2001.

Gunnings, Patrick J.: *Hayek, Free Banking, and the Commodity Money Syndrome: Toward A Praxeological Theory of Credit and Money*. Feng Chia University, Taichung 1999.

Gwartney, James D., Stroup, Richard L., Sobel, Russell, S. and McPherson, David: *Economics: Private and Public Choice* (10th edition). South-Western College Publishing, Mason 2003.

Hahn, Albert L.: *Volkswirtschaftliche Theorie des Bankkredits*. Mohr, Tübingen 1920.

Hahn, Albert L.: The Effects of Saving on Employment and Consumption. *Journal of Marketing*,1946, 11 (July), 35–43.

Hahn, Frank: *Money and Inflation*. The MIT Press, Cambridge 1985.

Hall, Margaret W.: Early Bankers in the Genoese Notarial Records, *The Economic History Review*. 1935, 6(1), 73–79.

Hamilton, Alexander: *Report on a National Bank*. 1790.

Hawtrey, Ralph G.: *Good and Bad Trade*. Constable, London 1913.

Hawtrey, Ralph G.: *Currency and Credit*. Longmans, London 1919.

Hawtrey, Ralph G.: The Tenth Annual Report of the Federal Reserve Board, *The Economic Journal*, 1924, 34(134), 283–86.

Hayek, Fridrich A.: *Prices and Productions.* London: Routledge & Kegan, 1931.
Hayek, Fridrich A.: Money and Capital: A Reply. *The Economic Journal*, 1932, 42(166), 237–49.
Hicks, John R.: Automatists, Hawtreyans, and Keynesians. *Journal of Money, Credit and Banking*, 1969, 1(3), 307–17.
Hicks, John R.: IS-LM: An Explanation. *Journal of Post Keynesian Economics*, 1980/81, 3(2), 139–54.
Hildreth, Richard: *The History of Banks.* Hilliard, Gray & Company, Boston 1837.
Howells, Peter and Keith Bain: *The Economics of Money, Banking and Finance. A European Text* (3rd edition). FT Prentice Hall, Harlow 2005.
Huang, Jing-Zhi and Ming Huang: How Much of Corporate-Treasury Yield Spread Is Due to Credit Risk? In: 14th Annual Conference on Financial Economics and Accounting (FEA), Texas Finance Festival. 2003.
Humphrey, Thomas M.: The Theory of Multiple Expansion of Deposits. What it is and whence it Came. *Economic Review (Federal Reserve Bank of Richmond)*, 1987, 73(2), 3–11.
Humphrey, Thomas M.: Rival Notions of Money. *Economic Review (Federal Reserve Bank of Richmond*), 1988, 74(5), 3–9.
Humphrey, Thomas M.: Price-Level Stabilization Rules in a Wicksellian Model of the Cumulative Process. *Scandinavian Journal of Economics*, 1992, 94(3), 509–518.
Innes, Mitchel A.: The Credit Theory of Money. *The banking Law Journal*, 1914, 31(Dec./Jan.), 151–68.
International Financial Reporting standards. IASB, London 2009.
Kaldor, Nicholas: *The Scourge of Monetarism.* Oxford University Press, Oxford 1982.
Kaldor, Nicholas: How Monetarism Failed. *Challenge*, 1985, 28(2), 4–13.
Keynes, John N.: *The Scope and Method of Political Economy.* University of Cambridge, Cambridge 1890.
Keynes, John, M.: The Prospects of Money, *The Economic Journal*, 1914, 24(96), 610–34.
Keynes, John M.: *A Treatise on Money*. Macmillan, London, 1930.
Keynes, John M.: *A Monetary Theory of Production*. Macmillan, London 1933.
Keynes, John M.: *The General Theory of Employment, Interest and Money.* Macmillan, London 1936.
Keynes, John M.: The General Theory of Employment. *The Quarterly Journal of Economics*, 1937, 51(2), 209–223.
King, Mervyn A.: The Inflation Target Five Years on. *Bank of England Quarterly Bulletin*, 1997, November, 434–42.

King, Mervyn A.: Changes in UK Monetary Policy: Rules and Discretion in Practise. *Journal of Monetary Economics*, 1997, 39(1), 81–97.
Knapp, Georg F.: *The State Theory of Money*. London, Macmillan 1905.
Kohn, Meir G.: *Finance Before Industrial Revolution: An Introduction*. Working Paper. Dartmouth College, Hanover 1999.
Kohn, Meir G.: *Early Deposit Banking*. Working Paper. Dartmouth College, Hanover 1999.
Kohn, Meir G.: *Bills of Exchange and the Money Market to 1600*. Working Paper. Dartmouth College, Hanover 1999.
Kohn, Meir G.: *Merchant Banking in the Medieval and Early Modern Economy*. Working Paper. Dartmouth College, Hanover 1999.
Kohn, Meir G.: Payments and the Development of Finance in Pre-Industrial Europe. Working Paper. Dartmouth College, Hanover 2001.
Koo, Richard C.: The Holy Grail of Macroeconomics: Lessons form Japan's Great Recession. John Wiley & Sons, Singapore 2008.
Laidler, David (ed): *Foundations of Monetary Economics I – III*. Edward Elgar, Cheltenham 1999.
Laughlin, Laurence J.: *The Principles of Money*. Scribner, New York 1903.
Laughlin, Laurence J.: The Quantity-Theory of Money. *The Journal of Political Economy*, 1924, 32 (3), 265–81.
Levin, Andrew T., Fabio M. Natalucci and Jeremy M. Piger: The Macroeconomic Effects of Inflation Targeting. *Federal Reserve Bank of St. Louis Review*, 86(4), 51–80.
Lavoie, Marc: The Endogenous Flow of Credit and the Post Keynesian Theory of Money. *Journal of Economic Issues*, 1984, 18(3), 771–97.
Lavoie, Marc: Credit and Money: The Dynamic Circuit, Overdraft Economics and Post Keynesian Economics. In: Jarsulic, Marc (ed): Money and Macro Policy. Kluwer-Nijhoff, Boston 1985.
Lavoie, Marc: *Foundations of Post-Keynesian Economics*. Aldershot, Edward Elgar 1992.
Lavoie, Marc: The Credit-led Supply of Deposits and the Demand for Money: Kaldor's Reflux Mechanism as Previously Endorsed by Joan Robinson. *Cambridge Journal of Economics*, 1999, 23(1), 103–13.
Lavoie, Marc: On the Full Endogeneity of High-powered Money: Lessons from the Canadian Case. In: The Monetary Theory of Production. Benevento, University of Sannio 2003.
Leijonhufvud, Axel: Three Items for the Macroeconomic Agenda. *Kyklos*, 1998, 51(2), 197–218.
Lerner, Abba P.: Functional Finance and the Federal Debt. *Social Research,* 1943, 10(1), 38–51.
Lerner, Abba P.: Money as a Creature of the State. *The American Economic Review*, 1947, 37(2), 312–17.

Lewinsky, Jan S.: *Money, Credit and Prices*. P.S. King & Son, London 1929.
Macleod, Henry D.: *The Theory and Practice of Banking I-II*: Longman, Brown, Green and Longmans, London 1855–56.
Macleod, Henry D.: *Lecture on Credit and Banking*. Longman, Green, Reader and Dyer. London 1882.
Macleod, Henry D: *The Theory of Credit I-II*. Longmans, Green, Reader, and Dyer. London 1893.
Maeda, Eiji, Bunya Fujiwara, Aiko Mineshima, Ken Taniguchi: *Japan's Open market Operations under the Quantitative Easing Policy*. Working Paper. Bank of Japan, Tokyo 2005.
Maureen, Burton and Raymond E. Lombra: *The Financial System and the Economy. Principles of Money and Banking* (4th edition). South-Western College Publishing, Cincinnati 2005.
Mayer, Thomas and Steeven M. Sheffrin (ed): *Fiscal and Monetary Policy*. Edward Edgar, Cheltenham 1995.
Mehrling, Perry: *Understanding Fischer Black*. Columbia University, New York 2000.
Mehrling, Perry: Economists and the Fed: Beginnings. *Journal of Economic Perspectives,* 2002, 16(4), 207–18.
Michener, Ron: *Money in the American Colonies*. EH.Net Encyclopedia 2003.
Mill, John S.: *Principles of Political Economy*. J. W. Parker, London 1848.
Minsky, Hyman P.: Central Banking and Money Market Changes, *The Quarterly Journal of Economics*, 1957, 71(2), 171–87.
Minsky, Hyman P.: Private Sector Asset Management and the Effectiveness of Monetary Policy: Theory and Practice. *Journal of Finance*, 1969, 24(2), 223–38.
Minsky, Hyman P.: The Financial Instability Hypothesis: An Interpretation of Keynes and an Alternative to "Standard" Theory. *Nebraska Journal of Economics and Business,* 1977 16(1), 5–16.
Minsky, Hyman P.: *Can "It" Happen Again? Essays on Instability and Finance*. M.E. Sharpe, Armonk 1982.
Minsky, Hyman P.: *Stabilizing an Unstable Economy*. Yale University Press, New Haven 1986.
Minsky, Hyman P.: On the Non-Neutrality of Money. *Quarterly Review (Federal Reserve Bank of New York),* 1993, 18(1), 77–82.
Mises, Ludwig: *Theorie des Geldes und der Umlaufmittel*. Duncker & Humblot, München 1912.
Mises, Ludwig: *Geldwertstabilisierung und Konjunkturpolitik*. Fischer, Jena 1928.
Mishkin, Frederic S. and Stanley G. Eakins: *Financial Markets and Institutions* (3rd edition). Addison-Wesley, Reading 2000.

Mishkin, Frederic S.: *The economics of Money, Banking and Financial Markets* (7th edition). Addison-Wesley, Boston 2004.

Mitchell, Innes, A.: What is Money? *Banking Law Journal* 1913, May, 377–408.

Mitchell, Innes, A.: The Credit Theory of Money. *Banking Law Journal* 1914, 31, 151–68.

Miyanoya, Atsushi: *A Guide to Bank of Japan's Market Operations.* Working Paper. Bank of Japan, Tokyo 2000.

Mizen, Paul (ed): *Central Banking, Monetary History and Practice.* Edward Edgar, Cheltenham 2003.

Moore, Basil J.: Wages, Bank Lending, and the Endogeneity of Credit Money. In: Jarsulic, Marc (ed): Money and Macro Policy. Kluwer-Nijhoff, Boston 1985.

Moore, Basil. J.: Contemporaneous Reserve Accounting: Can Reserve be Quality-Constrained? *Journal of Post Keynesian Economics*, 1984, 7(1), 103–113.

Moore, Basil J.: *Horizontalists and Verticalists: The Macroeconomics of Credit Money.* Cambridge University Press, Cambridge 1988.

Moore, Basil J.: Money Supply Endogeneity: "Reserve Price Setting" or "Reserve Quantity Setting"? *Journal of Post Keynesian Economics,* 1991, 13(3), 404–13.

Moore, Basil J.. Reconciliation of the Supply and Demand for Endogenous Money. *Journal of Post Keynesian Economics*, 1997, 19(3), 423–28.

Morgan, H. Wayne: The Origins and Establishment of the First Bank of the United States. *Business History Review*, 1956, 30(4), 472–92.

Munro, John H.: *Monetary Policies, Guild Labour-Strife, and Compulsory Arbitration during the Decline of the Late-Medieval Flemish Cloth Industry, 1390 – 1435.* Working Paper. University of Toronto, Toronto 1998.

Munro, John H.: *Wage-Stickiness, Monetary Changes, and Real Incomes in Late-Medieval England and the Low Countries, 1300 – 1450: Did Money Really Matter?* Working Paper. University of Toronto, Toronto 2000.

Munro, John H.: *Postan, Population, and Prices in Late-Medieval England and Flanders. Working Paper.* University of Toronto, Toronto 2002.

Munro, John H.: *The Monetary Origins of the 'Price Revolution': South German Silver Mining, Merchant-Banking, and Venetian Commerce, 1470–1540'.* Working Paper. University of Toronto, Toronto 2003.

Musella, Marco and Carlo Panico (eds): *The Money Supply in the Economic Process: A Post Keynesian Perspective.* Edward Elgar, Aldershot 1995.

Nell, Edward J. and Willi Semmler (eds): *Nicholas Kaldor and Mainstream Economics: Confrontation or convergence?.*St. Martin's Press, New York 1991.

Nelson, Edward: T*he Great Inflation of the Seventies: What Really Happened?* Working Paper. Federal Reserve Bank of St. Louis, St. Louis 2004.
OBrian, Yueh-Yun C.: *Reserve Requirements Systems in OECD Countries.* Working Paper. Federal Reserve Board, Washington, 2007.
Original pronouncements. Accounting Standards as of June 1, 2005. John Wiley & Sons, New York 2005
Papadimitriou, Dimitri B. and L. Randall Wray: The Economic Contributions of Hyman Minsky: Varieties of Capitalism and Institutional Reform. *Review of Political Economy,* 1998, 10(2), 199–225.
Partnoy, Frank: A Revisionist View of Enron and the Sudden Death of 'May', *Villanova Law Review*, 2003, 48(4), 1245–1280.
Pollin, Robert: Two Theories of Money Supply Endogeneity: Some Empirical Evidence. *Journal of Post Keynesian Economics*, 1991, 13(3), 366–96. .
Rabin, Jack and Stevens, Glenn L. (eds): *Handbook of Monetary Policy.* Marcel Dekker, New York 2001.
Rasche, Robert H.: Demand Functions for Measures of U.S. Money and Debt. In: Proceedings of the Board of the Governors of the Federal Reserve System. 1990, 113–172.
Redlich, Fritz: Jacques Laffitte and the Beginnings of Investment Banking in France. *Business History Review,* 1948, 22(4–6), 137–60.
Redlich, Fritz: Banking in Mediaeval Bruges: A Review. *Business History Review*, 1949, 23(2), 109–12.
Redlich, Fritz and Webster M. Christman: Early American Checks and an Example of their Use. *Business History Review,* 1967, 41(3), 285–302.
Redlich, Fritz: The Role of Private Banks in the Early Economy of the United States. *Business History Review*, 1977, 51(1), 90–93.
Romer, Christina D. and David H. Romer (eds): *Reducing Inflation.* University of Chicago Press, Chicago 1997.
Richards, R. D.: The Evolution of Paper Money in England. *The Quarterly Journal of Economics,* 1927, 41(3), 361–404.
Robertson, Dennis H.: *Money.* Cambridge University Press, Cambridge 1922.
Robertson, Dennis H.: *Banking Policy and the Price Level.* P.S. King & Son, London 1926.
Robertson, Dennis H.: Theories of Banking Policy. *Economica*, 1928, 23, 131–46.
Rochon, Louis-Philippe.: The Creation and Circulation of Endogenous Money: A Circuit Dynamic Approach. *Journal of Economic Issues*, 1999, 33(1), 1–21.
Rogoff, Kenneth: *Deflation: Determinants, Risks, and Policy Options – Findings of an Interdepartmental Task Force.* IMF, Washington 2003.
Roover, Raymond de: Money, Banking, and Credit in Medieval Bruges. *The Journal of Economic History*, 1942, 2(Supplement), 52–65.

Roover, Raymond de: The Lingering Influence of Medieval Practices. *The Accounting Review*, 1943, 18(2), 148–51.

Roover, Raymond de: The Medici Bank Financial and Commercial Operations. *The Journal of Economic History*, 1946, 6(2), 153–72.

Roover, Raymond de: The Scholastics, Usury, and Foreign Exchange. *Business History Review*, 1967, 41, 257–71.

Rousseas, Stephen: *Post Keynesian Monetary Economics*. M.E. Sharpe, Armonk 1986.

Schaling, Eric: *Institutions and Monetary Policy*. Edward Edgar, Cheltenham 1995.

Schumpeter, Joseph A.: *Theorie der wirtschaftlichen Entwicklung*. Duncker & Humblot, Leipzig 1912.

Schumpeter, Joseph A.: The Explanation of the Business Cycle. *Economica*, 1927, 21, 286–311.

Schumpeter, Joseph A.: There is Still Time to Stop Inflation. N*ation's Business*, 1948, 36, 33–35, 88–91.

Schumpeter, Joseph A.: *History of Economic Analysis*. George Allen & Unwin, London 1954.

Schumpeter, Joseph A.: *Das Wesen des Geldes*. Vandenhoeck & Ruprecht, Göttingen 1970.

Sechrest, Larry J.: *Free Banking: Theory, History, and Laissez-faire Model*. Quarum Books, Westport 1993.

Shilling, A. Gary: *Deflation*. McGraw-Hill, New York 1999.

Skaggs, Neil T.: Henry Dunning Macleod and the Credit Theory of Money. In: Cohen Avi J., Hagemann Harald, and Smithin John (eds): Money, Financial Institutions and Macroeconomics. Recent economic thought series. Kluwer Academic Publishers, Boston 1997.

Skaggs, Neil T.: Debt as the Basis of Currency: the Monetary Economics of Trust – Special Invited Issue: Money, Trust, Speculation and Social Justice – Part 2: Trust and Money. *The American Journal of Economics and Sociology*, 1998, 57(4), 453–68.

Skaggs, Neil T.: Changing Views: Twentieth-Century Opinion on the Banking School-Currency School Controversy, *History of Political Economy* 1999, 31(2), 361–92.

Smith, Adam: *An Inquiry into the Nature and Causes of the Wealth of Nations*. 1776.

Smithin, John N.: *Controversies in Monetary Economics*. Edward Elgar, Cheltenham 2003.

Staiger, Douglas, Stock, James H., and Watson, Mark W.: The NAIRU, Unemployment and Monetary Policy. *Journal of Economic Perspectives,* 1997, 11(1), 33–49.

Steuart, James: *An Enquiry into the Principles of Political Oeconomy*. 1767.

Stiglitz, Joseph E.: *Money, Credit, and Business Fluctuations*. The Economic Record, 1988, 64(187), 307–22.
Strong, Benjamin: Federal Reserve Control of Credit. *Quarterly Review (Federal Reserve Bank of New York)*, 1989, 75th Anniversary issue, 6–14.
Svensson, Lars E.O.: *Evaluating Monetary Policy*. Working Paper. National Bureau of Economic Research, Cambridge 2009.
Svensson, Lars E.O.: *Monetary Policy wij Judgement: Forecast Targeting*. Working Paper. National Bureau of Economic Research, Cambridge 2005.
Syed, Ahmad: Is Money Net Wealth? *Oxford Economic Papers*, 1970, 22(3), 357–61.
Taylor, W. G. Langworthy: The Source of Financial Power. *The Journal of Political Economy*, 1905, 13(3), 368–88.
Taylor, W. G. Langworthy: *The Credit System*. Macmillan, New York 1913.
Teichova, Alice, Ginette Hentenryk and Dieter Ziegler (eds): *Banking, Trade and Industry: Europe, America and Asia from the Thirteenth to the Twentieth Century*. Cambridge University Press, Cambridge 1997.
Thornton, Henry: *An Enquiry into the Nature and Effects of the Paper Credit of Great Britain*, J. Hatchard, London 1802.
Tobin, James: *Commercial Banks as Creators of Money*. In: Carson, Deanne (ed): Banking and Monetary Studies. Richard D. Irwin, Homewood 1963.
Tooke, Thomas: *An Inquiry into the Currency Principle*. Longman, Brown, Green, and Longmans, London 1844.
T*ransmission Mechanism of Monetary Policy*. Bank of England, London 1999.
Usher, Abbott P.: The Origins of Banking: The Primitive Bank of Deposit, 1200–1600. *The Economic History Review*, 1934, 4 (4), 399–428.
Vatter, Harold G. and John F. Walker (eds): *History of the U.S. Economy since World War II*. M.E. Sharpe, Armonk 1996.
Wagner, Helmut (ed): *Current Issues in Monetary Economics*. Physica-Verlag, Heidelberg 1998
Walsh, Carl E.: *Monetary Theory and Policy* (2nd edition). MIT Press, Cambridge 2003.
Warburg, Paul M.: Central Bank of the United States. *American Economic Association Quarterly*, 1909, 10 (1), 338–58.
Wee, Herman van der: International Business Finance and Monetary Policy in Western Europe, 1384–1410. *Business History Review*, 1969, 43, 372–80.
Wee, Herman van der: Structural Changes and Specialization in the Industry of the Southern Netherlands, 1100–1600. *The Economic History Review*, 1975, 28(2), 203–21.
Weintraub, Sidney: *Keynes, Keynesians, and Monetarists*. University of Pennsylvania Press, Philadelphia 1978.

Wheelock, David C.: *Monetary Policy in the Great Depression and Beyond: The Sources of the Fed's Inflation Bias.* Working Paper. Federal Reserve Bank of St. Louis, St. Louis 1997.

White, Horace: *Money and Banking.* Ginn, Boston 1896.

White, Lawrence H.: *The Theory of Monetary Institutions.* Blackwell, Oxford 1999.

Whitesell, William: *Tunnels and Reserves in Monetary Policy Implementation.* Working Paper. Board of Governors of the Federal Reserve System, Washington 2003.

Wicksell, Knut: *Interest and Prices.* Kelley, New York 1898.

Wicksell, Knut: *Lectures on Political Economy.* Vol. 1. General Theory. Routledge & Kegan Paul, London 1901.

Wicksell, Knut: *Lectures on Political Economy.* Vol. 2. Money. Routledge & Kegan Paul, London 1906.

Wicksell, Knut: The Influence of the Rate of Interest on Prices. *Economic Journal,* 1907, 17(66), 213–20.

Wicksell, Knut: Stabilizing the Value of Money. A Means of Preventing Crises. In: Wicksell, Knut: Selected Essays in Economics. Routledge, London 1908.

Willis, Henry P.: *The Theory and Practice of Central Banking.* Harper & Brother, New York 1936.

Wilson, James: *Capital, Currency and Banking.* The Economist, London 1847.

Withers, Hartley: *The Meaning of Money.* Smith and Elder, London 1909.

Withers, Hartley: *Money.* Benn, London 1927.

Wojnilower, Albert M.: The Central Role of Credit Crunches in Recent Financial History. *Brookings Papers on Economic Activity*, 1980, 2, 277–339.

Woodford, Michael: *Monetary Policy in a World Without Money.* Working Paper. National Bureau of Economic Research, New York 2000.

Woodford, Michael: *Interest and Prices: Foundations of a Theory of Monetary Policy.* Princeton University Press, Princeton 2003.

Woodford, Michael: *Central Bank Communications and Policy Effectiveness.* Paper. Columbia University, New York 2005.

Wray, L. Randall: *Money and Credit in Capitalist Economies: the Endogenous Money Approach.* Edward Elgar, Northampton 1990.

Wray, L. Randall: Commercial Banks, the Central Bank, and Endogenous Money. *Journal of Post Keynesian Economics*, 1992, 14(3), 297–310

Wray, L. Randall: Keynesian Monetary Theory: Liquidity Preference or black box horizontalism? *Journal of Economic Issues*, 1995, 29(1), 273–82.

Wray, L. Randall: *Understanding Modern Money: The Key to Full Employment and Price Stability.* Edward Elgar, Cheltenham 1998.

Wray, L. Randall: *Seigniorage of Sovereignty?.* In: Rochon, Louis-Philippe and Rossi, Sergio (eds): Modern Theories of Money: The Nature and Role of Money in Capitalist Economies. Edward Edgar, Cheltenham 2003.

www.ingramcontent.com/pod-product-compliance
Ingram Content Group UK Ltd.
Pitfield, Milton Keynes, MK11 3LW, UK
UKHW021843100926
8556IPUK00019B/1012

9 783631 591185